ENGAGING
—*the*—
CIVIL WAR

Chris Mackowski and Brian Matthew Jordan, Series Editors

A Public-History Initiative of Emerging Civil War
and Southern Illinois University Press

IMAGINING WILD BILL
JAMES BUTLER HICKOK IN WAR, MEDIA, AND MEMORY

Paul Ashdown and Edward Caudill

Southern Illinois University Press
Carbondale

Southern Illinois University Press
www.siupress.com

Cover illustration: photograph of David T. Wright, courtesy of and copyright
     by Kimber Heineman, used with permission of David T. Wright.

Library of Congress Cataloging-in-Publication Data
Names: Ashdown, Paul, 1944– author. | Caudill, Edward, 1953– author.
Title: Imagining Wild Bill : James Butler Hickok in war, media, and
     memory / Paul Ashdown, and Edward Caudill.
Other titles: James Butler Hickok in war, media, and memory
Description: Carbondale : Southern Illinois University Press, [2020] |
     Series: Engaging the Civil War | Includes bibliographical references
     and index.
Identifiers: LCCN 2019050547 (print) | LCCN 2019050548 (ebook)
     | ISBN 9780809337880 (paperback) | ISBN 9780809337897 (ebook)
Subjects: LCSH: Hickok, Wild Bill, 1837–1876. | Hickok, Wild Bill, 1837–
     1876—In mass media. | Hickok, Wild Bill, 1837–1876—In literature
     | Peace officers—West (U.S.)—Biography. | Frontier and pioneer
     life—West (U.S.) | West (U.S.)—Biography.
Classification: LCC F594.H62 A74 2020 (print) | LCC F594.H62 (ebook)
     | DDC 978/.02092 [B]—dc23
LC record available at https://lccn.loc.gov/2019050547
LC ebook record available at https://lccn.loc.gov/2019050548

Printed on recycled paper ♻

This paper meets the requirements of ANSI/NISO Z39.48-1992
     (Permanence of Paper). ∞

For Barbara, who survived it
For Lance, who inspired it
For Danny and Robby, who lived it

Contents

Gallery of illustrations beginning on page 125

Acknowledgments

We gratefully acknowledge the able assistance of Sylvia Frank Rodrigue, Jennifer Egan, and Wayne Larsen at Southern Illinois Press; copy editor Ryan Masteller; Niki Kirkpatrick at the University of Tennessee, Knoxville; Chris Mackowski at St. Bonaventure University; and Brian Matthew Jordan at Sam Houston State University.

A Note on Terminology

We use "press" primarily to mean newspapers and magazines. "Publishing" is the better term for book production. "Mass press" is a term that has been around since the 1830s. "Media," "mass media," "popular media," and "popular culture" are later, more inclusive terms. We use them primarily to mean the entertainment functions of radio, television, film, new media, and the twentieth- and twenty-first-century press and publishing industries.

We use "myth" in two senses. The less important, but more common, sense is as a false story. The other, more important, concept is "myth" as transcendent truth grounded in the ideals of the cultural imagination. Mythologist Joseph Campbell famously defined myth as a "public dream," while a dream is a "private myth." A myth, in the sense we use it, serves a purpose. It is a story the public "dreams up" and chooses to believe, or is led to believe, in order to make sense of things and bind a community together. It is an agreed-upon idea, often implicitly so, such as the value of an individual, the exceptionalism of the American experience, or the "new world" as a worldly Eden. Media, as we see them, are myth-making machines. The post–Civil War press in urban America was the proverbial melting pot of national myth and ethos. A "legend," as we use the term, is a good story, at least partially or potentially true, but lacking evidence and without the deeper symbolic structure of a myth.

We use "West" to denote a region and "Wild West" to mean a slogan, an idea, an image. We use "Native American" as a preferred modern term but "Indian" when appropriate to the time or context we are writing about. No one writing for the popular press in the nineteenth century referred to "Native Americans," and the term was rare through much of the twentieth century. When possible, we identify Native American tribes in preference to "Indians."

ENGAGING
—*the*—
CIVIL WAR

For additional content that will let you engage this material further, scan the QR code on this page. It will take you to exclusive online material and related blog posts at www.emergingcivilwar.com.

A QR scanner is readily available for download through the app store on your digital device. Or go to www.siupress.com/imaginingwildbill for links to the digital content.

Imagining Wild Bill

✤ Introduction

Wild Bill Hickok liked to tell stories, and one day in Springfield at the end of the Civil War he told Lt. Col. George Ward Nichols a whopper as big as Missouri. What Hickok left out, his friends added and embellished. Nichols scribbled all of it down in the diary he had carried with him during William Tecumseh Sherman's March to the Sea through Georgia the previous autumn. The fantasy the colonel concocted appeared in a national magazine some seventeen months later, making Wild Bill so famous as a gunfighter that some men wanted to kill him. Nine years later, one man did. Almost a century and a half later, we're still telling tales about Wild Bill—imagining him all over again—and we still don't know who he really was or what we want him to be.

Historical records on Western characters such as Hickok reveal a sharp contrast between the probable historical reality—"probable" because unassailable records are scant—and the mediated history. Barring an improbable unearthing of a lode of Wild Bill primary documents, we know as much now as we will ever know about that real, historical Hickok. The vein of Hickok lore appears to be unimaginably deep and rich, however. He remains instantly and universally recognized, not so much for what he did as for what has been presented about him.

Our purpose is not to find a misunderstood James Butler Hickok or add much new information about his enigmatic life story. Rather, we must explain how his story was imagined and interpreted, primarily by journalists, especially those doubling as novelists, screenwriters, biographers, and historians. Our interest is more in the legend than in the man, the mythic nimbus projected by the media and not the cold-eyed countenance staring from the many striking photographs of Wild Bill. We consider historiography as much as history, mythobiography as much as biography, and secondary as well as primary sources. Those secondary sources immerse Hickok history in the brine of popular culture.

Hickok lived, mostly in obscurity, from 1837 to 1876. Only in his last decade did he become a celebrity. The storytellers had to discover what his life meant to a mass audience. Imagining that story meant fitting it into a marketable frame of reference. In the fall line of history, where the documentation disappears, the cultural river keeps flowing to the churn of media and imagination below, and continues onward. Over the falls of history, more imaginative sources of information—newspapers, magazines, fiction, film, folklore, theater, poetry, and pageantry—mix with, and sometimes take over, academic history. And the farther downstream one gets, the less one realizes what has shaped the river. At the falls, history and biography stop, and myths and memories begin.

We've explored aspects of the media mythmaking process in previous books about Civil War–era figures: Sherman, John Singleton Mosby, Nathan Bedford Forrest, and George Armstrong Custer. Their paths crossed often. Mosby fought Custer in Virginia; Sherman fought Forrest in Mississippi, Tennessee, and Georgia. Sherman's aide and chronicler, Nichols, discovered Hickok, who scouted for Sherman on a Western expedition. Hickok scouted for Custer too, and Custer wrote about him. Mosby was sent to Colorado and Nebraska as a federal agent to help settle a range war involving powerful cattle barons. Hickok participated in the first widely publicized walkdown gunfight—an 1865 showdown in the town square in Springfield, Missouri—with Davis "Little Dave" Tutt. It became the prototype for walkdowns in hundreds of Western films and novels. But Forrest, the future Memphis slave trader, may have preempted him with a battle against four miscreants in Hernando, Mississippi, in 1845 when Mississippi and Tennessee defined the West.

Their reputations rose and fell with the times. Sherman, arguably a military realist who shortened the Civil War, has been linked to the German blitzkrieg campaigns, the Vietnam War, and genocidal policies toward Native Americans. Custer, a Civil War hero, disobeyed orders and sacrificed his command at the Little Bighorn, his vainglorious "Last Stand" immortalized by a beer company's lithograph displayed on the wall in hundreds of taverns. Mosby was lauded by Churchill, mythologized by Melville, despised by Custer, condemned by the press, and branded a political traitor by the South. Forrest was condemned for starting the Ku Klux Klan and praised for ending it. Denounced as the butcher of Fort Pillow, he was hailed as a military genius, praised and denounced as a Southern apologist. The equestrian statue above his grave in a Memphis park was removed in 2017. Soon thereafter, monuments and memorials were tumbling down all over.[1]

As the nation resumed its expansion, the popular press was about to make gunfighters both the agents and enemies of civilized morality. The Civil War hastened the transformation of the vast landscape beyond the Mississippi River. Out of the war came public fascination with the Wild West, itself a press invention. The frontier violence that presaged the Civil War in "Bleeding Kansas" and other Western states and territories continued after the formal ending of hostilities. The West in 1861 was a vast garrison state occupied by some ten thousand federal soldiers. By 1865, not just Native American tribes but also Mormons, Mexicans, the Emperor Maximilian and the French, and disgruntled Confederates had to be watched. Ordinary outlaws and potential troublemakers needed to be "controlled" not just by army units and militias but also by the "lawmen" of popular imagination. The gunfighter-hero was a short-lived icon of the post–Civil War West, when tensions and animosities still ran high. The war lasted about four years, but in memory, like the gunfighter and the Western, it has lasted much longer.[2]

While Hickok fought for the Union during the Civil War, he fits better within an expanded framework of the Civil War *era*. He was peripheral to the war, even in the West, but not to the era. The war created Hickok, and its aftermath provided the helium that inflated his reputation. If he didn't win the war singlehandedly, he later won the West on television, in the movies, and in popular culture. Some Western historians have claimed that Civil War histories constrain the war era geographically and chronologically. They have viewed the conflict as more continental than Eastern in scope, beginning perhaps with the annexation of Texas and the Mexican War and ending with Reconstruction in 1877, or even later. They have drawn attention to the West as central to a proper understanding of the war and its legacy. Richard Maxwell Brown, for example, posited a "Western Civil War of Incorporation" beginning about 1850 and ending about 1920 with the consolidation of federal power in the West. Elliott West's work on cultural pluralism rebranded the Civil War era as "Greater Reconstruction" (1845–77). William Pencak called "Civil War" a self-congratulatory term that fit the romance of reunion trope. It was not used widely until the twentieth century, and even then it competed with "War Between the States," the preferred term in the South. He proposed "Era of Racial Violence" (1854–77) as a more useful term. These chronologies and arguments about periodization are worth discussing, but not here, except to say that Hickok and the Wild West were products of the time and place, existing under the umbrella of that historical period spanning the whole continent and more than half a century—not just a few decades, territories, and states in midcentury.[3]

Our focus falls within the expansive literature called "historical memory," or "public memory," a scholarly inquiry inspired by sociologist Maurice

Halbwachs with his studies, beginning in 1925, of collective memory. Pierre Nora's *Realms of Memory*, in the abridged English translation in 1996, has been influential in memory studies in the United States along with Michael Kammen's *Mystic Chords of Memory: The Transformation of Tradition in American Culture* (1991). We locate our work more specifically at the intersection of Civil War memory and the memory of the West. Civil War memory has shifted over time, beginning with journalist Edward A. Pollard's *The Lost Cause: A New Southern History of the War of the Confederates*, which he claimed was "a severely just account of the War based on contemporary evidence." Revisionist studies have been published ever since, highlighted by such works Robert Penn Warren's *The Legacy of the Civil War* (1961), David W. Blight's *Race and Reunion: The Civil War and American Memory* (2001), and Caroline E. Janney's *Remembering the Civil War: Reunion and the Limits of Reconciliation* (2013).[4]

Blight claimed the Civil War had been turned into a national romance of unification, reconciliation, shared glory and sacrifice. Slavery as cause, crisis and calamity was left out. "American tragedies, after all, demand happy endings," according to Blight, who also studied the politics of history's relationship to collective memory. Blight viewed collective memory "as a set of practices and ideas embedded in a culture, which people learn to decode and convert into their identities." Janney saw less reconciliation among whites than Bright did, especially in the Southern "Lost Cause" memory of the war. She argued for the complexity of Civil War memory. Those discussions continue among Civil War historians and usually come to the forefront in the public sphere when controversies about Confederate monuments boil over in the news media.[5]

The public memory of an individual—such as Custer or Hickok—in the context of the Civil War era and its legacy has been the special focus of our work. The memory of a person, of course, is different from the memory of a time, like the Civil War, or a place, like Kansas or the West, but is shaped by both time and place. The Hickok biographers haven't had much interest in complexity, memory, or the Civil War. They address place, although not so much the way place shapes the public memory of Hickok or the way stories about Hickok helped create the "Wild West." Lacking substantial evidence, they too often have fallen back on personal recollections, tall tales, dime novels, scattered newspaper and magazine articles, and previous flawed biographies without fully interpreting the process and politics of myth creation and the popular culture that reimagines Hickok's legacy and keeps it alive as part of the collective memory.

Especially relevant to our study is Matthew Christopher Hulbert's *The Ghosts of Guerrilla Memory: How Civil War Bushwhackers Became Gunslingers in the American West*. Hulbert drew attention to guerrilla warfare along the Kansas-Missouri borderlands and explained how bushwhackers and robbers such as Jesse James were "stripped of their Confederate context," removed from their outlaw past, and refitted for the Wild West. Together with other Western figures on the margins of the war, including Hickok, who fought against the bushwhackers, the border men became "gunslingers and cowboys in American popular culture and historical consciousness" and were elevated into heroic or mythic figures. As Hulbert looked for Civil War guerrillas in Missouri and Kansas, he did not traipse along the familiar roadways but ventured into the recesses of public imagination and recollection, which he found in sites of memory and popular culture.[6]

Mass media scholars, too, have been active in memory research. Janice Hume summarized this research, including ours, in "Memory Matters: The Evolution of Scholarship in Collective Memory and Mass Communication," published in 2010. Our work draws upon this research thread—which we believe has been neglected by most historians of memory—but makes some distinctions. The primary purpose of popular media has always been to sell, not memorialize. As a result, these outlets have a legitimate claim to helping create memory, if by no other measure than simply having access to a vast audience and being the culture's eyes and ears. These materials were written for a wide, popular audience, and so they must be congruent with the popular imagination in order to create public memory, which becomes mixed up with marketing. For example, fans of the 1950s television show *The Adventures of Wild Bill Hickok* were likely to remember that the show was sponsored by Kellogg's Sugar Pops. We draw on the work of film, literary, and popular culture scholars to assess the multitude of Hickok-inspired movies, television, and radio shows and novels that have entertained audiences for well over a century.[7]

This media approach has also been of interest to scholars of cognition who examine the interface between technology and memory in a variety of fields. "Where does the spectator end and the screened media event begin? What are the boundaries?" asked D. W. Pasulka. "It's as if our imaginations have become exterior to ourselves, existing out there in our media, and our media then determines what is in our heads." Several of the sources we cite discovered and then imagined Hickok through the movies. What the public knows about Hickok, the Wild West, and the Civil War likewise comes from that exterior imagination, an archive of images that merge into memory. Closely related to collective memory and cognition studies is an expanding body of work on mythology in journalism and mass media that gained momentum in the 1950s with studies by Roland Barthes and Marshall McLuhan.[8]

Enough hokum has been written about Hickok to humble the relatively few historians and biographers who have ventured to parse the man from the malarkey. Their work was not easy because the public had been sold a fantastic story that was far more appealing than reality. Journalism and elite fiction, too, sometimes got lost in the literary landscape, just as settlers, soldiers, travelers, and facts were swallowed up in the expanse of territory. "The air of fiction and romance that surrounds Wild Bill is so rich that even the authenticated facts about him do not seem credible," observed Kent Ladd Steckmesser. Hickok, unlike Custer or Sherman, was mytho-historic before he *was* a myth, which is to say that his myth *preceded* what little history and biography could make of his life. He had to live up to a grandiose myth he didn't intentionally create, and it may have been the myth that killed him in 1876 in now-storied Deadwood.[9]

At the center of this myth and our investigation is the journalist—doughty, courageous, benighted, maligned, and making a living in whatever medium offered financial rewards, an unintentional worker in the salt mines of memory. Hickok came along well before the inchoate press had any pretension of objectivity, responsibility, or professionalism, or even much separation from the fictive landscape of the novelist. Journalists told stories in whatever medium would pay them a wage or a royalty. If newspapers and magazines gave writers an audience, and publishers compensated them with a fair share of advertising and circulation revenue for their labors, then journalists found stories to sell. If the press wasn't buying or paying enough for fact-inspired content, the scribblers embellished their stories for the fiction market. The better the story, the easier it was to enlarge and peddle to willing publishers. Later media workers sought other platforms for their work.

Along with the outlaws and outliers, the runaway Western mythology needed to be rounded up and collared. The press was there to do the job. Newspaper and magazine journalists, many of whom had covered the Civil War, reported fact-inspired accounts of frontier shootouts and then embellished stories for the dime-novel industry, largely an East Coast enterprise geared to a mass market of all ages and class strata. Soon the accounts became interchangeable. Dime novels brought the West to the East—not the West of endless grasslands, arid summers, and painfully cold winters endured by people huddling in sod houses, but a West of gunfighters, grizzlies, and galloping horses. The West was slowly civilized—at literary pen point—in penny papers and dime novels well before the patina of civility became reality.

Hickok was a prototype of the dime-novel Western gunfighter, a some-time-lawman, gambler, scout, spy, dandy, and showman whose legend lived in tall tales and outright falsehoods. His myth needed the West and a tradition of violence, but perhaps even more it needed the East, where publishers thrived on crime, cowboys, bloodshed, and romance. Hickok was good on all counts. He was a legend not so much for his few exploits as for his image. For the press, Hickok was a good story, a Civil War hero, a gun-slinging gambler cleaning up the cow towns, administering justice, and supposedly romancing an idealized woman of the West, Martha "Calamity Jane" Canary, a virago who was anything but the ideal of nineteenth-century womanhood. Publishers knew how to deal with Wild Bill—embrace and enhance. But the culture didn't yet know what to do with the outlaws and social outcasts who fled west. In 1876 and for subsequent generations, Hickok's postmortem recreation into an icon of the West helped keep alive the national myths. Hickok was nearly inconsequential in terms of how he personally affected the West, but he was monumental as a figure central to its myth.

As a tale of heroism and tragedy, Hickok's story served many masters. Facticity was not one of them. Consistent themes pile up around Hickok to fertilize the myth. There are also some great anecdotes—that he had killed the brother of the man who shot him, that he was trained in the ministry, or that he secretly married Calamity Jane. Among the most common errors are the number of men he killed (hundreds), his exaggerated shooting power (miraculous), details of his assassination (so-called, and not a homicide), his survival of numerous and egregious gunshots (a "superman"), the origins of his nickname (malleable), and the details of particular fights (spectacular).

As the postwar culture violated the landscape with railroads, logging, and mining, it did violence to people and ravaged the ideal of an American Eden with popular entertainment. The culture that moved west was already versed in bloodshed. One lesson of the Civil War was that violence solved the problems of secession and slavery, ending the institution if not the blight of racism. When the reunited nation faced other issues after the war—Native Americans and predatory outlaws impeding the settlement of the West; striking workers and anarchists confronting the empire-building industrial base—it had the solution at hand: men with guns. Also available was the vehicle for communicating the effectiveness and morality of such a solution: newspapers, magazines, and dime novels. Popular entertainment, such as *Buffalo Bill's*

Wild West, raised gunplay to an art form, coloring it with drama, purpose, and artisanship—the fast-draw artist and the sharpshooter.[10]

From the dusty streets of a cow town to the digitized mixed reality of modern America, violence became the fast track to fame. It is a staple of prime-time television and blockbuster cinema. One can become a celebrity via slaughter. Faux condemnation often met real-life killings, as evidenced by thousands of online viewings. Hypocritically, audiences and news media denounce the act, but "share" it and headline it. In making the actor a celebrity, the act is celebrated. Wild Bill and other gunfighters were glorified as mass entertainment. Such a carnival of bloodletting became a staple of mid-nineteenth-century publishing, when dime novels and penny papers found an eager audience for such tales, and lasted into the twentieth and twenty-first centuries, when cinema, television, and new media thrived and continue to thrive on violence. From its beginning, the World Wide Web was compared to the Wild West, a ubiquitous metaphor.

Hickok only sporadically brought some temporary order to Western outposts, such as Abilene, while attempting to profit from disorder and lack of regulation when it suited him, as in Deadwood. What eventually brought order to the West was not the rogue gunfighter but cultivation, government intervention, communication and transportation systems, economic necessity, and community initiative, which sometimes included vigilantism. The public conception of the Wild West, however, owed more to the celebrity culture that made heroes and pariahs out of outlaws, lawmen, explorers, inventors, entrepreneurs, politicians, and prophets than it did to the broader cultural, demographic, regulatory, and economic forces transforming the landscape.[11]

Pure celebrity, cheekily defined by Washington *Post* writer Bob Thompson as "widespread public recognition in the absence of significant accomplishment," was around long before Hickok. Historians point to frontiersmen Daniel Boone and Davy Crockett as among the first American celebrities whipped up by newspapers. James Kirke Paulding wrote a play inspired by newspaper stories about Crockett's antics. James H. Hackett produced and acted in the play *The Lion of the West* in New York in 1831, then took it on the road. The play was an inspired parody of tall tales spun by and about the Tennessee congressman, and it garnered international success. Crockett became even more famous with the publication of an unauthorized biography in 1833 and by his death defending the Alamo in 1836, a year before Hickok was born. No Western character had a longer or more storied media afterlife.[12]

Hickok was quite different. Crockett, too, supposedly had fantastic shooting and bear-fighting abilities, but he was not remembered for improbable fast-draw kill totals. Crockett liked being famous. Hickok had cause to regret his celebrity. Hickok was murdered. Crockett was a martyr. His violence was the violence of the "wild frontier." Despite this, Crockett was initially reluctant to fight in the Creek War and thought of himself as peaceable. Wild Bill came out of the Civil War and found himself among the seminal characters in American celebrity violence. His story was rooted in the imagined Wild West, a make-believe frontier drawn from writers' imaginations and aimed at audience fantasies at the cusp of modernity and beyond. This was where the story was simplest and most appealing. It was also the place where movie plots and TV series found ready-made material, simple story lines initially unencumbered by nuance. During the 1960s the Marx Toy Company, responding to the popularity of television Westerns, introduced a line of action figures in its Best of the West series. Hickok, although more of an ambiguous presence in history, warranted a white-hatted action figure along with Custer, Buffalo Bill, and Wyatt Earp. Jesse James and Billy the Kid got black hats that bleached white over time as their reputations shifted.[13]

When author Wallace Stegner peeled back the layers of the Western story, he found it was not the six-gun or mobility that defined the region, but aridity. People of the West, especially those out beyond the 100th meridian, were mobile because of aridity. Another kind of aridity has guided perception not just of the West but also of American society—an aridity of the soul. Hickok was a good example of such moral aridity, although he sometimes was a critical and bloody civilizing force. Popular culture made Wild Bill iconic and heroic even when he stood atop a steep slope littered with the talus and scree of raw violence. He was not alone. The cultural attraction to the stories of such "misunderstood" characters as the psychopathic Billy the Kid exemplified the embrace of violence. Actors Paul Newman and Robert Redford made outlaws Butch Cassidy and Harry Longabaugh into lovable mischief-makers in a 1969 movie. Antisocial lawlessness became a virtue, not just in the West but also in modern America, as the society eagerly followed the stories of individuals who committed crimes, became survivalists, and evaded authority in the wilderness. It was the mythic rebel spirit brought to life, independent from and in defiance of authority. For his part, Hickok was a rebel but no Rebel. His defiance didn't extend to political rebellion.[14]

The problem for writers trying to sort out fact from fiction has been that, as journalist and historian Christopher Knowlton pointed out in a review of a recent Hickok biography, "freed from their mythification, these jackalope-like gunslingers emerge for the most part—Bat Masterson being the exception—as shiftless, talentless young men with poor educations and lousy career prospects, whose scruffy, Hobbesian lives play out exactly as you might expect." Hickok personified pragmatic violence, which, like moral war, was bloody but purposeful. Ironically, such icons of violence and advances in technology—the gun—eventually civilized Western communities in the public mind, making them fit for habitation and democracy. So gunmen made the region civil, curing lawlessness with bloodletting, effectively stemming violence with firearms. The antisocial folk hero was necessary, and was cast in the mold of the loner who meted out justice.[15]

When journalists took control of Hickok's life and legacy, they never let go. Like the West, the story was largely empty, a wild landscape with a lot of space to fill, and a receptive audience. Hickok's life was one of aimlessness until the journalists imposed a certain order. By giving Hickok a largely false identity he could live into, the press created narrative boundaries, giving him and his story some consistency and direction when he became a lawman. That made him more than just a gunman, an agent of justice and order, a paragon of manliness, a paladin of individual freedom. His badge made his gambling, drinking, debauchery, and wanderings just elements in a story that could fit formulas or adapt to new narrative possibilities.

Hickok's story has been told many times. The first wave of biographies cast Hickok as more legend than man. Then came Joseph G. Rosa, Hickok's most comprehensive biographer, who was relentless in correcting previous errors and digging up what additional facts could be verified about Hickok's life. The result was *They Called Him Wild Bill: The Life and Adventures of James Butler Hickok*, first published in 1964. Rosa claimed that Hickok emerged "as a man and *not* a legend." Without the legend, however, the man would have vanished from public memory, not Wild Bill but just J. B. Hickok, teamster, scout, and card player. His life might have been longer but of no particular interest to the public.[16]

That legend, like a parable, allegory, drama, or myth, resonated with something an audience recognized. It was a satisfying story, facilitated by elements of suspense, irony, tragedy, heroism, sacrifice, aspiration, defeat, success, conflict, struggle, purpose, and levity. A story, E. M. Forster said in a famous 1927 lecture at Cambridge, only has one merit: "making the audience want to know what happens next. And conversely it can only have one fault: that of making the audience not want to know what happens next." The art of telling such a story and making it stick is the work of the imaginer. Imagining does not necessarily mean making something up. Rather, it means assembling elements in a powerful narrative form.[17]

The downtown history museum in Springfield, Missouri, a site of public memory, features a 360-degree painting of the square. Based on old photographs and drawings, the painting reveals what Springfield looked like in 1865. Visitors may enter an oval room overlooking the modern square. Within this immersive exhibit, they can fire a replica of the gun Hickok used in the fight with Davis Tutt. They can try to make the shot Hickok made, but without the bullet, the blood splatter, the taking of a life, or the murder trial. "We would never want to shoot at a person, so the figure of Tutt in the painting will fade to a target," a museum official said. The visitors keep coming to this Wild West, where they may partake of a violent story, one killing after another, a story that shows we are not yet done with Wild Bill Hickok.[18]

In chapter 1, we take a brief look at Hickok's life. We've left out most of the bear fights, stunts, massacres, shooting displays, spying missions, stabbings, winking horses, escapes, romances, and exhumations—or anything for which there is attenuated evidence, scant probability, or solely prurient interest. Chapter 2 examines Hickok in the press and puts the press in context. Chapter 3 explores the dime-novel industry that took over where the press left off, sending Hickok's story east. Chapter 4 examines the other side of biography—fiction and literature, all the stories from Hickok's life, factual or not, reimagined as entertainment, and so labeled. Chapter 5 carries the stories over to the movies, and chapter 6 continues with radio and television. In chapter 7 we track the "Hickok Hunters" who have followed the story—and changed it—to Deadwood. In chapter 8 we offer conclusions. In an epilogue, we assess the biographies and histories that have been written about Hickok and examine his place in the history of the West.

1. ❧ Strange Ripples: A Brief Life Story

> It was some strange ripples they got when God dropped Bill Hickok
> into the pond.
>
> —Pete Dexter, *Deadwood*, 1986

Even the generally accepted date of James Butler Hickok's birth, May 27, 1837, is disputed due to a missing page in a family Bible and rival claims by relatives. Throughout his life, there was confusion about the correct spelling of his surname, and, later, he was more commonly known by a name he was not given at birth. Just how he acquired that sobriquet is also in doubt. Hickok was born in Homer, Illinois, which still exists in La Salle County, but its name also was changed, to Troy Grove, around the time the Civil War began. Not even Hickok's gravesite in Deadwood stayed put.

Hickok's paternal forebears came from England in 1635, first settling in Connecticut. His parents were from Vermont and New York. La Salle County was settled primarily by New Englanders in 1832 after the Black Hawk War, many of whom were abolitionists. They found fertile land drained by the Illinois River and its tributaries that was slightly higher than the surrounding prairie. The Hickoks arrived in 1836, operating a store in the Green Mountain House and, later, a farm near the Little Vermilion River. The Illinois and Michigan Canal passed through the county, spurring commerce along its towpaths. The family home was a sanctuary along the route of the Underground Railroad.[1]

The abolition movement, the Civil War, Reconstruction, and Western settlement circumscribed Hickok's life. He came of age in the middle of a frontier state described as "the fractured Union in a mirror: divided in its allegiance, north and south, by its own sectional slant." Slavery in the territory wasn't officially abolished until 1848, although full emancipation did not occur until the middle of the Civil War. On November 7, 1837, a mob murdered Elijah P. Lovejoy, the abolitionist editor of the Alton, Illinois, *Observer*. In response to this and other outbreaks of "wild and furious passion,"

Abraham Lincoln, recently elected to the Illinois House of Representatives, urged "reverence for the Constitution and law" and denounced "mobocratic spirit." In 1851, Lincoln tried a case before the Illinois Supreme Court in La Salle County. An opposing attorney was Stephen A. Douglas, who later led the fight to repeal the Missouri Compromise through the 1854 Kansas-Nebraska Act. On August 21, 1858, Lincoln was back in the county for the first of the Lincoln-Douglas Debates.[2]

Hickok had grown up on the frontier in the vortex of the coming storm. He was born a Union man, and he died a Union man. His parents, William and Polly, had taken risks to help escaping slaves, many of whom were aided by nearby Quaker settlements. Runaway slaves crossed the Mississippi River to Quincy, Illinois, and moved through western Illinois to Mendota in La Salle County. From Troy Grove, the fugitives followed a stagecoach route about forty-five miles north along Kilbuck Creek to Lindenwood, Illinois. Slaves were quartered in a dry earthen cellar hidden beneath the floorboards of the Hickok home. Bounty hunters, kidnappers, and marshals roamed the county looking for fugitives. Family stories told of narrow escapes, times when James and his father eluded bounty hunters by whipping their team down backcountry roads at night while slaves cowered in the bed of a wagon.[3]

Hickok's legendary facility with guns came early, not unusual for a frontier lad. He purchased his first weapons in the late 1840s with earnings from farm labor and often practiced firing them in the woods. Nothing is known about the type of guns he used, although biographer William E. Connelley stated, without sources, that they were "a good rifle and a Colt's revolving pistol" and that Hickok became "the best shot in his part of Illinois." Biographer Richard O'Connor added that Illinois was "the cradle of the West's top guns. Wyatt Earp and Bat Masterson, among others. . . ." That odd factoid, unlikely to usurp "Land of Lincoln" as the state slogan, would seem to enhance Hickok's marksmanship by putting him in fast company, although later research has determined that Masterson was born in Quebec. Biographer Joseph Rosa just claimed Hickok had "an inborn fondness for handguns." Rosa sensed a "desire for loneliness" on Hickok's part and a self-confidence that grew out of this love of weapons. The description too easily fits the myth of the lonesome gunfighter, so beloved by Western storytellers and mythmakers.[4]

Hickok's father died in 1852, and for several years James helped to run the family farm and worked as a towpath driver. By June 1856, Hickok had lit out for the Kansas Territory by way of St. Louis. Ten miles north of the city, the Mississippi meets the Missouri, the continent's longest river, spilling from the northern Rockies and tumbling across the dry prairies. Hickok made his way upriver to Fort Leavenworth, which, even now, "symbolizes the frontier," in the words of journalist Robert Kaplan. "As the most important fort in the West, the place from which the first group of white settlers moved into Indian country, it was the starting point for what would one day be called Manifest Destiny," close to where the Oregon and Santa Fe Trails separated, and the staging point for the transcontinental railroad. The territory was in turmoil with competing pro-slavery and free-state legislators raising militias supported by outside forces. On May 21, 1856, pro-slavery forces had burned and looted businesses and the putative free-state governor's residence in Lawrence. John Brown, several of his sons, and a few other men retaliated by killing five pro-slavery settlers at Pottawatomie Creek. Hickok possibly became involved with the free-state Jayhawkers as sectional rivalries erupted into civil war, and a degree of order was not restored until the intervention of federal troops.[5]

In 1858, Hickok ran a farm and served as a constable for the town of Monticello. Later in the year he began driving for Russell, Majors, and Waddell, the freight and passenger transportation company that initiated the Pony Express mail service in April 1860 and closed it down just nineteen months later. The service lost money and was rendered obsolete by the transcontinental telegraph. Like Hickok, the Pony Express looms large in Western mythology, well out of proportion to its significance. The company famously advertised for fearless bantam orphans able to race ponies over sixty-mile segments through Indian country, shrinking the travel time from Missouri to California. The brawny Hickok, however, primarily was a long-haul stagecoach driver.[6]

A Seedling of Truth

In late 1860 or early 1861, Hickok suffered some type of injury that caused the company to assign him to less strenuous labor at Rock Creek Station, located in the Nebraska Territory along the Oregon Trail. Word got around that a bear, the favorite tall-tale opponent of any aspiring frontier hero, had mauled Hickok in Raton Pass, New Mexico Territory. At Rock Creek he was party to a notorious quarrel that left three men dead and shaped his reputation as a gunfighter, although just what happened is conjecture.[7]

The trouble started when David McCanles, formerly a North Carolina sheriff, acquired the Rock Creek property and leased it to the stage company, which then made a deal to purchase the station. Horace Wellman was appointed superintendent of Rock Creek Station before running afoul of

McCanles, who demanded payments on the lease and purchase. There was additional trouble with Wellman's father-in-law, who may have stolen some equipment from McCanles.

McCanles also had friction with Hickok, who had arrived in March and worked around the station as an assistant stock tender. On July 1, Hickok became acting superintendent of the station in Wellman's absence and probably had a relationship with Sarah Shull, who had accompanied McCanles to the Nebraska Territory from North Carolina. McCanles's common-law wife objected to Shull's presence near the station, and McCanles warned Hickok not to see her.

Wellman returned on July 11, and tensions escalated the next day when McCanles, his cousin James Woods, McCanles's twelve-year-old son William Monroe, and James Gordon, an employee, confronted Wellman at his home. Several accounts claim that Hickok hid behind a curtain and fatally shot McCanles at the door, then shot Woods, who was clubbed to death by Wellman or Mrs. Wellman. Someone shot Gordon, who was chased about four hundred yards down a creek by four men, including Hickok, one of whom blasted Gordon with a shotgun. William Monroe fled and, in the 1920s, gave several versions of what happened.

Returning to the station, Hickok encountered Joe Baker, who protested that he no longer worked for McCanles. Hickok clubbed him anyway with the barrel of his pistol. Although it is not clear that the victims were even armed, the killers were tried and acquitted. Hickok soon left Nebraska and returned to Kansas. Later stories spread by Lt. Col. George Ward Nichols and others claimed that McCanles was the leader of a gang that supported the Confederacy. "Out of this seedling of truth grew the legend of a 'massacre at Rock Creek Station,' which was the foundation of the picturesque fable that represents Hickok's life to most people," O'Connor concluded.[8]

Hickok's role in the Civil War is murky and often fantastic, based less on facts and more on stories told by Hickok, early biographers, journalists, and dime novelists. Because his duties primarily included scouting, spying, sharpshooting, and driving wagons, documents are scarce and stories prone to invention and exaggeration. Once established, information gaffes become indelible as well as important in establishing Hickok as an American myth. The facts might not have been enough. One later writer accepted stories that Hickok may have killed one hundred men in the war because it would be hard to prove that he did not, given his clandestine movements. Accordingly, his war service "added laurels to his reputation" and inflated his heroism.[9]

Hickok's first service probably came as a scout with Brig. Gen. Nathaniel Lyon's "Army of the West" in Missouri. Lyon's fifty-six hundred Union troops moved out of Springfield and, on the morning of August 10, 1861, attacked more than fifteen thousand Confederate forces under Maj. Gen. Sterling Price and Brig. Gen. Benjamin McCulloch at Wilson's Creek, some fifteen miles from the town. Lyon was killed; Union forces retreated and finally withdrew from Springfield. Hickok came under artillery fire while skirmishing during the early stages of the fighting. He may also have done some sharpshooting as the battle unfolded.[10]

By the end of October, Hickok was driving army supply wagons in and around Sedalia and Rolla, Missouri, for quartermasters. He continued driving at least through the next summer, hauling some loads into northwestern Arkansas for advancing troops. This was precarious work because slow-moving, supply-laden military wagon trains could be shot up, captured, or burned by Confederate cavalry. Some reports claim that Rebel forces captured a wagon train Hickok was leading from Fort Leavenworth, Kansas, to Sedalia, Missouri, in the spring of 1862. Hickok said he escaped after a gun battle and made it to Independence, Missouri. While there, he stopped a mob from killing a friend who ran a saloon. A woman supposedly shouted "Good for you, Wild Bill," during the incident. The name stuck, as did the story, which like most everything else associated with Hickok had multiple versions. Another claim was that Hickok rounded up some soldiers from Kansas City, recaptured the wagons, and eventually made it to Rolla. He continued to work as a wagon driver until September 1862.[11]

Hickok was employed by Brig. Gen. Samuel R. Curtis, the commander of the newly created Army of the Southwest, to help scout Confederate positions in southwest Missouri and northwest Arkansas. Stories had Hickok spying in Yellville, Arkansas, in 1861. In January 1862 Curtis assembled a team of scouts, some disguised in Confederate uniforms, to reconnoiter Rebel territory. Hickok assumed leadership in some of the probes and wore a captain's uniform. Tales of Hickok's exploits circulated, including escapes, ambushes, the capture of important dispatches, and gun battles with pursuing soldiers. Whatever the truth of these excursions, Curtis moved toward Springfield on February 7 while Price and McCulloch retreated into Arkansas to regroup under the command of Maj. Gen. Earl Van Dorn south of Fayetteville. On March 7 Van Dorn led some eighteen thousand Confederates to envelop Curtis's eleven thousand Federals at a plateau called Pea Ridge about ten miles northeast of Bentonville. After two days of fighting, the Federals drove the Confederates from the field. If Hickok was at the Battle of Pea Ridge, he joined in one of the Civil War's major Western fights. According to the prolific and highly imaginative Illinois-born journalist and Hickok biographer J. W. Buel, Hickok killed thirty-five men while sniping from a single position behind a log in Cross Timbers Hollow. Buel also implausibly claimed that Hickok shot and mortally wounded McCulloch from a distance of more than two miles.[12]

In March 1864 Hickok worked briefly as a special policeman and detective in Springfield under the authority of the provost marshal. In April, Capt. Richard Bentley Owen, an assistant post quartermaster, hired Hickok as a scout. He may have spied on Price's Confederates by joining their ranks as they advanced into Missouri from Princeton, Arkansas, bound for St. Louis and Illinois. Before the incursion was checked by Curtis and Maj. Gen. Alfred Pleasonton at Westport (now part of Kansas City), Missouri, on October 23, Confederates were said to have recognized Hickok, who slipped away and reached Union lines. The battle was the last major combat west of the Mississippi. Some twenty-eight thousand troops were engaged.[13]

During the remainder of the war, Hickok continued scouting Confederate positions. From Cassville, Missouri, Hickok reported to Brig. Gen. John B. Sanborn in Springfield on February 10, 1865, that he found no more than a dozen Rebels in any squad he saw during a frigid ride to Camp Walker, Arkansas, and Spavinaw Creek in Indian Territory. Sanborn suggested he go to Yellville, locate Confederate colonel Archibald S. Dobbins's cavalry, and return to Springfield. No more was heard from Hickok until the end of the war, when a teamster claimed he spotted him riding by a supply train approaching Fort Zarah, near present day Great Bend, Kansas, and hollering "Lee's surrendered! Lee's surrendered!"[14]

Shootout in Springfield

Hickok stayed in Springfield in 1865 and spent much of the summer gambling. Discharged soldiers had money to spend, so a man who knew his cards could profit from the heedless assurance of the callow gambler. New army recruits in the smaller postwar army were rowdy, undisciplined, and eager to make their fortune in the West. William F. "Buffalo Bill" Cody, in his suspect autobiography, claimed he watched Hickok playing cards in Springfield. Although Hickok appeared "sleepy and inattentive," according to Cody, he eyed his companions warily and appropriated the pot after drawing his gun and pointing it at a crooked gambler who had been slipping cards into his hat.[15]

During his sojourn in Springfield, Hickok killed Davis "Little Dave" Tutt, whom he likely met in Yellville during the war. Hickok may have had a relationship with Tutt's sister, and Tutt may have been Hickok's rival for the affections of another woman, Susannah Moore. A dispute arose over a gambling debt, and Tutt took Hickok's watch for security. Hickok warned Tutt not to show up on the streets with the watch, but they met on the public square on the evening of July 21. Shots were exchanged and Tutt, who was wearing a linen duster that may have compromised his dexterity with his pistol, fell to the ground, mortally wounded. The distance between the contestants was in dispute—fifteen paces, fifty yards, one hundred yards—depending on sources. Hickok was arrested two days later, charged with manslaughter, tried, and acquitted. Twenty-two witnesses testified during the three-day trial. The judge, C. B. M'Afee, had commanded the army post at Springfield during the war. The case turned on M'Afee's instructions to the jury. If Hickok used all reasonable means to avoid the fight, he could be acquitted. That was the law. But frontier law, or the unwritten "Code of the West," said Hickok was right to stand his ground if he knew that Tutt was aggressive and dangerous, had made previous threats, and was advancing on Hickok with his gun drawn. The jurors believed it was a fair fight.[16]

The Springfield, Missouri, *Weekly Patriot* took exception, blaming witnesses who "failed to express the horror and disgust they felt, not from indifference, but from fear and timidity." This template image of a passive citizenry watching the "walkdown" in the street has been reprised in numerous classic film sequences and television episodes. The killing of Tutt remained controversial, fanned by an out-of-town writer's fascination with Wild Bill.[17]

On or about September 11, 1865, and just weeks after the Tutt trial, Hickok awaited the results of the election for Springfield marshal, for which he was a candidate. However, he fell short of the first-place finisher by forty-four votes. He had the second highest total among five candidates, and the notoriety of the shooting and trial may have cost Hickok the job. The defeat coincided with a far more important event in Hickok's life, for he was about to meet George Ward Nichols. The thirty-four-year-old army lieutenant colonel, journalist, and novelist was in Springfield with Maj. Gen. Andrew Jackson Smith, who had commanded the Sixteenth Corps that surprised and defeated Nathan Bedford Forrest at the Battle of Tupelo a year earlier. Nichols interviewed Hickok and wrote a sensational article about him that was published in *Harper's New Monthly Magazine* in 1867. The article made Hickok famous.

Early in 1866, Richard Bentley Owen brought Hickok to Fort Riley, Kansas, as a deputy U.S. marshal to help round up government horses and mules, as well as a few deserters who had wandered off. The fort was soon to be reached by the Union Pacific Railroad, and it would also serve as the home of the Seventh Cavalry, a newly formed regiment under George Armstrong Custer. Before he met Custer, however, Hickok met William Tecumseh Sherman, who hired him as a guide. Sherman arrived at Fort Riley in May on his way to Omaha, Nebraska, and then St. Paul, Minnesota. Hickok accompanied Sherman's party as far as Omaha and then returned to Fort Riley. He continued scouting with the Seventh Cavalry at least through July 1867. During this time, he recommended Cody for a scouting job. Meanwhile, Hickok quickly was becoming one of the most famous gunfighters in the West as copies of Nichols's article reached a national audience.[18]

Murder, Lust, and Highway Robbery

The war left deep scars in the West, especially in the border states. Nichols claimed in the *Harper's* article that in September 1865 tranquility had come to the Southern states east of the Mississippi. He said that people living in Georgia and the Carolinas welcomed the restoration of order "and it would have been safe for a Union officer to have ridden unattended through the land." In southwestern Missouri, however, there were "old scores to be settled." Historian Thomas Spencer said the Civil War had created a "culture of violence in southwest Missouri for the remainder of the nineteenth century." The Regulators, also known as the Honest Men's League, was a vigilante group active in Springfield and the Missouri Ozarks in 1865 before formally organizing in 1866. On June 1, 1866, some 280 Regulators rode into Springfield. This show of force was not meant to deter ex-Confederates, some of whom were among the Regulators, but bandits, bushwhackers, horse thieves, outlaws, and "hard characters" taking advantage of the breakdown in order regardless of their wartime affiliation. Nichols said that Smith had told him in Springfield that some four thousand former Confederates had been shot or hanged by the Regulators, an absurdly high figure that just showed the multiplier effect of vigilante actions. Historian Richard Maxwell Brown estimated that about half of all vigilante groups killed no more than four people, and such was the total claimed by the Regulators in Greene and Christian Counties by June. A less violent pro-Union group called the law-and-order committee had also formed, and Nichols identified Hickok with this group. The law-and-order men and the Regulators were most likely to divide between Republicans and Radical Republicans, rather than between Republicans and Democrats.[19]

Party affiliations elsewhere generally ran along former battle lines, with Confederates and Southern sympathizers identifying with the Democratic Party. The Texas outlaw John Wesley Hardin, for example, was a Democrat. In extreme cases, war resistance by former Confederates evolved into outright antigovernment banditry against the politicians, merchants, railroad and mining interests, banks, land barons, and express companies who had persecuted them after the war, entities who were often backed by the dreaded Pinkerton detectives. Jesse and Frank James, who had fought with William Quantrill's Raiders in Missouri, claimed that Union soldiers had killed their brother and shelled their family home after the war.[20]

In July 1869, Hickok took office as sheriff of Ellis County, Kansas. Hays City needed a law-and-order man, given that the main businesses were saloon-keeping, prostitution, and gambling. The cow town had twenty-two saloons and one grocery. The town's proximity to Fort Hays added more strife. In general, the presence of army posts throughout the region exacerbated tensions, especially when former adversaries mingled in saloons. Hickok was thought to be the man for the job, having served as deputy U.S. marshal and army scout, and was appointed on August 23. He commonly quieted unruly cowboys by clubbing them with a gun rather than shooting them. But he did shoot two men as town marshal and county sheriff.

Though good at keeping the peace without subtlety, Hickok lost an election and left town. He spent time in Topeka, but a brawl hastened his departure for Kansas City. Hickok went on to Jefferson City, Missouri, returned to Topeka briefly, and then came back to Hays City. On July 17, 1870, he was involved in a barroom altercation with soldiers from the Seventh Cavalry. A sergeant from Fort Hays who claimed to have witnessed the incident said that Pvt. Jeremiah Lonergan and Pvt. John Kile were in the town without permission. Lonergan grabbed Hickok from behind and wrestled him to the floor. Kile rammed the muzzle of his pistol against Hickok's head and squeezed the trigger but the gun misfired. Hickok pulled out one of his own pistols and shot Kile and Lonergan. The wounded Lonergan fled, and Kile died the next day. The Junction City, Kansas, *Weekly Union* reported that after the shooting, Hickok "made for the prairie and has not been heard of since."[21]

After some appearances in circuses and Western shows, Hickok made his way to Abilene, a rowdy cattle town located at the northern end of the Chisholm Trail. The city was named after a biblical region traditionally held to be the burial place of Abel, victim of the first murder. Hickok became the town marshal on April 15, 1871. That year six hundred thousand cattle were driven up the trail from Texas across Indian Territory to be shipped from the Kansas Pacific Railroad terminal in Abilene to meatpacking centers in Kansas City and Chicago. "It was the point where the north-and-south cattle trail intersected the east-and-west railroad. Abilene was more than a point," according to historian Walter Prescott Webb. "It is a symbol. It stands for all that happened when the two civilizations met for conflict, for disorder, for the clashing of great currents which carry on their crest the turbulent and disorderly elements of both civilizations—in this case the rough characters of the plain and of the forest." As each herd of longhorns clambered into Abilene, the town's seventeen saloons, twelve dance halls, and six hotels welcomed another dozen droughty drovers, cowboys, horse wranglers, chuck-wagon drivers, and camp cooks, all ready to let off steam after a journey of more than a thousand miles.[22]

In the years immediately after the Civil War, the *Western News* in Detroit, Kansas, reported that seventeen men were murdered in Abilene. Seven were slain "through the influence of fancy women and six were slaughtered through intemperance and drunken rows, the remaining four being murdered outright in cool hand-to-hand fights. Murder, lust, highway robbery and prostitutes run the town day and night." Abilene was like many other cow towns of the period, initially constructed to receive and transport cattle and to cater to the men who drove them. The town was dusty in dry weather and muddy when it rained, and drinking, gambling, and whoring were among the mainstays of its early economy. Abilene was the place where archetypal cowboys first came to national attention. When they came to town, it meant profits; it also meant the shattering of peace and civility to others, recalling the unhealed wounds of the recent conflict. Though violence was part of every cow town's existence, the mayhem threatened the established order and business. But it was tolerated, within limits—that's where the lawmen, such as Hickok, came in.[23]

In 1868, Kansas passed a law banning "vagrants, drunks, or former Confederate soldiers" from carrying pistols, knives, or other deadly weapons in the state. Even if unenforceable, the law made clear what the legislature thought of the former men in gray and their sons and little brothers, especially Texas cowboys who were bringing the cattle north from the former Confederate state. In Abilene, the Texans hung out at the Alamo Saloon on the south side of town, where they raised as much hell as possible at the end of the cattle drives. On June 24, the city council added its own ordinance banning firearms in the city, and Hickok was determined to enforce it.[24]

Hickok was marshal of Abilene for just under seven months. He was fired December 13, ostensibly for budgetary reasons, and more probably because of politics involving saloons, gambling dens, and brothels in the Texas end of town. He was rumored to have been pocketing kickbacks from gambling interests. Abilene, however, was in the process of becoming civilized—albeit slowly. During Hickok's time in Abilene, he met Agnes Lake, the respectable widow of a professional clown who owned and managed a traveling circus. A romance developed and eventually led to matrimony. Hickok was best known in Abilene for shooting a Texas gambler, Philip Coe, in a gunfight during which Hickok unintentionally killed a theater security guard, Mike Williams. The bouncer had rushed around a corner to assist Hickok, who was too fast on the draw. He and Hickok apparently were friends; however, Williams, a former bartender, was not a deputy, as press reports claimed.[25]

Hickok's next movements are uncertain. He may have been involved in the murder of three Indian chiefs. He may have been in Boston in 1872 to gamble and give interviews, boosting his new celebrity. He may have been in Colorado for a time, then Kansas City, then Niagara Falls, back to Kansas City, and then on to Springfield. He was seen in places he never was and was in places he was never seen. Such were the dubieties of fame. On July 27, 1873, Hickok made his first appearance with *The Scouts of the Prairie*, the forerunner of *Buffalo Bill's Wild West*. *Scouts* was a stage play adapted by Ned Buntline (Edward Judson) from dime novels he had written about the West. Hickok was not suited for the stage life, however. Cody liked having the celebrity on the playbill, but Hickok feared performing for the audience and considered show business fatuous. In March 1874 he left the show from Rochester, New York.[26]

Hickok was mentioned in newspapers in Topeka, Kansas City, and Denver as he passed through during the summer of 1874, and in September he was in Cheyenne, Wyoming Territory. It's assumed that he came to Cheyenne to try his hand at prospecting after Custer discovered gold in the Black Hills. Hickok remained in Cheyenne until the fall of 1875. Stories had begun circulating about Hickok's eye troubles, gambling, and general dissipation. In June he had been charged with vagrancy, and by November he had left the city, only to return within a few months to marry Agnes, who was there visiting friends. The couple spent a short time in Cincinnati with her family, but Wild Bill's mind was on the Black Hills, not on domesticity. He traveled to St. Louis to organize an expedition, returned to Cheyenne, and by late June departed for Deadwood with his friend Charlie Utter, along with four other men.[27]

The Other Shore

Hickok had no way of knowing as he pulled out of Cheyenne with his party's two wagons that Custer and 267 men riding with the Seventh Cavalry had been slain along the Little Bighorn River. Both Hickok and Custer would be remembered in popular culture as Indian fighters. In Custer's case, the Little Bighorn eclipsed Custer's generalship at Gettysburg and other Civil War engagements. Hickok's gunfighter reputation overshadowed his poorly documented Indian fighter narrative, but it was lodged in the Wild West mythology nonetheless. On the day Custer died at the Little Bighorn, and little more than five weeks before Hickok was murdered, the New York *Herald* commented on the irony of fighting the frontier war as the nation was celebrating its centennial. The occasion marked the nation's progress, but the "war" with the Indians seemed to draw the nation back to the past.

> The Indian, even now, is as much of a romance to us as the caliphs of the "Arabian Nights." We do not know him. We never see him. . . . We question if one in twenty, even of our educated people, could tell where the Apaches, the Utes or the Sioux inhabit. We know in a vague, half-informed way, that out in the vast expanse beyond the Mississippi there still wanders a remnant of those savage men who once ruled and dwelt there.[28]

That commentary also came on the day the *Herald*'s correspondent was killed with Custer at the Little Bighorn. For a short time, news of the disaster directed the nation's attention to the Montana Territory, the Lakota and the Cheyenne, and the continuing Indian wars.

Whenever and however the news of Custer's death reached him, Hickok may have had misgivings about his own undertaking. Before sunset on August 2 he would be dead, and two of the greatest icons of the West would have crossed to what Hickok called "the other shore." Hickok's party, composed of a man known only as "Pie," Charlie and Steve Utter, and "White-Eye" Anderson and his brother, Charlie, reached Fort Laramie on the Platte River, about ninety miles from Cheyenne. After resting, they joined a wagon train heading toward the Black Hills. Accompanying them were several prostitutes, with colorful names like Sizzling Kate, Dirty Emma, and Big Dollie. They soon took on another strange companion, a bibulous twenty-year-old who had caused trouble at the army post and in Cheyenne, where she recently had been tried and acquitted on a charge of grand larceny. She was called Calamity Jane, and her name would forever be linked to Wild Bill's, although they knew each other little more than a month. By most credible accounts, Hickok wanted nothing to do with her.[29]

The Black Hills rise from the Great Plains to a maximum elevation of more than seventy-two-hundred feet at Black Elk Peak. From a distance, they appear as a dusky streak, then slowly emerge in viridian splendor except where charred and serrated. John Ames described the hills as "a high altitude island of timber surrounded by level, barren, treeless plain." Custer's 1874 expedition to the Black Hills had triggered both a gold rush and a war uniting the Lakota Sioux and their Cheyenne allies. By 1876, the Black Hills had yielded some $2 million in gold, and eight hundred gold miners a week were coming to Deadwood Gulch to make their fortune. Supposedly, when Hickok looked toward Deadwood Gulch from the edge of the Black Hills, he had a premonition, or maybe a wish, that he would die there. High above Deadwood—one of the valley's elongated, splintery settlements, prone to floods, fire, and tornadoes—is Mount Moriah Cemetery, the lofty necropolis where Wild Bill would soon be interred after his thanatological journey, and Calamity Jane would join him there, uninvited, in 1903. Hickok and his companions arrived in town on or about July 12 after a brief stop in Custer City. A decade later, a Dakota Territory journalist said that he had seen Hickok in Custer City in 1876. He upbraided Hickok for lodging in the area with "his crew of depraved women."[30]

Determining Hickok's behavior and movements in Deadwood during the approximately three weeks he was there is a challenge for biographers. It makes a better story if Hickok truly knew his days were numbered, and what better place to die than in a place called Deadwood? He wrote a letter tinged with irony to Agnes on July 17: "I don't expect to hear from you but all the same I no my agnes [*sic*] and only live to love hur [*sic*] never mind Pet we will have a home yet then we will be so happy. . . ." Those who were in Deadwood at the time were tempted years later to remember seeing him in public, even when they didn't. Not having a Hickok story to share with interlocutors would be tantamount to having slept through a performance of *Our American Cousin* at Ford's Theater in Washington on the evening of April 14, 1865. Hickok sightings and doings multiplied over the course of twenty days and the next century and a half. Rosa noted that Hickok "would have needed a year to do all the things he is supposed to have done." There was talk that Hickok was going to be made marshal and would shut the doors of the gambling dens he so regularly frequented. Hickok may have found prospecting for gold unproductive and arduous, which may have drawn him to the card tables where he thought the chance of a quick strike was better. But they weren't better, and he lost money.[31]

On the afternoon and early evening of August 1, Hickok played cards in Nuttal and Mann's No. 10 Saloon. Earlier in the day he had written Agnes, "[I]f such should be we never meet again, while firing my last shot, I will gently breathe the name of my wife—Agnes and with wishes even for my enemies I will make the plunge and try to swim to the other shore." That evening Hickok seemed to be enjoying himself at the card table. A new player, known as John "Broken Nose Jack" McCall, joined in and fared badly, as did William Rodney Massie, a former riverboat pilot. Hickok, enriched at McCall's expense, stood him the price of supper, about seventy-five cents, and retired.[32]

Not much has been learned about the man who would end Hickok's life the next afternoon. McCall showed up in the Black Hills not long before Hickok arrived, taking the alias Bill Sutherland. Why he took an alias is unknown. It was later established that he was about twenty-five years old. Stories got around that McCall had been a rustler and a buffalo hunter, and he said that he had been a mail carrier and a miner. Soon after noon on August 2, Hickok, dressed in a Prince Albert–style frock coat, entered the No. 10, took an available chair, and joined a card game in progress. Tradition holds that Hickok always sat with his back to a wall to protect himself against being shot from behind. Such precaution might have been mere superstition or habit. Hickok may not have been unusual in wanting to protect his back and flanks in an environment where cards, wagers, liquor, and hot tempers could be combustive. Even McCall preferred sitting with his back to a wall, according to a reporter from the Cheyenne, Wyoming, *Daily Leader* who interviewed him on August 30. On August 2, however, Hickok grudgingly deferred to Charles Rich, who already had the protected position. Hickok had met the gambler in Cheyenne, and one story had Hickok helping to break up a fight after Rich had proved a bad loser. Had the favored position been as important to Hickok as legend implies, he could have left the game, or given Rich an argument. Instead, he took a chair to Rich's left, leaving himself open to an attack from behind. He could see the front door but not a smaller door to the rear. Hickok again requested that Rich switch places with him. Rich declined, joking with Hickok about his anxiety.[33]

To Hickok's left sat the saloon's proprietor, Carl Mann. Massie was seated across the round table. As the game of poker progressed, Massie was relieving

Hickok of some of Massie's losings from the previous evening. Intent on assessing his cards, Hickok took no particular notice of McCall, who had entered the saloon through the front door and made his way to the bar, edging his way behind him. Hickok's final words, as some remembered, were directed at Massie: "The old duffer—he broke me on the hand." At about 3 o'clock, McCall fired a .45 Colt revolver behind Hickok's head. Hickok jerked, remained inert for a few moments, then tumbled backward to the floor. The bullet tore through Hickok's brain, exited through Hickok's right cheek and penetrated Massie's left wrist. Massie initially thought Hickok had shot him before realizing, with the others, that Hickok was dead. Ellis T. "Doc" Peirce, a barber called to the scene to examine the body, supposedly later noted the cards Hickok had been holding. Tradition, without evidence, says that the cards were a pair of aces and a pair of eights, and either a queen or a jack, the proverbial "dead man's hand." It's unlikely anyone at the blood-and-brain splattered table, or anyone arriving at the unsecured crime scene within minutes or hours, took notice of cards, even if they had fallen in a tight and recognizable pattern instead of scattering. After-the-fact irony may gild the legend, but it's still hogwash.[34]

McCall's trial in Deadwood commenced on August 3, only one day after the shooting. The Chicago *Inter-Ocean's* report, published on August 18, depicted McCall as possessing an "animal countenance," as he apparently faced jurors and the court with "nonchalance and bravado." He was found not guilty, a result the *Black Hills Pioneer* condemned. Due to the legal technicality of Deadwood still being on land ceded to Sioux Indians more than a decade earlier, a new warrant was issued, McCall was re-arrested in Laramie City, Wyoming, re-tried, found guilty, and hanged in Yankton, Dakota Territory, on March 1, 1877.

The jury foreman for the first trial was a newspaperman, Charles Whitehead, of Kansas City, Missouri, in effect putting the press even closer to hearing evidence and passing judgment in a central episode of Hickok's myth and its place in public memory. The Kansas City *Times* correspondent apparently was reporting on the gold strikes in the Black Hills for the newspaper. He returned to Kansas City in 1877, later reporting for papers in Colorado and Wyoming before drifting again back to Kansas City.[35]

Just a year after Hickok's death, Elmer Baldwin, a former Illinois state senator, published a history of La Salle County, which had not forgotten its favorite son. Hickok, wrote Baldwin, "was more than a match for the

roughs he met on the debatable ground between civilized and savage life."
That much, with the exception of his murderer, was certain. Less certain
were the details, which drew upon myth and memory. Hickok, Baldwin
continued, "is said to have often killed his man; at one time he is said to
have killed four in sixty seconds—they were on his track seeking his life."
At least that's what they say.[36]

2. ❊ Hickok and the Press: A Durable Story

My memory tells me only of those old days as they appeared at the time and they are not being viewed as a distant era, which seems inclined to make heroes out of desperadoes.

—John Plesent Gray, 1940

Before Wild Bill charged out of the mythic West, he oozed from the pens of Eastern journalists. He was a better story than person, as often is the case with legendary figures. The West caught hold in the American imagination via the growth of mass media in the nineteenth and twentieth centuries, and spread in the nineteenth century through rail and telegraph. People and ideas moved more quickly and voluminously than they once had, if not always harmoniously. There was a lot of space to fill—both geographically and in the pages of newspapers and magazines. Burgeoning Eastern cities, paradoxically, fired a growth in the idea of a wide-open Wild West. Bigger cities meant more newspapers and magazines, larger circulations, and markets for an idea. The West and Western figures were good material, not just the tales of mountain men and gunfighters but the real West of fantastic landscapes, cross-continental railroads, and grand opportunities.[1]

The main-street shootout found its genesis in nineteenth-century newspapers and became an entertainment mainstay in post–World War II American cinema. In such Western towns as Deadwood and Abilene, nineteenth-century newspapers condemned the rowdiness and violence, and in the next century cashed in on their tourist appeal. Hickok—hired to curb the mayhem at various times and places—was part of it. The cause of disorder and presumptions about how to fix it were a natural part of social discourse in nineteenth-century America. In the press as well as the larger community, attacks on order and civil society were often attributed to "outsiders." In coastal cities, and Chicago and St. Louis, this meant immigrants, and newspapers were predictably xenophobic. In the West, the search for order assumed a similar taint, with the outsiders being outlaws, rowdy cowboys, and Indians. Gamblers, prostitutes, and saloon owners seemed to occupy a gray area. They were not "outsiders" when they were central to the economies of so many towns and territories. But neither were they the foundation for a civil, god-fearing community. This put Hickok in an odd spot with the public and in newspapers. He was a part of the incivility—a gunman, gambler, drinker, and womanizer. But he was also part of the solution, which itself might be uncivil in that it was commonly violent, perhaps fatal. His presence affirmed the existence of lawlessness, perhaps to a rampant degree. He was the promise of order, even if through bloodshed. For reporters, Hickok was central to identifying what was wrong, or uncivil, in a community. He also was an exciting narrative.[2]

A Hunger for Heroics

The public was ready for Hickok's story. Earlier tales of Boone, Crockett, and Natty Bumppo had captured the public imagination, so figures such as Cody and Hickok found a ready and receptive audience. The primitive—the frontier—has an undeniable allure in the national imagination, not just in popular entertainment but also in the intellectual air. Alexis de Tocqueville provided intellectual respectability for the general fascination with the West and the frontier, whose stock only went up more after Frederick Jackson Turner's pronouncement on its centrality to defining the American character in 1893. That allure continued to be affirmed in venues as diverse as prime-time television and academic conferences crowded with historians. In postbellum America, it was more than a growing audience and a booming publishing industry, both of which were necessary to spawning the Hickok myth. Dime novels, books, magazines, and newspapers were all feeding a hunger for Civil War heroics that made escape from the ills of the moment much easier. In this context, Hickok's war deeds were greatly exaggerated as he assumed the role—in print—of a man of courage and conviction.[3]

As the dominant force in news and information in the era, the Eastern press led the national agenda, which included the perception of the West and figures such as Hickok. The modern market for entertainment violence was at work in the nineteenth-century press, too. Although twentieth-century Americans may have believed violence and gunplay won the West, there is little evidence to support such a view. The main-street shootout was an uncommon event in nineteenth-century cattle towns and gold-rush settlements. This is not to say the region did not contain its share of violence, but it was no more violent than the rest of the country. When image and historical reality collide, image has the advantage.

Hickok attracted press interest even before the Civil War was under way. The coverage of the McCanles shootout began to appear in August 1861. The Chicago *Tribune*'s four-paragraph rendering, which was attributed to the Nebraska City *News*, said the "noted desperado" McCanles had "organized a band of secessionists" who attacked and intended to "murder" the occupants of the station at Rock Creek. "Mr. Heacox," a misspelling in several other publications' accounts of the incident, killed all three of the men involved in the attack. The story also gave credit to two other men in defending the station, although Hickok supposedly did all the killing. They were subsequently acquitted of any crime, the *Tribune* reported. A similar, nearly identical account was credited to the Leavenworth *Times* of August 16, with one also running in the Burlington, Iowa, *Weekly Hawk-Eye* placing the same blame on the "terrible affray."[4]

As to why a few gunfights won such inordinate attention, violence and contradictions are dramatic and inevitably newsworthy. In the West, wildness was menace and promise. Hickok had the menace of a killer, the promise of law and order. The inherent contradiction was irresistible to newspapers East and West. The West was a place of purification and redemption, and cow towns of brothels and bars. "Lawless" may imply the need for violent, sinful men to bring order and civilization—men like Wild Bill. As historian Roderick Frazier Nash pointed out, the Exodus story created a "tradition of going to the wilderness for freedom and the purification of faith." Enthusiasm for wilderness developed in Europe "among those surrounded by cities and books." In America, similarly, the attraction of the wild began among those who did not have to confront the wilderness—or the "wild" men—as a pioneer, but among reporters, writers, artists, even tourists. Enthusiasm for frontiers, wilderness, and gunmen emanated from libraries, publishing houses, and newsrooms in the East.[5]

The end of the Civil War was the right time for building a mythic character out of Hickok. The war had redefined the nation, which was growing geographically and as an ideal with the approach of the centennial. Bold and self-reliant frontiersmen who would civilize untamed areas were good symbols of America, especially its individualism and exceptionalism. A good vehicle for such ideals was the West. Steering that vehicle was a post–Civil War press that saw tremendous growth. The number of daily newspapers grew 78 percent in the 1880s, while evening newspapers, which were seen as the workingman's paper, grew an incredible 112 percent. In that decade, daily circulation grew 135 percent, reaching more than 8.4 million daily. In addition, national magazines emerged, and readership exploded. The growth of the press meant more reading and increased demand for material to fill the pages. When newspapers started finding characters such as Hickok, they did so in a narrative to win audiences. That was a business necessity—they needed readers and so appealed to the values of readers, reinforcing the heroic myth of the gunman, the individualist, the frontiersman, and the civilizer.[6]

The postwar years witnessed an important transition in the press, which was putting more emphasis on event-centered news as opposed to the traditional, long-form narrative style that nevertheless remained important. In addition, the appeal to a wider audience meant courting a mass audience, in effect competing for bigger audiences, often as much with sensation as with facticity. This changing press and audience had an important impact on news about such figures as Hickok. Railroads, the telegraph, and faster printing all contributed to news being cheaper and more widely available. As the press shifted to more entertaining material and away from political polemics, it was no longer a matter of reading about someone congruent with an audience's partisan inclinations, but someone interesting—like Wild Bill.

Nichols and *Harper's*

George Ward Nichols, the journalist who made Hickok famous in 1867, was born in Tremont, Maine, in 1837 and came of age in Boston. An adventurous young man, he lived for a time in 1855 and 1856 among members of the Shawnee, Delaware, and Wyandot tribes. The fighting in Kansas drew him to the West, where he wrote reports for newspapers on the growing crisis. When he had had enough of Kansas, he went to Paris at the age of twenty-two to study art and music. After returning to the United States, Nichols covered the arts for the New York *Evening Post*. In 1862 he joined the army and served as an aide under Maj. Gen. John C. Frémont at the rank of captain. He joined William Tecumseh Sherman's staff in 1864 and wrote a journalistic account of his commander's famous March to the Sea. Rushed into print as the war ended, *The Story of the Great March from the Diary of a Staff Officer* sold sixty thousand copies and quickly went through more than two dozen printings. Nichols's book aggrandized Sherman and anticipated the mythmaking treatment Nichols would give Hickok after meeting him in Springfield.[7]

Nichols relied heavily on anecdotes and interviews with characters he met in order to provide a colorful and marketable account of the march. Although his style was common to the journalism of the era, Nichols pushed the limits of credibility by repeating long stories told by dubious sources. His description of Sherman was hagiographic: "[He] is terribly in earnest in his method of conducting the war, but he is neither vindictive nor implacable. . . . Yet there is a depth of tenderness, akin to the love of woman, behind that face which is furrowed with the lines of anxiety and care, and those eyes which dart keen and suspicious glances. Little children cling to the General's knees and nestle in his arms. . . ."[8]

The mythmaking became even more evident as Nichols made Sherman a symbol of America. The New York *Times* praised the book's "spirit-stirring narrative." Few men "have so harmoniously united common sense and genius as General Sherman. He can hardly be styled a representative man, but he is altogether original, and is, at the same time, a pure outgrowth of American civilization. . . . There is nothing European about him. He is a striking type of our institutions, and he comprehends justly the National Idea."[9]

As he arrived in Springfield, Nichols was finishing a novel inspired by Sherman's March. *The Sanctuary: A Story of the Civil War,* published in 1866, was characteristic of most post–Civil War romances-of-reunion written in a swoon of breathless, cloying prose. Three sets of lovers struggled to survive the war while wounded and weary men searched for lost brothers, noble women tried to rebuff lusty war profiteers, and slaves wreaked revenge on treacherous white siblings. Sherman was a modest and unselfish soldier who preserved the Republic as the holy "sanctuary" of a united people.[10]

Nichols's star was ascending, and he anticipated more success with *The Sanctuary.* In Springfield, he saw a chance to interest Harper and Brothers, his New York publishers, in a new character he might write about for *Harper's New Monthly Magazine*, a literary journal founded in 1850. The magazine had published works by Charles Dickens, William Makepeace Thackeray, and Herman Melville. Perhaps Nichols envisioned blending the gushing, imaginative prose of *The Sanctuary* with the documentary narrative style that had worked well for him in *The Story of the Great March*. If so, documentary truth was an immediate casualty, and the wound was mortal. Nichols claimed to have heard about "William Hitchcock" and his exploits from soldiers who had fought in the West, "and the hero of these strange tales took shape in my mind as did Jack the Giant Killer or Sinbad the Sailor in childhood's days," he wrote. Introduced to Hickok by Capt. Richard Bentley Owen, called in the article "Captain Honesty," Nichols gave an imaginative description of "Wild Bill," stressing his manly stature and womanly sensitivity and grace, belying his claim that the scout undoubtedly had killed "hundreds of men." The latest was Davis Tutt.[11]

Owen was one of Nichols's sources for the gunfight, as well as for some of the stories of Hickok's exploits as a Union scout and spy in the Civil War. Whether or not the name Captain Honesty was ironic, the article's dime-novel prose did nothing to inspire credibility. Nor did Nichols's interview with Hickok, who spun amazing tales of his Civil War heroics in a peculiar backwoods patois. Nichols was especially eager to hear the Rock Creek story, which he said had come to him from a regular army officer who arrived on the scene within an hour and had seen Hickok standing over the bodies of ten dead men, shot, hacked, and slashed to death. Nichols listened to Hickok's account of the bloodbath, "conscious of its extreme improbability." Told in advance he was in mortal danger of being shot, Hickok confidently replied, "Who's a-goin to kill me? There's two can play at that game." He said he went up against the M'Kandlas gang [*sic*] of "desperadoes, horse-thieves, murderers, regular cut-throats," terrors of the border. Hickok enumerated the shootings and stabbings that befell him as he battled ten-to-one odds. The colonel listened, open to hearing a good war story, then capitulated. "[O]ne who has lived for four years in the presence of such grand heroism and deeds of prowess as seen during the war is in what might be called a 'receptive' mood. Be the story true or not, in part, or in whole, I believed then every word Wild Bill uttered, and I believe it to-day."[12]

And there we have a myth, true or not, believed because a writer is "receptive." Despite the fact that some less-gullible Western newspaper editors disputed Nichols's story when it appeared in *Harper's New Monthly Magazine* in February 1867, the tale resonated with Eastern newspaper readers. The thirteen-page, double-columned spread was punctuated by nine extravagant wood engravings of unlikely scenes and events, which probably did even more to charm and amuse readers than Nichols's text. By year's end, more tales about Wild Bill the fearless scout and Indian fighter were in print to meet the demand. The Springfield *Weekly Patriot* demurred, regretting the loss of veracity: "These little rivulets in the monthlies, weeklies and dailies, all run into and make up the great river of *history* afterawhile [*sic*]; and if many of them are as salty as this one, the main stream will be very brackish at least." Nichols's story, and Hickok's storytelling, marked the true beginning of the Wild West and inspired celebrity journalism. In 1868 Nichols married Maria Longworth, heiress to a wealthy Cincinnati family, and became something of a celebrity himself. While working as an art critic for the New York *Times* in 1877, he published *Art Education for Industry*, a reformist response to concerns that the machines of the industrial age were replacing people.

He and his wife were active in the American arts and crafts movement and the manufacture of art pottery. He later served as president of the Cincinnati College of Music until his death in 1885.[13]

Nichols seemed a peculiar, if not ironic, conceiver of the Hickok myth. As an artist, he understood imagery, form, and representation. That Nichols feared the machine is not surprising given the industrialized warfare he saw with Sherman. "Where our footsteps pass, fire, ashes, and desolation follow in their path," Nichols wrote in his diary. But Hickok, the lone scout and gunman on the frontier, stood in contrast to the sixty-two-thousand-man industrial-strength army Sherman had marched across Georgia. Nichols saw something he wanted to see in Hickok. One possibility came from Sherman himself, who had written his brother, Senator John Sherman, about his frustration during the campaign. The March to the Sea, he wrote, was "a big Indian war," which the general first had experienced as a second lieutenant during the Seminole War in Florida in 1840. He lamented that Confederate "sharp-shooters, spies, and scouts, in the guise of peaceable farmers, can hang around us and kill our wagonmen, messengers, and couriers." Hickok, the Indian fighter and scout, fought like an Indian and knew his enemy, a man who would be useful in Sherman's campaigns in the West. Nichols listened, imagined, took it all in, and wrote about it.[14]

Biographers assumed Nichols tried to write a serious profile of an interesting character, another Sherman, perhaps, but wasn't up to the task. It's possible Nichols intended the story as parody, a send-up in the American tall-tale tradition, a bit of Western travel journalism for the amusement of Eastern readers, and Hickok might have been an eager collaborator. Or, perhaps Nichols played the Eastern sophisticate having some fun at the expense of a frontier yokel. Maybe he was the Eastern tenderfoot out of his depth in the West. Or, an editor at *Harper's* may have found the story amusing and embroidered it further. Just two months earlier, *Harper's* had published a piece by Mark Twain, so it was open to humor. There is yet another possibility. By turning Hickok into a heroic scout, Nichols may have been attempting to generate some favorable press for the postwar army in the West. The whole interview could be interpreted as a publicity stunt. Nichols arrives in uniform accompanied by a general, who is on a "tour of inspection." Jaunty Union veterans saunter down the streets of the drowsing town, which is filled with indolent loafers. "Captain Honesty" points out the splendid Hickok and starts spinning tales. The captain is joined by a lieutenant who calls Hickok "the most remarkable character I have met in four years of service." The lieutenant tells war stories about Wild Bill, who embellishes them further. But the story turns out to be less a brief for the army and more a rowdy ballad acclaiming Wild West mythology.[15]

Nichols was a better writer than the Hickok story would suggest, especially when writing about art. As published, however, the story strikes every false note. Take, for example, the prolixity of Hickok's remarks. This long-windedness is entirely at odds with Hickok or the character who later emerged in Western fiction, film, and television. Hickok's friend Joseph "White-Eye" Jack Anderson recalled that "Bill didn't talk much but he always said something important." As literary scholar Jane Tompkins noted in her study of the genre, the Western "is at heart antilanguage. Doing, not talking is what it values." The Hickok of the Nichols interview is out of character. Nichols's Hickok does plenty and never shuts up about it. Even when he brushes off one of Nichols's questions, he dilates interminably. "I don't like to talk about that M'Kandlas affair," said Hickok, who does just that for more than eleven hundred words of direct quotation. The kind of language he uses is unlikely to strike fear in the hearts of grizzled Civil War veterans bellying up to the bar in a border town: "There was a few seconds of that awful stillness, then the ruffians came rushing at both doors. How wild they looked with their red, drunken faces and inflamed eyes, shouting and cussing! But I never aimed more deliberately in my life."[16]

Nichols gave Hickok a frontier dialect but was inconsistent in quotation, as if the effect was being forced. Hickok's few surviving letters show that he had only a rudimentary education and difficulty with spelling, punctuation, vocabulary, and grammar, but nothing indicates he was the garrulous bumpkin Nichols described. Nor do the foolish anecdotes Nichols provides, as for example Hickok's horse, Black Nell, winking, dropping to the ground on Hickok's signal, and climbing atop a billiard table. After the article was published, the *Weekly Patriot* called Nichols a bibulous faux colonel "who was here for a few days in the summer of 1865, splurging around among our 'strange, half-civilized people,' seriously endangering the supply of lager and corn whisky, and putting on more airs than a spotted stud-horse in the ring of a county fair. *He's the author!*" If that assessment is true, it's easy to believe that Nichols was having his way with Springfield, Missouri, and Wild Bill. In 1876, Hickok was in Cincinnati with his wife Agnes. If he called on Nichols, neither ever mentioned it.[17]

Historian Pamela Haag cited the Nichols article as "the trope for the Western gun hero." Many newspapers recognized the nonsense but appreciated the appeal. The article continued to be referenced throughout Hickok's lifetime and even after his death as the foundation of his legend. Although the article got a lot of attention, that did not mean it was taken as fact. The editor of the Springfield *Patriot* said Nichols "cuts it very fat" with the facts in talking about Hickok's feats with arms. But it was good reading. The wide response, pro and con, meant a higher profile for Hickok. Appropriately, the first dime novel about Wild Bill, in July 1867, used for its cover the same wood cut that appeared in *Harper's*, in which Hickok was shooting it out with the McCanles gang. It's not surprising that Nichols's account would inspire more sensation, given the market and the competition for audience. DeWitt's *Ten Cent Romances*, after the July 1867 number, published another Hickok tale only five months later.[18]

Perhaps the best testament to the article's popularity was its longevity and use as a reference point. The Chicago *Tribune*, a year later, published a letter about an article it had run on January 24, implying Hickok had a role in a bank robbery. The letter writer defended Hickok's honor, citing his military service and the sketch in *Harper's*. "Haycock" was known as an "honorable and upright man." The article at issue referred to the person in the *Harper's* article and misidentified the bandit as Hickok. A rather romanticized view of frontier America appeared in the *Daily Ohio Statesman* in August 1868. It noted the handsome Wild Bill, pretty much parroting the physical description given in *Harper's*, and credited with sending many an Indian to the "happy hunting ground." A theater advertisement appeared in numerous newspapers as Buffalo Bill's production was touring in the Midwest and East in the 1870s. Headlined "Wild Bill" along with "Texas Jack," the advertisement touted the "remarkable scout" as "described in *Harper's Magazine*" of 1867. In Kansas, the Saline County *Journal*, five years after the Nichols article appeared, was much less complimentary of Hickok, deeming him "a gambler, a libertine and a rowdy." But the journal credited *Harper's* with launching his fame: "[E]ver since his achievements were narrated in *Harper's' Magazine*, three or four years ago, Wild Bill's star has been ascending. . . ." In Vermont, six years after the article's publication, the *Essex County Herald*, in an article attributed to the New York *Sun*, had a mixed verdict, calling Hickok "one of the most remarkable men this country has produced. . . . Deemed one of the most reckless desperadoes ever known even among the roughest class of frontiersmen. . . ." Getting the marshal's job in Abilene was due in part to local authorities "who had read his story, and thought Mr. Hickok possessed of just the heroic qualities required for the perilous position." Up to that point, the most detailed story of Wild Bill had been in *Harper's*. The description of physical attributes and temperament followed Nichols, as did another article in 1872 from the Chicago *Tribune,* which in a review of Custer's *Life on the Plains* lauded Hickok's manliness.[19]

Harper's was an ideal place to start the legend. The magazine was relatively new, having launched in 1850. It reached a circulation of fifty thousand within six months of its introduction and was up to two hundred thousand by the start of the Civil War. Its success was a matter of English serials, illustrations, and eclectic material that included sentimental fiction, travel writing, science, history, and biography. *Harper's* published popular American writers and artists, as well as feeding their popularity, including Theodore Dreiser, John Muir, Mark Twain, Frederic Remington, Winslow Homer, and Jack London. Those names included a few of the foremost popularizers of the great American West. It only made sense, given the magazine's newfound marketing trend, to seize on such a character as Hickok. *Harper's Weekly* was not very political, most of that being left to *Harper's Monthly,* whose strongest rivals included *Scribner's Monthly, Graham's, Putnam's,* and the *Atlantic.* In the context of the dime novels and other illustrated newspapers and magazines, Hickok's dashing portrait was a natural. Even a competitor and critic, *The Nation,* in 1866 said that *Harper's* may be considered "an index to the literary culture and general character of the nation."[20]

Fantasies and Fabrications

If the press invented Wild Bill, it did so in 1867. The year began with the Nichols article and ended with the dime novel *Wild Bill's First Trail.* In between, Henry Morton Stanley's interview with Hickok had appeared in the St. Louis *Weekly Missouri Democrat,* and the first Wild Bill dime novel appeared in midsummer. Stanley further polished Hickok's reputation, especially as an Indian fighter, and attempted to tamp down the exaggerations in Nichols's article, affirming that Hickok was "the very reverse of all we had imagined." He soon added more fantasies and fabrications to the emerging mythology, however. Stanley claimed that Hickok told him he'd killed "over a hundred, a long ways off," but never killed a man without good cause. Hickok certainly knew the number was nonsense and that Stanley probably knew also. But the latter had a story to write, an audience to please. Stanley was an accomplished journalist in his own right, but in this case he was following Nichols's example. Hickok also spun a tale of killing five men in his hotel room in Leavenworth, Kansas Territory—in self-defense, of course. Stanley said Hickok was "an inveterate hater of the Indians," and "woe to the Indians who cross his path." He found Hickok "one of the finest examples of . . . frontiersman, ranger, hunter and Indian scout."[21]

The Welsh-born Stanley became most famous for the line—which may have been a fiction by Stanley—of "Dr. Livingston, I presume," supposedly delivered upon finding Dr. David Livingston in what is now Tanzania in November 1871 after an arduous seven-hundred-mile journey through tropical forests. The line was first reported in the New York *Times* on July 2, 1872. Stanley's celebrity stemmed in large part from his travels and subsequent reports. He had immigrated to America at age eighteen and enlisted in the Confederate Army. In 1862 he fought at Shiloh, where he was taken prisoner, and joined the Union army in June of the same year. After becoming ill, he was discharged following only three weeks of Union service. In July 1864 he joined the navy, becoming perhaps the only person to have served in both Union and Confederate Armies and the U.S. Navy. In 1867, he went to work for New York *Herald* publisher James Gordon Bennett, who sent him on several overseas assignments. Like Nichols, Stanley found Hickok a handsome, deadly, fair-minded gunman. However, he reported an even more deadly man than had Nichols, and endowed him with greater eloquence. Nichols and Stanley set in motion the transformation of a minor celebrity into a gunfighting legend. Unlike Buffalo Bill Cody—also known as a scout, hunter, frontiersman, and Indian fighter—Hickok was not inclined to parlay his minor notoriety into major celebrity. Nichols and Stanley did that for him.[22]

Bloodshed made gunfights newsworthy, even more so by the fact that they were unusual but spectacular events. Had shootouts been common, perhaps they would not have been so newsworthy. Such things as the OK Corral or Hickok's main-street duel with Tutt were also in public view, making them credible and susceptible to enhancement not just by the participants but also by eyewitnesses, whether the latter were there or not. Prior to the *Harper's* article, Hickok was involved in only two actual notable gunfights. The McCanles fight did not get much national attention until after the Nichols account gave Hickok credit for killing ten men in that confrontation—with pistols, rifle butts, knives, and fists. Nichols attributed that story to Hickok.[23]

A longer story, which ran in September 1871 in the Clarksville, Tennessee, *Chronicle*, elevated Hickok's heroism. Headlined "Wild Bill's Story," the article had Hickok riding up to the station and being warned by the woman occupant that "M'Kandlas and his gang" were there. "There's ten of them and you've no chance. . . . M'Kandles was dragging poor Parson Shipleg on the ground with a lariat round his neck." Hickok supposedly recounted this version to the "Kernel," Nichols presumably, and admitted it was one of the "few times I said my prayers." Nichols detailed the killing of four, and Hickok finished off the remaining half dozen in a furious melee, his knife "striking and slashing." He claimed "eleven buckshot in me . . . cut in thirteen places." The exaggerated numbers, the multiple wounds, and the drama of the shooting and brawling more than ten years after the fact was almost certainly a matter of the *Harper's* article four and a half years earlier.[24]

The Hickok-Tutt fight achieved great infamy—well after the actual event. Its occurrence in July 1865 appears to have achieved scant attention in the press of the day. The event won more press attention after the swell of publicity following the *Harper's* article and the Stanley interview. The Tutt shootout was a high point in a narrative portraying Hickok as a fearless, dead-shot gunman, subsequently well established in Hickok lore. Nearly twenty years after Hickok's death, the Atlanta *Constitution*, in an unsourced feature, called him a gambler, scout, one who held an "intense antipathy to secession." The piece focused on two killings—Tutt in 1865 and Hickok in 1876. A recounting of the duel with Tutt and events that led up to the walkdown are familiar, ending with a paean to Hickok's marksmanship. "They were too far apart for Tutt. . . . But he didn't know Bill. He raised his gun and fired like a flash and Tutt dropped dead with a bullet in his head, fully 150 yards away. . . . The effect of such witchlike skills on the nerves of the crowd was too much. The general view seemed to be that the killing of Tutt was 'on the square.' . . ."[25]

The durability of the story was seen nearly eight decades later, when the Chicago *Daily Tribune* ran a feature on Hickok in 1944. According to this account, Tutt fired first "because Hickok was unwilling to appear the aggressor. But the second shot was Hickok's and Tutt fell dead." Following the established story line, Hickok then backed down a crowd of "Tutt's friends who were drawing their guns." A witness said, "Wild Bill never shoots twice at the same man—never has to," as though such street shooting were not terribly infrequent.[26]

The nature of Hickok's gunfights and brawls, some in the name of law and order, and the amount of coverage they received changed substantially after the *Harper's* article. As sheriff of Ellis County, Kansas, Hickok in August 1869 shot Bill Mulvey, who the Kansas City *Daily Journal of Commerce* said was among a "party of intoxicated roughs. . . . He attempted to shoot several citizens, and was determined to quarrel with every one whom he met, using the revolver freely, but fortunately injuring no one." Hickok's stint as sheriff resulted in another shooting a little over a month later, when he shot and killed Samuel Strawhun, whom Hickok apparently had clashed with in Ellsworth, Kansas. It appeared to have been another barroom brawl. Though accounts vary on where the shootout occurred, the Junction City *Weekly Union* put the fight in a "beer saloon," where Strawhun and companions were "on a spree." An eyewitness letter published in the Leavenworth *Daily Commercial* concluded, "Too much credit cannot be given to Wild Bill for his endeavor to rid this town of such dangerous characters as this Stranhen [*sic*] was." In these stories, Hickok was the good guy, fighting ruffians and toughs, keeping the peace. The image is in contrast to the occasional references to Hickok in other newspapers and concerning other events, describing him as a desperado, gambler, and drunk.[27]

The dime-novel Hickok continued ascendant. In at least eight different newspapers in December 1869, an Edward Judson feature on Hickok offered Wild Bill in a long account of more than three columns in the company of Buffalo Bill, who he met during the Civil War in Kansas. They later take on "Col. M'Kandlas" and Tutt, who missed out on the M'Kandlas [*sic*] fight because Tutt was too cowardly to accompany the others. Tutt and McCanles were in different times, different places, but fiction ignored that fact. Dime-novel publishers Street and Smith offered a subscription to their series, titled *Buffalo Bill, the King of the Border Men!* The papers in which it ran included the New York *Weekly*, Chicago *Daily Tribune*, the Charleston, South Carolina, *Daily News*, the Philadelphia *Evening Telegraph*, and the Richmond, Indiana, *Palladium*.[28]

The Phil Coe shooting in 1871 generated a different sort of coverage. It was a result not so much of the shooting itself as it was of Hickok's accidental killing of theater security guard Mike Williams. The Leavenworth *Weekly Times* said Hickok was attempting to quell a "riot," of which the "Texas gambler" Coe was part. Williams's death was an accident, it said. The Topeka *Commonwealth* said the troublemakers were attempting nothing less than assassination of the sheriff. That Hickok paid, remorsefully, the funeral expenses for Williams was widely noted, apparently confirming earlier tales of generosity and gallantry. Undoubtedly, he would have been affected by killing the security guard. As it was in this case, the news often was merely a paragraph or a one-sentence addition to a few paragraphs about Coe. But paying funeral expenses burnished the legend, which by now was a mixture of fearless gunman and frontier ruffian. He probably needed to be both, in fact, to do the law enforcement jobs that he signed on for. Not all was somber admiration, though. The Ottawa, Illinois, *Free Trader* reported, "Mr. Williams, we have no doubt, deeply regrets his inability to thank Wild Bill for his liberality."[29]

Hickok's detractors were abundant in the press in spite of heroic accounts by others. In a lengthy story in the Delaware, Ohio, *Gazette* in November 1869, a correspondent from the Columbus *Journal* fitted Hickok to a region of "wild and rough hunters, adventurers and desperadoes." Writing specifically about Hays City, Kansas, and Sheridan, Wyoming, the reporter portrayed the towns as "characteristic cities. . . . A couple of score of wooden shanties, nine-tenths of which are places for the sale of whiskey and resorts for gambling and kindred villainies. . . ." Hickok was sheriff of Hays City when the piece was written in October, but had lost the subsequent election on November 2. "Wild Bill is heartily hated" by the residents, in part because he was a Republican in a "radically Democratic" town. Many of his adventures were "fiction." The writer referred to Nichols, but added,

> [T]he bright particular star among the notabilities of this region of country, is one Wild Bill, whose name is reverenced among all cut-throatdom of the western border. . . . There is some question as to how and upon what this wonderful individual subsists. Such is his traditional thirst for human blood as might lead one to suppose that to be his favorite beverage, and that he feasts and revels like a buzzard on the flesh of the human species. . . . Wild Bill's usual drink is not blood but whiskey. His chosen diet is not fricasseed [*sic*] human hearts or human heads served up on the half shell; but invariably and simply whiskey. In short, Wild Bill lives on whiskey.[30]

Likewise, the *Weekly Kansas Chief* cited him as a man who "could sling a navy [revolver], drink whiskey or cheat at poker with any man thereabouts." The *Buchanan County Bulletin*, of Independence, Iowa, in a report from Great Bend, Kansas, said it was a place of a "few" respectable men, but "the larger portion are a rough, wild set of half-civilized ruffians, of which Wild Bill is a fair sample. . . ." One of the more severe indictments was in the Emporia, Kansas, *News*, which called him a "drunken, reckless, murderous coward, who is treated with contempt by the border men and who should have been hung years ago" for murder. Hickok comes off as a ruffian and desperado in as many instances as he is depicted as brave, generous, and heroic. In some cases, it was as though the newspaper could not figure out what to do with him. The Lancaster, Ohio, *Gazette*, in a brief item noted,

Here we meet the notorious ruffian and desperado known as Wild Bill. He is a man of fine proportions, over six feet tall. . . . His long and flowing hair is of a soft and silky texture, his hands and feet are beautifully modelled. His face is handsome. . . . He is said to have shot about 150 men, two of them within the last month in the little city of Hays. . . . That he is at liberty is no credit to the State of Kansas, and that he is sheriff of the county, adds a deeper dye to the local stain.[31]

Hickok's mixed reputation in Kansas may have tarnished his name in some newspapers, but he still had national stature. Custer was Hickok's most enthusiastic publicist. *Galaxy* magazine paid the former brevet general one hundred dollars for each article he wrote about his experiences in the West. He wrote about Hickok in 1872 in one of his first articles, republished in Custer's *My Life on the Plains* in 1874. Hickok was one of the scouts who served with Custer under Maj. Gen. Winfield Scott Hancock in 1867. Custer wrote that Hickok was "a strange character, just the one a novelist might gloat over." Hickok was already a fictional character when Custer knew him. He probably read the Nichols's article, with its homage to masculine perfection. Custer said that Hickok was "a Plainsman in every sense of the word, yet unlike any other of his class." Among scouts, Hickok was singular in appearance and reputation as an Indian fighter.

In person he was about six feet one in height, straight as the straightest of the warriors whose implacable foe he was. . . . His hair and complexion were those of the perfect blond. The former was worn in uncut ringlets falling carelessly over his powerfully formed shoulders. Add to this figure a costume blending the immaculate neatness of the dandy with the extravagant taste and style of the frontiersman, and you have Wild Bill . . . one of the most perfect types of physical manhood I ever saw.[32]

Custer might have been projecting much of his own press image on his buckskin scout. Hickok, if a bit larger in stature, had a physiognomy similar to Custer's, at least according to many generous descriptions of the general written by journalists. Of Hickok's courage, "there could be no question; it had been brought to the test on too many occasions to admit of a doubt. His skill in the use of the rifle and pistol was unerring; while his deportment was exactly the opposite of what might be expected from a man of his surroundings. It was entirely free from all bluster or bravado."

This hardly squares with the teller of tall tales depicted in the Nichols and Stanley profiles, as well as in many newspaper articles.

He seldom spoke of himself unless requested to do so. His conversation, strange to say, never bordered either on the vulgar or blasphemous. His influence among the frontiersmen was unbounded, his word was law; and many are the personal quarrels and disturbances which he has checked among his comrades by his simple announcement that "this has gone far enough," if need be followed by the ominous warning that when persisted in or renewed the quarreler "must settle it with me." Wild Bill is anything but a quarrelsome man; yet no one but himself can enumerate the many conflicts in which he has been engaged, and which have almost invariably resulted in the death of the adversary. I have a personal knowledge of at least half a dozen men whom he has at various times killed. . . .[33]

Although frontier justice and the law were often strangers, Custer was sure that jurors would have acquitted Hickok of any of the shootings attributed to him. Custer's wife, Elizabeth, also wrote glowingly about the scout her husband admired. She recalled Hickok as "a delight to look upon. Tall, lithe, and free in every motion, he rode and walked as if every muscle was perfection. . . . I do not recall anything finer in the way of physical perfection than Wild Bill when he swung himself lightly from his saddle. . . ."[34]

Hickok Dies, and Dies Again

Numerous false reports of Hickok's death also indicated his celebrity. The items were typically just one or two sentences. In 1869, such things ran from New York to Chicago to Phoenix to South Carolina and points in between. These sorts of stories appeared intermittently up to his actual death in 1876. Another flurry of death reports occurred in 1873. Some of those same newspapers turned the death stories into spoofs, such as one picked up in the Nevada Territory Goldhill *Daily Times*: "In order to quiet the variety of reports, 'Wild Bill' writes to a Kansas City paper admitting that he is dead." The White Cloud, Kansas, *Chief* ran a similar item a few days earlier. The Omaha *Daily Bee* noted that Wild Bill frequently was killed by newspapers.[35]

A number of these false reports were not complimentary of the now notorious gunman. The Richmond, Virginia, *Palladium* in 1873 led its one-paragraph report:

"A noted desperado known as 'Wild Bill,' who has killed dozens of men in frontier brawls, . . . met his death . . . in Kansas. . . ." The Clarksville, Tennessee, *Weekly Chronicle* called him a "noted Union spy bravo" who took pleasure in killing. An item lifted from the Kansas City *News* in March 1873 and republished variously detailed how earlier reports of Hickok's death were in error. It then reported, according to an "informant," that Hickok was killed, but many friends in Abilene, where the latest death occurred, "refused to believe" the report. Perhaps the most facetious item was a brief comment in the *Weekly Caucasian* of Lexington, Missouri: "At last we have ascertained the facts of 'Wild Bill's' death. He died in Uti, Switzerland. William Tell and Wild Bill were shooting nickels off Gesler's head, when Bill's pistol went off at the wrong end. The result is sad. (Sedalia *Bazoo*)." Such items affirm that Hickok was entertainment, in spite of his own disdain for being an entertainer. The degree of his celebrity is apparent in those reports that often referred to him only as "Wild Bill," omitting the last name, presumably because readers already knew of him. The accounts of his death in 1876 often described him as a plainsman, scout, or hunter instead of focusing on a checkered law enforcement career or looking to his more frequent occupation as a gambler. The gunman identity would grow with the years and the legend. It may have been a matter of language in entertainment media: "gunfighter" sounded more menacing and exciting than "plainsman."[36]

The first published account of Hickok's murder was August 5, 1876, in the Deadwood *Black Hills Pioneer*. A. W. Merrick and A. W. Laughlin began the Black Hills *Pioneer* only a couple of months before Hickok was killed in a saloon down the street. Merrick was soon on his own with the paper, as Laughlin stayed with the enterprise for only a short time. As the voice of the paper, Merrick probably served as a reflection of general sentiments in the town and of the times. He was rabidly anti-Indian, harped about the bias of the Eastern press toward the alleged uncivil atmosphere of the region, and was a booster of the town's economy. This all fit well with his conviction that the territory should be made part of the United States as soon as possible, any treaties concerning Native Americans be damned. Although the shooting of Hickok and trial of John "Broken Nose Jack" McCall turned out to be the most consequential event of the time for the settlement, the incident was initially played down. The Hickok legend loomed larger in the East, but the editor knew he was dealing with something more than the ordinary shooting of a hard-luck gambler in a local bar. That the story was relegated to the back page of the newspaper probably was more a matter of production than news values. At that time, news pages were typeset by hand, so the publication most likely was assembled from front to back, with the front-page material having been set first and the back-page stories bearing the latest news. A story about the saloon assassination of a gunman such as Hickok may also not have played well with potential investors from back East, as Merrick worked to convince such an audience of the economic potential of Deadwood—hence the back-page placement. This boosterism was consistent with Merrick's disdain for Native Americans. That the "civilized" residents of the community were dealing with the "savages" was part of affirming Deadwood's stability. The story made a point of showing "government" at work. There was a trial and due process, even if it had no legality. Even the jurors were named in the story.[37]

Perhaps the only real mystery to it all was not in premonitions of death or subsequent omens of bad fortune, such as the aces-and-eights hand, but why Hickok wasn't sitting with his back to the wall, as was his custom. The *Black Hills Pioneer* said that sitting with his back to the wall was "his rule for many years, since his career of law enforcement had developed a long list of men [who] swore they would shoot him at the first opportunity." Several newspapers reported Hickok's death premonition, as well as his sister's premonition of her brother's death. As for Hickok's premonition, which the Cheyenne *Daily Leader* reported at the end of August, the hindsight is suspect, but it does make for a better story, like the dead man's hand.[38]

The Chicago *Daily Tribune* used the death of Hickok to provide a slap at not only the man but also the region:

> . . . . Thousands of men, of a lower mental stamp, have flourished and died, along the line of country that claimed "Wild Bill," but not one ever to the distinction attained by this most remarkable loafer of his time, whose death is but a crystallization of his life, and whose life was spattered with great blotches of crime and deviltry. . . . [T]he good people around here were not displeased when they reflected that his eccentric and noisy code served to thin the ranks of the desperate and reckless characters that made the Western edge of civilization a gilded hall. . . . Almost always drunk, and ever ready for what he grimly termed "a frolic," he was hated and admired wherever his name was known. . . .[39]

The St. Louis *Post-Dispatch*, in nearly twenty paragraphs on Hickok's death, was full of praise. It reported that the "greatest of all Western scouts," whose aim was unfailing, even had on one occasion killed nine Indians single-handedly. The story got the name of the assassin partly right, in that it reported the killer was Bill Sutherland, one of the sobriquets used by McCall and the name reported in a number of news stories. The *Post-Dispatch* obituary included the caveat that the report of his death may not be true. "[T]here is a probability that the great scout will turn up sometime soon again . . . ready to fight or ply his old vocation, for he has been reported killed more than a score of times. . . ."[40]

Recounting and building the legend was helping it to gain momentum. The Ellis County *Star*, of Hays City, Kansas, noted that Hickok killed several men while in Hays City, but "acquaintances agreed that he was justified. . . . He never provoked a quarrel, and was a generous, gentlemanly fellow," feeding the idea of Hickok killing only when necessary. The *Chief*, of Red Cloud, Webster County, Nebraska, headlined the obituary "The Romance of Wild Bill's Life," one notable for his being a hunter, plainsman, scout, and marshal at several frontier towns.[41]

Back East, the Boston *Daily Globe*, apparently picking up the story from the Louisville *Courier-Journal*, ran a full-blown drama, nothing less—according to the headline—than "A Scene for a Word Painter." Hickok reportedly killed thirty-six men and was "the best pistol shot in the West." McCall was avenging his brother's death at Hickok's hand. Picking up details from the Chicago *Inter-Ocean*, the *Daily Globe* went on to recount the minutiae of the funeral procession. Altogether, it was both sympathetic and heroic. The New York *Sun*'s headline summarized its coverage and perspective: "A Dime-Novel Hero Dead/ The End of Wild Bill, the Notorious Border Desperado."[42]

Several newspapers used the obituary from the Kansas City *Times*, whose story was not flattering but was fairly balanced. It noted that he was a courteous gentleman— "when sober"—but that he "seldom allowed himself to drink to excess." He dressed well, had been praised by Custer, and was "every inch the frontier hero, as painted by the yellow back novelists [dime novelists]." In spite of the good looks and heroism, he faltered, as when he was arrested for vagrancy in Kansas City. The Kansas City *Times* account admitted he was something of a dime-novel product.[43]

Farther west, in the Denver *News*, he was the "noted scout, buffalo-hunter and plainsman," who kept comparative peace in Abilene and Wichita, having "shot to death many a man who resisted him." Tall and handsome, he went to the East to get into show business with Cody but drifted back to the West, meeting his end at the hand of a man seeking revenge for his brother's death. In the Chicago *Daily Tribune*, a one-paragraph, one-sentence item was headlined "The Avenger." The killer, it said, "alleges that Bill killed his brother at Fort Hayes, Kan., some years ago." The *True Northerner*, in Paw Paw, Michigan, showed the legend assuming a familiar form—a catalog of his killing, a man "who never missed his mark" but who was also a gentleman. The number Hickok killed was reported as a score. As for aggrandizing the killer, it could be seen in the remark "it is to be regretted that he himself was shot down 'without a show.'" In a brief recounting of the Tutt shootout, the challenger was shot through the heart: "Wild Bill never waited to see the effect of his shot, but wheeled on Tutt's friends, and asked if any more shooting was wanted by them. They appeared to be satisfied."[44]

West of the Mississippi, many obituaries were briefer, probably due to those being smaller newspapers and having fewer resources, such as wire or telegraph services, for running the longer stories. Picking up a story from the Cheyenne *Leader*, the Bozeman, Montana, *Avant Courier* charged that stories of seven or eight years ago about Hickok's exploits were hardly believable. "Contact with the man, however, dispelled all these illusions [about daring deeds], and of late years Wild Bill seems to have been a very tame and worthless loafer and bummer. Our city marshal ordered him out of town by virtue of the provisions of the vagrant act, only a few months ago." The moralistic account called him a liar and a drunk. "Years ago, before wine and women had ruined his constitution and impaired his faculties, he was more worthy of the fame which he attained on the border." It concluded, uncharitably, "and the world has not suffered anything like an irreparable loss."[45]

The news of Hickok's death often was only a one-paragraph gossip item. The one-, perhaps two-sentence items said little more than Wild Bill had been shot in a Deadwood saloon by McCall, who claimed he was avenging his brother. Hickok was noted as a scout of some prominence. There was nothing else in those short items.[46]

Even obituaries cited the *Harper's* article, whether or not they found Hickok praiseworthy. A Chicago *Tribune* correspondent recalled, "I have been sorry to see that only three writers that I now remember have regarded him as anything else than a lawless character who went about killing men for amusement and reputation." Those three were Custer, a "Mr. Webb" (probably William E. Webb) who wrote about Western Kansas, and Nichols. Wild Bill's reputation owed much to *Harper's*, according to the Las Vegas *Gazette*. He "became famous through the assistance of *Harper's*. He belonged to that class whose reputation has been made by deeds of violence and blood," including "getting the 'drop' on the victim, which in plain English means shooting an unarmed man. . . ." A lighter piece, picked up from the Chicago *Tribune* by the Abbeville, South Carolina, *Press and Banner*, cited *Harper's* in an anecdote about an unlikely combination of pistols and flirtation. A "fashionably dressed young lady—an Ohio girl—with a pretty face" sighted Hickok at the train station in

Hays City. "Bent upon his destruction, she made her way to where he stood, and discharged her weapons about as follows. 'Are you Wild Bill the *Harper's Monthly* tells about?' The astonished scout bashfully replied: 'I believe I am.' The mischievous eyes surveyed him complacently from head to foot, while their owner laughingly said: 'Are you? Why my papa told me to come out here and marry some great man like you.'" The result, reportedly, was that Wild Bill was "thoroughly frightened" for once in his life. Finally, she "bounded away to tell of her capture, and perhaps find other 'sons of the border' to conquer."[47]

In all, there was no single, consistent story line in the amalgamation of obituaries and death notices. Hickok was everything from hero to drunkard, meriting several columns of newsprint or perhaps only a sentence. A number of obituaries contained the elements essential to a mythic figure, including strong individualism, bravery, being fair minded, and decisive in the face of danger. No matter the slant—good guy or bad—his life was a story of drama and danger, genuine and exaggerated, replete with a bloody demise.

The "dead man's hand" fueled the aura of the mystery around a very straight-forward killing, although no evidence supported the fable. There were no contemporary references in the press to aces and eights or any other combination of cards in Hickok's hand. But the press did help elevate the story. Rosa thought it added to the confusion about the legend, but murkiness rarely harms the mystique surrounding a tall tale. The *Rocky Mountain News* in an undated issue printed a poem titled "Jacks and Eights—The Dead Man's Hand," which was reprinted more than a hundred years later in the Tombstone *Epitaph*. A dying, elderly rancher was gambling with a friend. As the rancher played his last hand, his friend called, and said:

> Now, watcher got? I'll call yer bluff
> Mine's deuces say ain't them enough?
> But the Parson's soul had passed away.
> He had cashed his chips, as the gamblers say,
> So they turned up his cards to see what he had
> Jim scowled as he said, "Say, I feel kinder bad,
> But I'm glad that he won, for he made a good stand."
> There were jacks and eights in the dead man's hand.[48]

3. ❁ Dime Novels: The West Conquers the East

> It is only the cheap stories, which you call dime novels, for which the demand is, and always will be inexhaustible, and which must be depended on for the regeneration of American literature.
> —Frederick Whittaker, 1884

The real-life Hickok, like Buffalo Bill Cody, was an ideal figure for adaptation to dime-novel tales of frontier derring-do—colorful, interesting, fast. Dime-novel characters provided templates for use by subsequent generations of media. The phenomenon began in Great Britain with the "penny dreadfuls." A few New York newspapers, including the New York *Herald*, carried similar material, often serialized. The term "dime novel" applied to more than just ten-cent pulp fiction and encompassed a wide range of mass-market material from 1860 to about 1910, with slim volumes selling by the millions for five cents to a quarter in a variety of formats. The major contribution of the genre to American culture may well have been the Western, with a fairly clear trajectory from dime novels to Zane Grey to Hollywood. No matter one's opinion of the high- or low-culture value of such material, it mattered by virtue of numbers and impact. In their heyday, some series consisted of more than a thousand titles and could go through ten to twelve editions, beginning with a print run of up to seventy thousand copies.[1]

English journalist G. K. Chesterton wrote a spirited defense of penny dreadfuls and similar "pulp fiction" in 1901. Such "romantic trash" was then under attack from moralists, churchmen, and jurists who thought the stories drove uneducated readers to violence or at least kept them from reading more morally uplifting literature. In judging such writing, "we have probed, as if it were some monstrous new disease, what is, in fact, nothing but the foolish and valiant heart of man." Chesterton made a distinction between popular fiction and literature, arguing that "literature is a luxury; fiction is a necessity." The penny dreadfuls were not literature but "the actual center of a million flaming imaginations." Stories about such stock fictional characters as

American cowboys were concerned with "adventures, rambling, disconnected, and endless," little different than the novels of Sir Walter Scott. Pulp fiction might be badly written, but "[b]ad story writing is not a crime." As a voice of the masses, the publications expressed "the sanguine and heroic truisms on which civilization is built; for it is clear that unless civilization is built on truisms, it is not built at all." For the average reader, the penny dreadfuls were "the great gaudy diaries of his soul," and "their driveling literature will always be a 'blood and thunder' literature as simple as the thunder of heaven and the blood of men."[2]

The dime-novel industry came about in the midst of cultural and techno-logical changes beneficial to the business. While the themes in the earliest tales were often congruent with classic standards of heroism and conquest, American ideas of individualism, exceptionalism, the progression from rags to riches, and the frontier gradually found their way into the stories. One of the most successful publishers of the cheap, popular fiction was Street and Smith's New York *Weekly*, which started publication in 1858 with serialized stories, running thirty to fifty thousand words. The Beadle and Adams publishing house introduced in 1860 what now would be recognized as the dime novel—brief paperbacks sold for only ten cents. The appeal to a downscale market was part of a cultural dynamic that gained momentum in the 1830s, when penny newspapers redefined "news" to be not just informative and opinionated but entertaining and inexpensive. The market for cheap books expanded greatly in the 1840s and 1850s as literacy increased and lyceums, debating societies, and libraries, especially in public schools, became common. These, in turn, enlarged the market for books.[3]

Hickok, Cody, and others simply came along at the right time. Numerous fiction and nonfiction series appeared from the 1830s to the 1850s, including foreign titles, until the International Copyright Act in 1891 made them less profitable. These precursors to dime novels were commonly pirated European books, which American publishers could set, print, and bind in paper covers within a day. The new modes of transportation by canal and rail added to the market. Just as popular, if not more so, as the established writers and novelists—including Charles Dickens and Edward Bulwer-Lytton—were the sensationalists, who appealed to adventure, patriotism, and some steamy romance. Not too steamy, however, given the mores of antebellum America, and moralism was part of the formula.[4]

Story papers anticipated the dime novel, usually appearing as eight-page weeklies, costing five to eight cents, and containing five to eight serialized stories of adventure, romance, and Westerns. Most were published in New York, Boston, and Philadelphia, which is significant because the American Western started on the East Coast, far from the geographic West but close to the nation's creative heart. Another manifestation was the short-lived pamphlet, fifty to one hundred pages, five by eight and a half inches, initially only twelve and a half cents, but forced out of business in 1845 as postal rates increased. It was the precursor for the Beadles, which was a series of four-by-six-inch pamphlets published in 1860.[5]

The *Police Gazette* was another forerunner to the dime novel in terms of lowbrow appeal, violent content and popularity. Not surprisingly, the editor, Richard Kyle Fox, had a newspaper background and knew the terrain of violent crime on which his magazine thrived. Like the later dime novels, it was formulaic, bloody, and awash in stereotypes of racial minorities, the British, cowboys, and some religious groups. The *Police Gazette* had the added appeal of illustrations. Texans were Fox's especial target. In 1879, a full 40 percent of the crimes reported in the magazine involved Texas, which was not wholly undeserving of the condemnation. He also detested pretense and injustice, two things the dime novels seemed to address—and find a way to correct—in nearly every issue.[6]

Beadle and Adams's first dime novel was *Malaeska: The Indian Wife of the White Hunter* by Ann Sophia Stephens. It sold more than three hundred thousand copies. Other publishers imitated the success, and by 1865 more than four million dime novel copies had been published, with sales of individual volumes running thirty-five to eighty thousand. Working in the seams of reality and in the corners of imaginations, Beadle and Adams had produced 3,668 issues by the end of the century, and Street and Smith 2,802.[7]

"Books for the Million"

Drifters, desperados and dead shots provided much grist for the booming publishing mills in the East. The decades after the war saw communication and transportation speed up, moving more goods, people, and information than ever. The telegraph had divorced human movement from communication several decades earlier, and telegraph lines followed the rapid growth of rail lines in the postwar years. Newspapers, magazines, and dime novels spread more information (and misinformation) to more people than ever before, thanks to those rail lines and improved, less costly mass-production printing technology. With increased literacy and access, the audience for reading material of all sorts erupted. Matching these new and larger audiences with demand meant the publication of content that was a bit more downscale. The enhancement of facts in the nineteenth-century press fueled the image of the savage killer, wild men of the plains, and gunfights on Main Street. It was an exciting time in the West, especially in the pages of newspapers and dime novels.

The place of the cowboy-gunslinger in American folklore is indebted to the dime-novel industry. Though detective stories, romances, and tales of pirates and soldiers were quite popular, the Western was the favorite of the lot, accounting for anywhere from two-thirds to three-quarters of the titles, a testament not only to a large market but also a fascination among all classes with the frontier West. Before 1875, wilderness was a common setting for the Western adventure. After 1875, Western action more frequently took place in small but growing towns that might need a little civilizing at gunpoint. Fighting Indians and outlaws was the hero's stock in trade, as he rescued damsels and saved the timid townsfolk from the menacing men in black. The dime-novel gunmen were only a step removed from gallant knights of earlier romance literature. Now, they were garbed in boots, hats, and dusty clothes, a look that became standard material for subsequent film and television productions. As civilizing these towns became a common theme in nineteenth-century writing about the Wild West, Eastern culture provided the civilizers: so, men from the East went West. Cody turned the mission into entertainment, replete with savages, shootouts, and stagecoach robberies. Almost all dime-novel authors were Easterners. The Wild West vision of the West was not the only view, but it exceeded and dominated all others.[8]

Colorful characters who went "out West" became legends thanks to sensational journalism and dime novels. Hickok's legend, as it evolved, was also deeply indebted to *Buffalo Bill's Wild West* and the dime-novel successors. The dime-novel Hickok character was similar to that of Buffalo Bill, whose character was created by author Edward Judson. The immediate market was young men and women, primarily craft and factory workers and servants. The broader appeal was not restricted to working classes. Urban professionals, including clerks and shopkeepers, as well as farmers and their families in more rural areas read the books. Beadle and Adams had a slogan that addressed the issue succinctly: "Books for the Million!" The influx of immigrants expanded the market, especially among Irish and Germans, which is attested to by series such as the Ten Cent Irish Novels and George Munro's Die Deutsche Library. Frederick Whittaker, who later wrote a sensational and worshipful biography of Custer, was a writer of dime-novel literature. He stated that mass-appeal novels were for a "great people," perhaps as much a reference to democratic instincts as deference to audience. As further testament to the popularity of the cheap literature, they were shipped to Civil War camps in bales, via freight cars, wagons, and waterways. They were among those items that Confederate and Union pickets swapped across lines. The novels were so popular that one publisher, in order to thwart overcharging of enlisted men for the volumes, printed the picture of a ten-cent coin on the cover.[9]

From about 1860, fifty heroic years of pages were filled with battling bad guys and Indians, saving imperiled ladies, and slaying the occasional beast. Like newspapers, the works were made cheaply in order to be read and discarded. The cowboy as fast-draw artist became a stock character. It was this inaccurate image credited largely to Beadle and Adams that later gave rise to the cinema's dandily dressed gunmen, which included Hickok.[10]

The first Wild Bill dime novel was the progeny of George Ward Nichols's article, which was not much more constrained by facts than the dime novels it would inspire. Journalist Thomas Picton, writing under the name Paul Preston, had written *Wild Bill, the Indian-Slayer*, printed by New York publisher Robert M. DeWitt as one of his DeWitt's Ten Cent Romances in July 1867. *Wild Bill's First Trail*, ostensibly told by Wild Bill himself, appeared in December. The dime novel was "edited" by "Col." Chris Forrest, a pseudonym for William Osborn Stoddard, a journalist for the New York *Examiner* who had been one of Abraham Lincoln's White House secretaries. Hickok, as narrator, warned the reader in advance that he may have stretched the facts a bit, a disclaimer likely ignored by readers who had devoured Nichols's fantasy and wanted more. "A good many things that I have to tell didn't happen to me, or in my sight and hearing, but I got them pretty near first hands, as a general thing, and even if I didn't I shan't spoil my yarn by leaving them out if they chance to fit well. If anything doesn't suit you, just bear in mind that I'm telling the story. . . ."[11]

A Taste for Violence

No wonder Hickok found lots of space in nineteenth-century newspapers. Dime novels helped fire a cultural obsession with mayhem and killing that has run from the heroic gunmen such as Wild Bill, with his triple-digit body counts, to Sam Peckinpah's 1969 bloodbath Western *The Wild Bunch*, along with its ever gorier sequels and imitators. American literature, journalism, entertainment—and culture in general—were and are enthralled with violence and killing. Hickok was part of a long tradition that embraced killers and killing. "If it bleeds, it leads" is a newsroom cliché. Killing is popular and profitable in news as well as entertainment, and while the media may change, the values do not. When Hickok exaggerated the number of killings, he was lionized, not assailed, even though most people, including journalists, knew the number was nonsense. It elevated his celebrity status and was in keeping with what came to be a storied American West that was colored with killers. Dime-novel plots and protagonists were often bloody but virtuous, traits passed on to their successors, the pulp fiction Westerns, cinema, and television. Moral killers proliferated. As Richard Maxwell Brown pointed out in *No Duty to Retreat*, "standing your ground" rather than retreating for the sake of human life was not merely a behavior but an expression of cultural mores that dated back to the Wild West, and probably to Wild Bill's shootout with Davis Tutt. A casual perusal of dime-novel titles reveals devotion to overt violence or the suggestion of it: *The Black Avenger of the Spanish Main; or, The Fiend of Blood: A Thrilling Tale of Buccaneer Times*; *The War Cloud; or, Life for Life*; *Buckskin Sam, the Scalp Taker*. And so on.[12]

Historian David Hamilton Murdoch credited Nichols with "the literary rehabilitation of the frontier psychopath." Given the quick acceptance and widespread repetition of the tales, there may not have been much rehabilitating to do. Public embrace of the killer came quickly and easily, as the account was reprinted widely and even expanded upon. As a sometime lawman, Hickok may have been justified in the eyes of the readership. Ostensibly, he was acting for law and order, hardly a psychopath. At other times, as in the Tutt killing, the jury found him acting in self-defense. Historically, the court of public opinion largely has not just exonerated Hickok but idolized him for the deed.[13]

Even when the killings appeared inexcusable, the press seemed to find a rationale. Newspapers contrived stories about Jesse James and his gang becoming Robin Hoods of the West, sharing their loot with people in need, especially widows and orphans. There was no evidence he ever did such a thing, but it makes a better story. The idea of Hickok as a latter-day knight errant is fiction. If he did kill in self-defense, he was not defending the poor or aiding widows and orphans except in fiction. He supposedly did pay for the funeral of Mike Williams, the security guard he inadvertently killed. Men such as James, Hickok, Billy the Kid, and John Wesley Hardin were further enshrined when they died as a result of betrayal or being shot in the back. Treachery compounded the tragedy, elevating it from merely a killer meeting a just end. In the dime novel, killing was mixed with morality. Erastus Beadle disallowed "all things offensive to good taste . . . , subjects or characters that carry an immoral taint . . . , and what cannot be read with satisfaction by every right-minded person, young and old alike." The offenses included drinking, smoking and swearing. But not killing.[14]

Beadle and Adams published at least nine titles about Hickok, including *Wild Bill's Gold Trail*; *Wild Bill's Sable Pard*; *Wild Bill's Trump Card*; *Wild Bill's Weird Foe*; *Wild Bill, the Pistol Prince*; and *Wild Bill, the Wild West Duelist*. In addition to dime novels by Beadle and Adams and other publishers citing Wild Bill in the title—his notoriety assuring strong sales—hundreds more included Hickok as a supporting character. He was likely to turn up in any saloon or along any trail to supply a few pages of action. An accurate tally is complicated by the problematic definition of a dime novel. Hickok appeared in story papers, serializations, and pamphlets, some of which were republished in different formats or in the same format at a later date. Furthermore, only four appeared before Hickok's death. Like Custer, Hickok was more famous in death than in life. And there was the apocryphal moment of his demise: where Custer was often shown as the last man standing, guns blazing on a hilltop, Hickok had the "dead-man's hand."[15]

In *Wild Bill's Last Trail*, which appeared four years after Hickok's death, Judson's account of Hickok's last days had elements that were both peculiar and predictable in terms of dime-novel content. Hickok was killed at a card table, but there was no mention of the dead-man's hand. The morality came into play with Judson's constant reminder that drink and gambling were the downfall of men, including Hickok. Otherwise, the story was replete with romance between a beautiful woman and a desperado, Indians, treachery, and even a ghost that caused Hickok to faint. Although Judson apparently never met Hickok, a tale did circulate of Judson going west for just that purpose (no city ever named) and finding Hickok in a saloon. Judson approached his hero too brashly, according to legend, exclaiming, "There's my man," and "I want you." Hickok drew his pistol, ready for the worst. In spite of Judson's retreat and his explaining who he was and affirming that Hickok was his Indian-fighting hero, Hickok gave Judson twenty-four hours to get out of town. Judson did. Subsequently, Judson's view of Hickok was mixed—the heroic gunslinger/lawman on the one hand, great material for a dime-novel protagonist, and a drunkard and gambler on the other. That meant a character with regrets whose appearance on the receiving end of a story with a revenge motif was appropriate. The story also offered what became standard fare in many Westerns and crime stories—getting out of town in a prescribed amount of time, with sundown and twenty-four hours becoming popular deadlines.[16]

Before getting out of town, Judson managed to gather some tales from Hickok pals Cody and Texas Jack Omohundro about Hickok's exploits. Judson transferred some of the feats to Cody, perhaps in retaliation for being tossed from town so easily and unheroically, at least according to legend. If the tale is true, it may shed light on Judson's depiction of Hickok vacillating from heroic to wimpy, turning him into a desperado and wanton killer, and actually fainting in a part of *On the Death Trail; or, The Last of Wild Bill*. Horace Hickok, brother of James, in 1880 wrote the New York *Weekly*, which had published the story, accusing Judson and the newspaper of depicting James as a desperado and coward, characterizations that were nothing short of slanderous. A few weeks later, publishers Street and Smith printed a letter from Cody, who supported Horace's accusations. Although Judson died in 1886, the story that so offended Horace Hickok did not. *Wild Bill's Last Trail* was republished in 1896.[17]

Wild Bill's First Trail had promised Indian fighting and buffalo hunting. It did so, and also included a love story and a revenge plot. As if buffalo hunting were not enough, there was a bear attack à la Crockett when the hunter draws a knife to finish the job. In the cast of characters, Wild Bill was not the lead but instead the scout for a party hunting down a band of Indians. The details of the setting were fuzzy ("the upper Arkansas"), as were the particulars about the tribes involved (Comanches, Chocktaws, Cherokees, and "Coyotes" were named). Actually, Wild Bill did not appear too often, and a more skeptical reader might wonder if he was just a selling point in the title. Much action took place in the Indian camp. In spite of Hickok's minimal presence, the story is still a rollicking adventure of Indian attacks, rescuing the kidnapped lady, and hunting.[18]

Not Wicked, but Wild

Wild Bill, the Indian Slayer: A Tale of Forest and Prairie Life also pitted Hickok against savage Indians. In *Wild Bill's First Trail*, the author took time to point out the evils of alcohol. In *Indian Slayer*, Wild Bill moralized, "I have been wild, but wicked never. . . . I've the blood of many a man on my hands, but I never killed save in a fair fight. I never shot a white man, unless he drew a bead on me, and as for Indians, I've always given 'em a white man's show." This racist Hickok was clad in a buckskin hunting shirt and described as a chivalric "species of knight." There was even a gunfight scenario that mimicked the real-life showdown with Tutt, down to the detail of the bad guy trying to "pack Bill's watch." There was nothing original in the story, just a brave and noble hero, an expert horseman and marksman, keen on upholding justice and well versed in woodsman's skills. Judson found Hickok similarly useful in *Wild Bill's Last Trail*, which reminded readers not to drink or gamble. Hickok was not heroic in this story, but he was used as a tool to moralize in the tale of revenge and treachery. Judson used Hickok's name to sell an adventure that had little to do with the exploits of the real-life Wild Bill. Another story of blood, revenge, guns, and justice emphasized Hickok's pistol prowess. *Wild Bill, the Pistol Dead Shot: or, Dagger Don's Double* was a dime novel only in the sense of genre, because although it ran in Beadle's dime library, it was not published as a bound edition.[19]

This tale pulled another successful and popular dime novelist to the Wild Bill group, Prentiss Ingraham, a former Confederate army colonel and soldier of fortune. But the story and the action were along the lines of the other Hickok stories—adventure and action. The title summed up the plot. As for the supposed code of the gunfighter, *Wild Bill, the Wild West Duelist* depicted Wild Bill and a villain back to back, pistols raised, prepared to pace off in a fashion befitting the knights of the American West. Cody was credited with authorship, but any of a number of house writers might have written the tale.[20]

Anything so popular had to generate detractors, who for the dime novels arose as early as the 1870s and 1880s. In 1886, the Massachusetts Legislature outlawed "criminal news, police reports, or accounts of criminal deeds, or pictures and stories of lust and crime." They meant dime novels. Anthony Comstock's campaign in the 1870s was aimed in part at dime novels and story papers. He was the primary influence in passage of what came to be called the Comstock Law, passed by Congress in March 1873. His target was obscenity and sexuality, broadly defined and construed as anything that might corrupt one's morals—or offend Anthony Comstock. He had the editor of a story paper arrested in 1872 and successfully prosecuted book dealers in the 1880s for selling "criminal story papers" and stories of "bloodshed and crime." A New York Assembly bill in 1883 stated, "[A]ny person who shall sell, loan, or give to any minor under sixteen years of age any dime novel or book of fiction, without first obtaining the written consent of the parent or guardian of such minor, . . . guilty of a misdemeanor, punishable by imprisonment or by a fine not exceeding $50." The bill did not pass, but it captured the essence of Comstock's fears. In an account of his troubles, "Traps for the Young" (1883), he called dime novels and their kin "Satan's efficient agents."[21]

The objections to dime-novel content may have gained a bit more credence toward the end of the century as authors began to substitute completely fictional characters, such as Deadwood Dick, and real-life outlaws for the likes of Hickok, Cody, and frontier legend Kit Carson. The characters became more lurid, the acts more sensational, and law and order less the driver of the plot than simple action. Increased competition and the demand for more material drove writers and publishers to new extremes in order to stay in business. The mainstream press also objected, though perhaps as much for economic as prurient reasons, given the great success of the dime novels.[22]

Newspapers found plenty of opportunities to assail dime novels. Much of the criticism came via stories of crime, which were blamed for corrupting young minds. A linear cause and effect was often drawn from dime-novel "addiction" to the young readers' crimes, which included murder, robbery, burglary, kidnapping, arson, vandalism, and even stealing chickens. Non-felonious offenses included running away, usually westward, and the breakup of families. The Atlanta *Constitution* and the Chicago *Daily Tribune* called reading the novels an addiction, one that even resulted in mental illness and hallucinations. In newspapers from San Francisco to New York, the immorality of the genre was unquestioned. The New York *Times*, among others, called for stopping the sale of dime novels. The New York *Tribune* declared the literature "how to" manuals for committing crime, in this case arson. The San Francisco *Chronicle* wrote that a twelve-year-old boy injured himself in a bear hunt after being inspired by a dime-novel story.

The Atlanta *Constitution* cited Hickok specifically in an article on "Dime Novels and Murder," in which a minister was quoted as saying, "our boys are tempted into evil ways by what they read." A quadruple-murder trial in Erie, Kansas, revealed "the intimate connection between dime novels and crime." Ironically, the *Constitution*'s crime scene description rivaled any dime-novel prose: "The floor was covered with blood, in which he [a neighbor] fairly had to wade. The ceiling was spattered and the walls stained. The old man Sells (the family's name) was lying on the floor with the whole back part of his head crushed in and his throat cut so deep that his head was almost severed from his body." The next victim also had a "crushed skull and her throat cut in the same manner. . . . Miss Ina Sells with the skull crushed and her throat cut from ear to ear. . . . The body of Willie Sells, with a large gash in his forehead, one of his eyes chopped out and his throat cut similar to the others." The accused had never been considered vicious, according to the article. However, "He has always been an inveterate reader of dime novels of the worst class, and has frequently expressed his desire to become a frontier hero; a 'Wild Bill,'

'Slippery Sam' or something of the sort." In light of the narrative, the killer apparently was not the only one to find dime novels an inspiration.[23]

In 1884, the New York *Tribune* charged that the novels had inspired three boys to rob their parents and head west. Dime novelist Frederick Whittaker, who lived in Mount Vernon, New York, replied to the *Tribune*, denying the accusation that dime novels were a bad influence. The paper printed his response. Whittaker said that he intended "to defend the class to which I belong. . . . The only writers who can make a living by literary labors alone are dime novelists." If Edgar Allan Poe were still alive, Whittaker wrote, "he would have been a writer of dime novels; for his prose stories have all the qualities which are required in a good dime, . . . It is only the cheap stories, which you call dime novels, for which the demand is, and always will be inexhaustible, and which must be depended on for the regeneration of American literature." Whittaker, notably, did not merely defend the genre but asserted the need for the sake of literature itself. Like the dime novels themselves, Whittaker implied a certain anti-elitism mixed with an egalitarian appeal to the common man.[24]

Writing dime novels frequently was a sideline for people who were earning a living as journalists, teachers, or clerks. Few made a career of it, but those few who did wrote profusely, quickly, and colorfully. Upton Sinclair, of later fame for his muckraking journalism and novels, claimed that in his dime-novel years, 1887–1902, he wrote as much as the collected works of Scott. William Wallace Cook said that for months at a time he wrote at the prodigious rate of two 30,000-word stories per week. Author Eugene Cook said there were three requirements of these writers: a tireless writing hand, a riotous imagination, and a good instinct for drama. As though to affirm Cook, Whittaker, who wrote for Beadle and Adams, said in 1886 that he was paid $3,200 for 16 novels a year, for topics as wide-ranging as pirates, Russian spies, and the Mexican frontier. Judson cranked out 300 to 400 dime novels, claiming to have once produced a 610-page novel in only 62 hours.[25]

A Profitable Sideline

Dime novelists' voluminous output was grounded in imagination, not experience or evidence. They did not generally concern themselves with such things as subject familiarity or firsthand knowledge of geography. Ingraham did personally know Cody and wrote some two hundred dime novels about him. Few of the authors managed to get west of the Mississippi River. One of the implications for the narrow range of knowledge was a limited story line. When a plot became popular, it endured, to the point of becoming an entrenched stereotype. The Hickok-Tutt duel demonstrated how an anomalous event, one hardly worthy of cultural devotion and praise, became a mainstay in the Western story.[26]

Although fictional, the dime novels were linked intimately to the journalism of the era. Writers worked in both fields, often concurrently. One journalist who was also a dime novelist noted a letter from his publisher, Street and Smith, that suggested he work less at trying to produce unusual plots and draw on newspapers, "which are teeming with material of this character," although probably more suited to detective and crime stories than cow-town shootouts and frontier knife fights. Many of the tales were anonymous, but these novelists, like journalists, wrote quickly and formulaically. Although the work usually did not generate much wealth for the writers, it was a profitable sideline.[27]

With many plots drawn from the daily news, and given the need to churn out the words, it's understandable that many dime novelists were newspaper journalists. Few better knew the seamy side of life. Journalists brought with them not only the ability to write fast and on deadlines but also a good sense of reality's sharp edges. Probably more for the urban detective tales than the frontiersman sagas, journalists were able to inject a street-level familiarity with the subject gained from everyday dealings with police and courts. Journalists knew audiences and understood as well as any group of writers how to appeal to the masses, young and old, highbrow and low. They could bring color to the drab and sordid events of daily life and give the bawdy house a patina of romance. They were not paid for originality, and were even instructed on stock plots and characters. The habit has continued into the twenty-first century with the popularity of television's dime-novel adaptations—"reality" series and dramatizations, "based on actual events," but mostly fictional.[28]

Edward Judson was imaginative, dramatic, and one of the few to make a career of dime-novel writing. A glimpse into his life and work is instructive in understanding the world of the hack writer of the nineteenth century. He was the sort of writer who originated and fueled the legends. Sensation abounded in both Judson's writing and his personal life. For Judson, writing was an opportunity, not a higher literary calling. He agreed with Nathaniel Hawthorne that mass-appeal fiction was rubbish, but it was affordable entertainment for common people. Judson claimed to be making at least $15,000 annually from his writing for Street and Smith, and this in an era when a skilled laborer or businessman would consider $1,300 a good yearly income. Of course, his figure is suspect because stretching the truth made him a great dime novelist.

Clay Reynolds, who edited a collection of dime novels that included stories about Wild Bill, noted some of Judson's other flaws: "That Judson was also a bigamist, a slanderer and blackmailer and notorious scoundrel, an inciter of riots and a fugitive from justice, and very possibly a murderer, an ex-convict, deadbeat, philanderer, and one of the world's greatest liars likely did not come up in conversation." He was married six or seven times and had a number of mistresses. A mob in Nashville, Tennessee, hanged him, but he was cut down before choking to death. That incident arose from a shootout with an irate husband whose wife Judson apparently attempted to seduce. Judson and the husband wounded one another. Trying to escape the lynch mob, Judson suffered a broken leg when he leaped from third-story hotel window. Even his military service was marred. He served with the First New York Mounted Rifles and saw action in only one minor skirmish in the Civil War, but it was enough to give him a story behind his limp. A war wound was a much more dramatic explanation than reality, which probably included sciatica and arthritis aggravated by his Nashville adventure. He was stripped of his rank—sergeant—and discharged after being jailed for desertion. Nevertheless, back in Baltimore his portrait showed him in a colonel's uniform. He adopted the honorific for the rest of his life.[29]

Judson and his dime-novel talent were at the center of events that elevated William Cody to showmanship and fame. Judson contrived the character and name "Buffalo Bill" in 1869 after a conversation the two had, and Cody assumed the dime-novel moniker and costume, both of which the hero needed. Judson also convinced Cody to take on an acting role—playing himself. Judson wrote a stage play, *The Scouts of the Prairie*, specifically for Cody when the new celebrity came East to Chicago in 1872, dashing off the script in only four hours after Cody agreed to it. The theater dramas and dime novels spawned the incredibly successful *Buffalo Bill's Wild West*, whose impact on the Eastern image of the West was immeasurable. It ran from 1883 until 1909—it changed management in 1894, when Barnum and Bailey took it over—and toured the United States annually, making its way to Canada in 1885 and Europe in 1887. The impact in the East was most important because the East was the heart of the publishing and entertainment industries.[30]

Although best known for his dime novels, Judson also produced magazines, broadsides, journalistic-style exposés, and lectured on temperance. Well before the dime-novel era, he was working on books that were journalistic only in that they flirted with facticity. *The Mysteries and Miseries of New York: A Story of Real Life* was supposed to warn people about the menace of drinking and gambling. In some ways, his work anticipated the next generation of muckrakers, some of whom used fiction based loosely on fact to address larger moral issues, such as Sinclair in *The Jungle*.[31]

But Judson was never one to get bogged down in evidence. Although writing voluminously about the West, he probably had never traveled west of the Mississippi prior to an 1868 trip, which may have been his only sojourn there. As for the story of his going to Dodge City to present Wyatt Earp and Bat Masterson with "Buntline Specials," it was pure fabrication, promoted largely by an Earp biographer. Judson also wrote about adventures at sea, fighting Indians, hunting and fishing, and the American Revolution, and he also produced travel guides, among other things. Judson's pen name "Ned Buntline" was taken from the term for the rope at the base of a ship's sail. The name grew out of an incident when Seaman Judson and a few of his shipmates, while serving in the U.S. Navy, stole a roast pig from the ship's captain during a cruise near Havana. Judson privately published the story in a pamphlet as "The Captain's Pig," which was attributed to Buntline. The captain happened upon a copy of the pamphlet, which infuriated him, but he could do nothing because the story was anonymous. Judson resigned from the navy in June 1842, apparently without the captain ever knowing Buntline's identity.[32]

Frederick Whittaker's eclecticism was comparable to Judson's, but he had a bit more credibility as he had written a biography of Custer, among other journalistic works. The book was more than complete in some respects, given that reality was highly enhanced and praise for the subject ceaseless. In addition to dime novels, he wrote for a number of newspapers and magazines. His family immigrated to the United States from England, where he worked briefly in a law office before embarking on his writing career. He served in the cavalry during the Civil War and sustained a wound in the Battle of the Wilderness in 1864. For his bravery, he apparently was promoted to brevet captain after the war, when he became a book agent. He found himself on the authorship end of the business in February 1870, when he started writing for *Frank Leslie's Illustrated Newspaper*. Whittaker spent the rest of his life writing for magazines and several Beadle and Adams publications. His Custer biography was his first work, written in short order considering that Custer had died at the Little Bighorn only the previous summer. Whittaker died ingloriously in 1889 when the pistol he always carried accidentally discharged.[33]

Prentiss Ingraham, who also authored plays, novels, and poems, was one of Beadle and Adams's most productive writers, churning out a couple of thirty-five-thousand- to seventy-thousand-word pieces monthly. He may have written as many as a thousand novels, and in 1900 he claimed credit for more than six hundred. He also published in *Family Story Paper*, *Nickel Libraries*, and the *Saturday Evening Post*. He allegedly wrote a volume for the *Half-Dime Library* in a day and night, and in only five days he wrote a *Dime Library* number. He reportedly was a ghostwriter for Cody, which would be appropriate given the numerous stories he had written about Cody for Beadle and Adams. Street and Smith also picked up the stories in its *Far West Library*, where the tales showed up in the 1918 catalog. Ingraham's designation of Hickok as the "prince of the pistoleers" became part of the Wild Bill myth. The moniker originally appeared in Ingraham's dime novel of 1891, *Wild Bill, the Pistol Prince*, which Frank Wilstach adapted to his 1926 biography.[34]

Dismissed by many as simple adventure books for boys, dime novels perhaps were guilty of unwarranted popularity and undeserved riches, which was not necessarily a virtue among the literati. Historian Richard Etulain credited Buffalo Bill more than others for the myth of the West. Cody may have invented the myth, but dime novelists created Buffalo Bill. The dime-novel industry saw more than 550 original works about Cody, with around 1,700 total when one includes reprints and retitled volumes. By the end of the century, Cody was a household name, along with Texas Jack Omohundro, Annie Oakley, and Buck Taylor, who were also part of *Buffalo Bill's Wild West*.

When Street and Smith serialized *Buffalo Bill, the King of the Border Men* from December 23, 1869, to March 10, 1870, it was the beginning of world fame for Cody and, to a lesser extent, Hickok. Cody had been known on the Plains for some years, but Judson's series and the New York *Weekly* made him an international name. The show was a resounding success in Europe, where it was to be part of the American Exhibition in London. When Cody's enterprise left America for London in 1886, it included 180 horses, 18 buffalo, 10 elk, 5 Texas steers, 4 donkeys, 97 Indians, 83 saloon passengers, and 38 steerage passengers. In London, Prime Minister William Gladstone toured the show's grounds, which also were graced by the prince of Wales and his family, who met Oakley and other performers. And a few days later, on May 11, even Queen Victoria took in a show. It was news across the country, especially since she had not attended a public performance since her husband's death twenty-five years earlier. Eventually, *Buffalo Bill's Wild West* drew kings of Belgium, Greece, Saxony, and Denmark, and the future German Kaiser. Crowds averaged around thirty thousand for the twice-daily performances, exceeding more than a million by the time the tour ended in October 1887. It was basically a staged dime novel.

With the American Exhibition and London behind him, Cody headed for Paris and its 1889 Universal Exposition, where the French president and more than ten thousand people showed up for the opening. From there, the show went to southern France, Spain, Italy, Germany, and back to England in 1890. The earlier affiliation with Cody was a factor in building Hickok's reputation. Because they were writing for the masses, Judson and other dime novelists have gone largely unacknowledged in terms of their impact on making Wild Bill and others so well known in national myth and culture. Colorful nicknames, in turn, were and continue to be great marketing devices.[35]

In Hickok's earliest appearance in a Judson dime novel—*Buffalo Bill, the King of Border Men*—Wild Bill was a sidekick who did the revenge killing for Cody. The novel used the West as a backdrop for a story about the Civil War in Kansas. In later novels, Buntline's protagonists became much more capable of murder and mayhem, but always for a good and just cause. Hickok changed too in later versions, suffering from nightmares and quaking at the thought of his own death, a plot device that would be used in later fiction about Hickok. Thus, the writers splattered the pages with rhetorical blood, gore, and psychobabble but preserved a pretense of morality.[36]

Even among outlaws, Hickok's exploits found a readership. The rancher and miner John Plesent Gray deposited a typed memoir with the Arizona Pioneers' Historical Society in 1940. After leaving the University of California at Berkeley, Gray had operated a ranch near Camp Rucker in the Chiricahua Mountains and claimed to have been on easy terms with the stage robber and rustler Billy Leonard and his gang. Leonard, according to Gray, was a New York watchmaker "much above his fellow rustlers in intellect and education." As a favor, Leonard converted Gray's long-barreled Winchester into a carbine with simple tools, and in gratitude Gray gave him a book he thought the outlaw would enjoy. Its title, as Gray recalled it, was *Life of Bill Hickok*. "He lost no time in getting his little bunch of followers together, and then spent the rest of the day reading to them. Bill Hickok was the hero, henceforth, of the rustlers. . . ." The book probably was J. W. Buel's *Life and Marvelous Adventures of Wild Bill, the Scout*, published in 1880, but it might also have been *Wild Bill's First Trail* or one of the many dime novels in circulation. Gray pondered why Hickok and other Western characters and places were splashed with romance when he remembered them quite differently. "My memory," he wrote, "tells only of those old days as they appeared at the time and they are not being viewed as a distant era, which seems inclined to make heroes out of desperadoes." Gray understood the limits of memory when it is appropriated by media and audiences. Leonard, however, didn't have long to enjoy his Wild Bill book. He was shot during a robbery in 1881 and died a few hours later.[37]

Taking Audiences Seriously

Although dime novels were dismissed as cheap thrills for the unwashed, they made a big difference in imagining Hickok. The story line prevailed, not just in mass media and histories but in the broader culture and the allure of guns and violence. Widely read, dime novels were important in creating the early gunslinger legends. When dime novelists of the 1880s, such as Ingraham, drew on Nichols's 1867 article, they had found a veneer of authenticity. This pseudoreality was adopted in subsequent generations of media. Elegantly and accurately stated by historian Pamela Haag, "Like Hickok, Buffalo Bill did not become a myth as much as he began as one."[38]

It was often the case, as the ever-present fretters about cultural decay worried, that dime novels were creating a false narrative. The critics missed the point, which was that writers such as Judson and Whittaker created great stories with wide, lasting appeal, and did so with Indian killing and high-noon walkdowns. Other media eventually absorbed dime novels, most immediately comics and pulp fiction books and magazines, where the focus was on entertainment, not factual reporting. Critics who assailed the disregard of fact and history were looking through the wrong lenses, the same way an idealist might misunderstand such modern platforms as reality television or talk radio—entertainment draws audiences, which attract advertising and dollars. The real insight of the dime novel was marketing and the use of the then-modern modes of transportation and communication. The writers cast their heroes in similar molds. Not one of them is unique, including Hickok, whose good looks, quick draw, Indian-killing prowess, horsemanship, and frontier skills could be found in any number of dime-novel personalities. What the dime novel did, essentially, was to create a successful character. Wild Bill was among the most durable.

Dime novels did not take Western history, sociology, or geography seriously. They did take their audience seriously, however. The Wild Bill that dime-novel writers created has endured for more than 150 years and across media platforms. The criticism of dime novels parallels that of the next century directed toward pulp fiction, cinema, and television, all of which moralists and the literati disdained in part because the work appealed to too many people.

4. ❈ A Country in the Mind: Hickok in Literature

> I tremble to think what the writers do after a body dies.
> —Pete Dexter, *Deadwood*, 1986

Popular literature offers a perspective different from history, biography, and autobiography. Stories reflect, create, and comment upon historical memory. Historical fiction, even when richly fact-based, imagines the past and is inherently ahistorical. History opens the past to the inquirer based on available records. The biographer documents a life story in a particular historical context. While some biographers take a suspect psychobiographical approach, the novelist has greater opportunity to explore the mind of the characters.

Western novelists departed from their mainstream literary peers and differed among themselves within the conventions of the emerging Western genre. Some stories continued in the dime-novel, pulp, and comic book traditions with derivative plots, stock characters, and vapid dialogue. Others sought more mythical, abstracted themes not rooted in a particular landscape or time, or they dabbled in fantasy. Westerns sometimes drifted into fact-heavy sagas strong on texture and tumbleweeds. Long and immersive, those Westerns usually got the atmosphere right but received little respect from reviewers and academics because they were not literary enough, nor were they as comfortably predictable as the pulps. Popular Westerns were closely tethered to audience expectations and desires. Westerns fell under a kind of bastardized journalistic genre, a pastiche of frontier newspapering. Frontier scribes showed up as characters in Westerns to add some faux-documentary authenticity or simply to allow the author, probably a former journalist, to ride merrily into town on a metanarrative horse. The essence of the Western, according to literary scholar Jane Tompkins, is death. "To go west, as far west as you can go, west of everything, is to die. Death is everywhere in this genre. Not just in the shoot-outs, or in the scores of bodies that pile up toward the narrative's close but, even more compellingly, in the desert landscape with which the bodies of the gunned-down gradually merge." Journalism is not far behind with its body counts, but the landscape is more likely to be urban wastelands as it is the empty, arid quarter.[1]

Dime-novel writers had a substantial impact on modern fiction, seen in the variegated works of Jack London, Ernest Hemingway, Ernest Haycox, Bertha Sinclair (B. M. Bower), Zane Grey, and Dorothy Johnson. James Agee, the magazine journalist, poet, and film critic who ventured with photographer Walker Evans into a distressed Alabama county in 1936 to write the Depression-era classic *Let Us Now Praise Famous Men*, was quickened by resonances of a primitive Western quest. In 1916, Agee had seen the first cowboy star, William S. Hart, who later played Hickok, on the screen at a movie theater in Knoxville, Tennessee, "with both guns blazing, . . . and the great country rode away behind him as wide as the world." The plight of the cotton tenant farmers Agee observed in Alabama was part of the fading memory of the Civil War and a growing national obsession with the decline of that "great country" in the West. "Frontier and Civil War nostalgia were interconnected," according to historian Barry Schwartz. Americans were already sentimental about the West and wanted to return to post–Civil War decades, which were not that far in the past but mythically distant. "The West of thirty-four years ago is now only a tradition," Carrie Adell Strahorn could write in 1911. "The picturesque wilderness with its marauding bands of Indians, with its lawless white men . . . and with its vast tenantless reaches of mountains and plains was a reality, with all the vast resources of the domain yet to be developed." Americans did not want to let go of the frontier and its potential. "They wanted to win it all over again, in the imagination," according to Tompkins.[2]

Whether or not they wrote Westerns or learned their craft by writing for the pulps or watching movies, something in the writers' work drew upon the idea of the West of popular mythology. Western fiction began in the 1820s with James Fenimore Cooper's *Leatherstocking Tales*. Just what constitutes a true Western is as debatable as how we define the West. "West is a country in the mind," Archibald MacLeish wrote in a 1955 *Collier's Weekly* article, "and so eternal." Westerns had proliferated during the dime-novel era from the Civil War up to about the time of Buffalo Bill Cody's death in 1917. After 1900, the Western slowly gained credibility in the hardback book publishing trade. Owen Wister's *The Virginian* (1902) was followed by Grey's *The Last of the Plainsmen* (1908) and *Riders of the Purple Sage* (1912) and Max Brand's *The Untamed* (1919).[3]

A Detour through the Pulps

The transition from the dime novel to literary respectability required a detour through the pulps. In 1919 Street and Smith converted one of its Western periodicals to a new seven-by-ten-inch format printed on woodpulp paper with a glossy enameled cover and retitled it *Western Story Magazine*. Initially a biweekly publication, *Western Story* soon became a weekly, still cost fifteen cents, and sold a half-million copies each week by 1921. By the mid-1930s, some two hundred "pulp magazines" were being published, the most popular of which were Westerns, with titles such as *Thrilling Western* and *Masked Rider*.[4]

During World War II, with paper in short supply, the pulps languished. *Western Story* folded in 1949 after 1,263 issues, and only a few titles continued into the 1950s. Several Western fiction magazines started up, but they failed to compete with paperback books and television. The last title bit the dust in 1981. Westerns were eclipsed for about 20 years after the war by some 150 different men's adventure magazines. These titles reflected the anxiety of the postwar period. Men returning from wartime service often found it difficult to adapt to civilian life. Wartime trauma had induced a particular kind of stress that played out in images of aggression more complex than the comparatively straightforward frontier shootout. Combat veterans had shared experience that sought release in everything from blood sports to stories of military life. Such titles as *Battle Cry* and *Man's Conquest* "aided in the general resocialization, or 'remasculization' of society" and also marked "a shift in the portrayal of women," according to magazine scholar David M. Earle. Eventually, the Westerns returned, transferring the postwar battle trauma of blood and death to a more familiar environment tinged with nostalgia for a slap-leather world of male agency. Tompkins saw this regress as a flight from language and interiority, the province of women. "Men would rather die than talk, because talking might bring up their own unprocessed pain or risk a dam burst that would undo the front of imperturbable superiority."[5]

Comic strips began appearing in American newspapers in the 1890s to boost circulation during the so-called newspaper war between the New York *World* and the New York *Journal*. The first color strips appeared in the *Sunday World* in 1894. Mass distribution through syndication boosted circulation into the millions. Western strips came later, with such titles as *Young Buffalo Bill* beginning in 1928 and *Red Ryder* and *The Lone Ranger* appearing in 1938. Many early strips evolved from popular movie serials. Comic books evolved from strips and brought color to what largely had been a black-and-white Western landscape in the movies and, before the mid-1950s, television. Although pulp fiction magazines were in decline, story lines easily could be repackaged in comic book form, the better to compete with more visual media, at least for a time. Early characters were superheroes without complexity. They began to change as the movies offered more revisionist plots.[6]

Avon Books was founded in 1941 to publish paperbacks before it moved into the comic book market at the end of World War II. It published *Wild Bill Hickok* comic books from 1949 to 1956, at which point Avon went out of business. Each bimonthly comic had multiple stories. A page of advertising offered readers a Daisy Air Rifle for $2.59, a throwing knife, an air pistol, a sling shot, a leather whip, a fencing set, and a ukulele, just what every young buckaroo needed to emulate Wild Bill in the neighborhood. The first issue, *Wild Bill Hickok, Frontier Fighter*, promised "True Stories from Official Files," which, judging from the content, meant Nichols, Buel, Ingraham, and Wilstach. The first story offered a fanciful interpretation of the McCanles incident.

"Old Grey Eagle" told young Hickok, "The land where the sun falls down needs strong young men, yellow-hair! It needs good young men who will keep the law and make others keep the law!" Never mind that they would settle on Indian land. Once in the West, Hickok won a shooting contest. "McCallan" and a partner thought his prize money was easy pickings, so they tried to jump him, only to get shot by the kid they thought was a tenderfoot. Next, McCallan's gang tried to rob the Overland Stage with Hickok driving, taking more casualties. On the trail, Hickok killed a giant grizzly with a knife. As he nursed his wounds at the Rock Springs station he was attacked by McCallan and nine men and took them all out, becoming "Wild Bill," in the story line at least, for the first time. It was the same old massacre tale with a few unimaginative name changes.[7]

Charlton, a publishing company that existed from 1945 to 1986, introduced a Hickok series that continued through 1959. The comics featured Wild Bill and Jingles, his sidekick from a popular radio and television series. Hickok also appeared in several issues of the *Classics Illustrated* series in 1954. Comic books had been under attack since the 1930s, culminating in televised hearings in New York in 1954 by the Senate subcommittee on juvenile delinquency. The hearings led to the formation of the Comics Magazine Association of America, which established a draconian code of ethics constricting what could be published. The industry never fully recovered. The number of titles dropped from 650 to about 250 by 1956. Among the survivors, Western comics lost popularity through the 1960s and gave way to a new line of superheroes and antiheros more in the spirit of the times. Hickok was made for the comics, but his time was up. He was a scant presence until reinvented for new media.[8]

As late as 1961, no general histories of the literature of the West had been published. The study of the literature of the South, in contrast, was in its ascendancy. Scholars may have looked for the West in the wrong places. E. C. Little had compared Hickok to Sir Lancelot in 1901. John Steinbeck thought American Westerns had their origin in the Middle Ages. "The American Western is the Arthurian Cycle. The King is the man who solves everything with a gun," Steinbeck said in 1960.[9]

Hickok was a very modern figure, a quasi-fictional character aware of his own fictions. Had he been an entirely fictional character in a novel, he might have been a Don Quixote, a knight-errant of the plains. Miguel de Cervantes was, according to the literary scholar Harold Bloom, "the inventor of a mode now common enough, in which figures, within a novel, read prior fictions concerning their own earlier adventures and have to sustain a consequent loss in the sense of reality." J. W. Buel, his first biographer, claimed to have written from Hickok's diary, which has never been found, if it ever existed. Inevitably, debunkers arose to reshape Hickok's image. William E. Connelley rebutted criticisms of Hickok in 1927, affirming that Kansas revered its heroes and would defend them against literary and historical attack.[10]

Times changed, and literary tastes changed with them. Revisionist Westerns and other adaptations became popular, beginning with *Hombre* (1961) by Elmore Leonard, Thomas Berger's *Little Big Man* (1964), and Charles Portis's *True Grit* (1968). Western writers invented characters or reimagined historical figures. Hickok died before most of the famous Western characters passed from the scene: Billy the Kid (1881); Johnny Ringo (1882); Jesse James (1882); Doc Holliday (1887); John Wesley Hardin (1895); Calamity Jane (1903); Butch Cassidy (1908); the Sundance Kid (1908); Bat Masterson (1921); Annie Oakley (1926); Wyatt Earp (1929). Hickok got an early start in the mythmaking business, just far enough back in time to be beyond the living memory of most writers of the 1920s. He and the West were imagined together. The revisionist writers discovered a more ambiguous figure, a manticore of contrasting parts, and a projection of current cultural and political concerns.[11]

When writers imagined Hickok, they faced a special challenge because most of what had been written about Wild Bill was already fiction. Even the most "realistic" Hickok novels were based on guesswork and exaggerations. With the fall line between fact and fiction hard to find, much of the fiction writer's inventive work was already done—selection became a matter of choosing which variant best engaged the restless audience. Because Hickok was a "real" character, tales of the great gunman had the implicit stamp of authenticity, as verified in the familiar example of the movie disclaimer: "based on a true story." Fictions had to outdo the biography, or else why bother with make believe? If the story fell short of the biography, an author's only recourse rested with getting details of landscape, historical background, weaponry, and anthropology right, creating plausible dialogue, and sometimes imagining Hickok's thoughts. Although the biographies improved, the earlier images and muddled history persisted, opening the door ever wider to fiction.

Like the dime novelists, many of the modern fiction writers began as journalists. They understood audiences and stories, wrote quickly to meet deadlines, liked to investigate, questioned authority, and observed or experienced violence. They had an eye for the telling detail and came in contact with a wide range of people—often denizens of the demimonde—who could be developed into characters. Writing magazine stories, reviews, books, and screenplays had the potential to provide additional income and the opportunity for apprenticeship. An interest in Western history and landscape could lead to a sideline in writing historical fiction. Established fiction writers in other genres could test the Western fiction market, which offered room for experimentation.

One of the earliest novels featuring Hickok was written by Emerson Hough, a lawyer who wrote for newspapers and national magazines. He had written favorably of Hickok as a lawman in *The Story of the Outlaw* in 1906, drawing on Buel. In *North of 36*, a 1923 novel stretching historical facts and probabilities, Hickok, as the virtuous sheriff of Abilene, helped a heroine elude rustlers on a cattle drive. Hickok supposedly wiped out the McCanles "gang" when it stole stock for the Confederate Army even before there was a Confederacy. The novel set the tone for much subsequent fiction by placing Hickok in the maelstrom of the Civil War and its aftermath.[12]

J. Allan Dunn, the author of *Wild Bill: A Western Story*, was born in England and graduated from Oxford. He came to the United States in 1893 and covered the Spanish-American War and the Russo-Japanese War for newspapers. He wrote prolifically for such magazines as *Wild West Weekly* and turned out popular novels syndicated in newspapers. Dunn had several pen names, writing *Wild Bill*, published in 1926, as Joseph Montague. The novel had two sections, each with chapter titles revealing the content and theme. The first section presented "The Modern Samson," which recounted the signature McCandlas [sic] incident, taken directly from Buel. Hickok was sure the "gang" was stirring up trouble with the Sioux on behalf of the new Confederate government and left eight bodies strewn about Rock Creek after he was attacked. At Pea Ridge, Hickok shot twenty-three charging Rebels and a general, apparently pausing to count the bodies. After the war, Hickok said he aimed "to do my share in boostin' the empire westward. Pacifyin' the Sioux, for one thing, an' I reckon thar's jest one way to do thet—over gun sights." He was off to a good start, with sixty-six kills, all in fair fights. [13]

John Peele Miles, an American journalist, wrote "Wild Bill Hickok, Super Gunman," a fictional series syndicated in several newspapers in 1928. He wrote more Hickok adventures for several issues of *Triple-X Western* in 1931. After service in World War I, he attended Columbia University and the Sorbonne. His writing appeared in the New York *Times*, the New York *Journal*, and United Press dispatches. He later worked as a publicist for American film director D. W. Griffith. Miles's stories became the basis for *The Great Adventures of Wild Bill Hickok*, a fifteen-chapter movie serial screened during 1938. The tales brought Hickok to a national audience. [14]

"A Sorry Way to Live"

Steve Frazee, a prolific pulp fiction writer and screenwriter, wrote a memorable short story about Wild Bill, "One Evening in Abilene," first published in 1955 and later adapted for television. The story added complexity to the Hickok character. Gideon Marlow, a New Englander who had come to Texas in 1846, was herding longhorns to Abilene during the year Hickok was marshal. Accompanying Marlow was his young nephew Caleb Starbuck. Like his late cousin, shot by Hickok on Texas Street the previous spring, Starbuck imagined himself a gunfighter. Marlow tried to dissuade Starbuck from bringing his guns to Abilene, which were prohibited in the town limits, and reminded him that his cousin had provoked Hickok, but Starbuck "was not willing to give a Yankee Marshal the benefit of any doubt." [15]

The Starbucks were an old whaling family. Frazee may have been thinking of Starbuck, the chief mate of the *Pequod* in *Moby-Dick*, who contemplated shooting Captain Ahab and turning back from the mad quest to kill the White Whale. In Frazee's story, Starbuck is the obsessed killer and Hickok a force of nature entirely instinctual in his killing. At the Alamo Saloon, Phil Coe asked Starbuck to remove his guns to comply with the Abilene ordinance. When Hickok tried to arrest him, Starbuck balked, but Coe stepped between them, allowing Starbuck to surrender his guns. Hickok left, "an insolent man with a graceful walk, who did not look behind him." Convinced he could outdraw Hickok, Starbuck was told by his uncle that he lacked the willingness to kill that was "born in Hickok, along with his utter fearlessness. Your skill with a pistol cannot stand against equal skill—and a complete lack of hesitation to murder without thinking." After Hickok shot Coe in a gunfight, Starbuck threatened to avenge him, but his uncle said the only way to do that would be by ambushing the marshal from a distance. "He's not a duelist, Caleb. You'll get no better than Coe when Hickok knows your mind," Marlow said. As Starbuck walked that night with his guns strapped on, he felt that dead men "rested very lightly in Bill Hickok's thoughts."

Marlow knew Hickok would never fight fair. He thought the whole affair was a trap. "The streaking of a rifle from darkness was a poor solution to a personal problem, but it was the solution that the country and the moment now thrust upon Gideon Marlow." As Hickok advanced toward Starbuck from the dark recesses of the street, Starbuck hesitated. Marlow tackled his nephew as Hickok fired. Starbuck took a bullet in his shoulder, but his life had been spared. He knew that he could never have bested Hickok, that "he was never born to be a killer." Marlow saw Hickok walking away, "erect, fearless, watchful and unchanged. Bill Hickok, Marlow was sure, would have to walk and live like that, hated and friendless, until someone who did not think like Marlow got the same chance Marlow had refused a few minutes before. It was a sorry way to live, Marlow thought."

This story departed from fictional depictions of Hickok as any kind of hero. His violence was preemptive and without feeling. Texas Street, demarking the district where the shooting occurred, represented a contested border between the Texas Confederates and the "Yankee Marshal." Although Starbuck was by blood a Yankee, he had crossed Texas Street by birth. Marlow had made a moral choice, saving his nephew not just from Hickok but from becoming like Hickok—hated, friendless, and damned.

The full impact of Thomas Berger's *Little Big Man* wasn't felt until after the film version was released in 1970. By then other revisionist films and novels had enlarged the Western landscape, reflecting the Vietnam War and the civil rights movement. Berger's picaresque novel was slow to find an audience or critical success, but it was later hailed as one of the greatest novels of the West, a new myth in a well-worn holster. Times had changed, and the myth of the West, riddled by revisionist bullets, needed patching up. Berger grew up in an Ohio mill town. After military service, he graduated from the University of Cincinnati. He worked as a librarian, was associate editor of *Popular Science*

Monthly, and wrote summaries for the New York *Times* and *Esquire*. *Little Big Man* was his third novel.[16]

Little Big Man began with a fatuous "Foreword by a Man of Letters," one Ralph Fielding Snell, who had transcribed tape-recorded conversations with the scout and gunfighter Jack Crabb shortly before he died at the age of 111 in a nursing home on June 25, 1953. His death occurred on the seventy-seventh anniversary of the Battle of the Little Bighorn, of which he claimed he was the only white survivor. Crabb's story had enough detail to warrant attention, although the unreliable narrator Snell suspected it might be a hoax. The Custer-hating Crabb claimed to have met Hickok in 1871. He was skeptical when told that Hickok had killed a half-dozen men at Rock Creek, because when he heard a "story of more than three against one and one winning, then you have heard a lie." Hickok, however, was no braggart, just a constant target and "a marvelous observer of anything which pertained to killing." Known throughout Kansas, Hickok remained controversial, "and you could get a sharp reaction on one side or the other, and there might have been more men killed in arguments about him than he himself ever sent under." Many believed that Hickok enjoyed killing and that those "who admired him liked this idea, for in any white population there is a vast number of individuals who have murder in their hearts but consider themselves too weak to take up its practice themselves, so they substitute a man like Hickok."[17]

Hickok tutored Crabb in gunfighting, but Crabb didn't see the point of it. "Gunfighting," he said, "was all idea when you got down to it, devoted to testing the proposition: *I'm a better man than you*. It might have been fair, for size and weight did not enter, and a midget was on the same terms as a giant, when they both held Colt's [*sic*]. But the question was, what did you establish when you found the better man?" Hickok was indifferent to killing. "Life to him consisted of doing what was necessary, endlessly measuring his performance against that single perfect shot for each occasion. He was what you call an idealist." Hickok accused Crabb of cheating at cards and forced him to square off for a gunfight in the street. Crabb won through trickery and declined to kill Hickok, but wouldn't give him any deference. "He would rather I had killed him than take pains to show I was basically indifferent to the fact of his existence so long as I could protect my own hide." He said he didn't reveal that he could have killed Hickok because he "wasn't going to give him no free advertisement of any kind. That was the trouble with them long-haired darlings like him and Custer: people talked about them too much." But then so did Jack Crabb.[18]

Snell weighed the credibility of his manuscript and reasoned that if any part of it could be verified, "then what precedes and follows has as great a lien on our credulity. If he knew Wild Bill Hickok, then why not General Custer as well? The case is similar when we suspect his veracity at a certain point: then why should he be reliable anywhere?" Berger bellied up to the same saloon bar as the journalist, the historian and his own fictional creation, the gullible academic, and ultimately the reader. Asked why he wrote Hickok into the novel, Berger said that Hickok was "universally regarded as the most iconic gunfighter, so having my character connect with him was a way of representing the whole gunfighter culture." No wonder Crabb pointed out that Hickok "referred to himself like he was an institution: . . . [He] could not let the noble firm of Wild Bill Hickok, Inc., be loosely dealt with."[19]

Dumas of the Pulps

Richard Sale best illustrated the continuing legacy of the dime-novel tradition in twentieth-century Western fiction about Hickok. Hailed as the "Dumas of the Pulps," Sale, born in 1911 in New York, sold his first story at the age of twelve and continued writing throughout his teens before studying journalism at Washington and Lee University and working on New York newspapers. In the 1930s and 1940s his writing appeared regularly in *Argosy*, *Black Mask*, and the *Saturday Evening Post*. His first novel was published in 1936. His short story "The Devil Made a Derringer," published in a 1938 issue of *All-American Fiction*, became the basis for the CBS television series *Yancy Derringer*, which Sale produced and wrote. *Yancy Derringer* was set in New Orleans after the Civil War, but stories had themes pulled from Westerns, thrillers, and spy dramas. Derringer, a former Confederate officer, served as a secret agent to help restore order in the city. He was always accompanied by his silent Pawnee companion Pahoo-Ka-Ta-Wah. By the time Sale's Hickok novel, *The White Buffalo*, appeared in 1975, he had written hundreds of novels, novelettes, serials, and short stories. At one time he was said to be the highest-paid pulp fiction writer. After 1944 he turned to B movies. He wrote or cowrote screenplays for thirty-six films and directed twenty-three, most notably *The White Buffalo* in 1977.[20]

Sale's novel came with a Lakota language glossary, references, and three pages of notes. He mined Richard O'Connor for stories about Hickok's early life. Sale said, "Most of the story is fact. As for the rest—who will ever know? The two hunters—red and white—who lived it have long since lost their shadows and gone to earth in that never-land known as the Old West, where legend was truer than truth." Hickok's history again gave way to his capacious myth. Sale offered what looked like documentary support for a trip to never-never land, most of which, he claimed, was factual, but the larger truth was to be found in legend. *The White Buffalo* embraced the largest legend of all, *Moby-Dick*, or in this case a one-ton albino buffalo, with Hickok and Crazy Horse in mad pursuit.[21]

The White Buffalo drew on folklore traditions about white animals. The Plains tribes had particular veneration for the rare white buffalo. With the buffalo in the northern herd close to extinction by 1882, such an anomaly would be even rarer. The southern herd was virtually extinct in 1875 after 3.7 million buffalo were slaughtered in just three years. Crazy Horse was said to have predicted that the coming of a sacred white buffalo would restore harmony to the land and herald a new age.[22]

Sale's novel began with Hickok recovering from the bear fight, suffering from rheumatism, bullet wounds, a cavity in his right hip from a Cheyenne war lance, a case of gonorrheal ophthalmia requiring his use of tinted blue spectacles, gambling losses, alcoholism, and violent nightmares about a phantom white buffalo. He was too old to drive stagecoaches, too blind to be a marshal, and too late to resume buffalo hunting. With scant prospects and stalked by gunfighters, Hickok learned that Custer had discovered gold in the Black Hills. Hickok hastened to Cheyenne by way of Abilene and Denver aboard the Kansas Pacific and Union Pacific Railroads. Traveling incognito, he was dreaming in his bunk when he discharged his two silver-plated navy Colt .44 caliber pistols into the unoccupied upper berth where he imagined his "angel of death," that "rarest of creatures, an albino buffalo. It looked to weigh more than two thousand pounds and its great pale hump rose seven feet high, towering over his own head by a full foot." In Abilene he learned that a hunter had shot what he believed was the last white buffalo, and that the skin had been sold to a buffalo hide yard.[23]

At Fort Fetterman Hickok learned that the Lakota and Cheyenne had hidden a herd of buffalo east of the Big Horn Mountains and that there was talk of a white buffalo near the Black Hills. He also found Poker Jenny, who ran a boardinghouse in which he had another meltdown following a dream. Hickok awoke and blasted the mounted head of a white buffalo, creating havoc in the boardinghouse. Nevertheless, Wild Bill assured Poker Jenny that he was a man of comity. "Oh, but surely you are. The most polite, the most civil shootist who ever blew out a man's brains," said Poker Jenny. Hickok acknowledged killing more than fifty men, and "every damned one of them deserved it, most of them being redskins." Hickok hated Indians, "Vermin-ridden lampoons of Man." He asked, "What kind of country would Illinois have been if left to their heathen rituals and sadistic tortures?"[24]

Crazy Horse, too, was hunting for the white buffalo, which he, like Hickok, had seen in a vision. Crazy Horse was the Lakota Chosen One, the "mortal enemy of the pale world." But first he had to find the body of his daughter, who had died from pneumonia. Her corpse reposed on a scaffold above Wounded Knee Creek. The Great Spirit told Crazy Horse that his daughter could not enter the Other World until he wrapped the child's body in the pelt of the white buffalo. He knew the beast could only survive in the high country, so he directed his hunt toward the Elk Mountains.[25]

There Crazy Horse met Hickok, who knew enough Lakota to hold council on deep topics such as history, death, religion, and race. Hickok concluded "that of the two quests for the white buffalo, the Indian's was the noblest, an unselfish act of filial love, beside which the shinking [*sic*] avarice of the whites faded into vileness. For them the dead buffalo would only mean money for gaming and red-eyed cock crowing. For the little squaw it would mean Heaven." Hickok imagined the possibility of a better world, "something that might have created a true and realistic peace with the Teton Sioux—some kind of live-and-let-live treaty based on mutual trust. A matter of national significance which—in his random life—he had never touched before." This despite his oft-stated aversion to Native Americans suggested that the fictional Hickok in this post-Vietnam novel was capable of moral enhancement, taking off the dark glasses as it were, although he said he had no time for morality. After Hickok and Crazy Horse killed the buffalo, Crazy Horse carried the pelt to his daughter's scaffold and Hickok sold the buffalo's skull to a hotel owner in Cheyenne. Such an ending served as a nod and a wink to those eager to hear the Dumas of the Pulps tell a good yarn in the hotel bar.[26]

A novel so cloying in symbolism inspired multiple interpretations, not necessarily what Sale intended but influential in the way the book and sub-sequent film were received. Dee Brown's *Bury My Heart at Wounded Knee: An Indian History of the West*, published in 1970, challenged myths about Native Americans and accelerated interest in revisionist Western fiction, often mixed up with concerns about Vietnam. *The White Buffalo* was written during a time when the American Indian Movement was a major media story. *The White Buffalo* tried to consolidate some myths through the partnership between the Indian-hating Hickok and the white-loathing Crazy Horse. They connected only through their similar vision of the blanched beast pursuing and goring them. For Hickok, the white buffalo represented guilt for his multiple slayings. Like Hickok, the white buffalo was an anomaly, a statistical freak with supernatural powers, and facing extermination. For Crazy Horse, the white buffalo was more explicitly a sacrificial religious object.[27]

As a discourse on racism and civil rights circa 1975, *The White Buffalo* was not encouraging. For Crazy Horse and Wild Bill, there could be no rapprochement. "You cannot understand," said Crazy Horse. "You are white." Crazy Horse was never going to be Wild Bill's Pahoo-Ka-Ta-Wah. Two myths might have met in real life—but they didn't. With fiction, it didn't matter. Sale was a master of pulp fiction and had an eye toward converting a novel into a movie script. No matter how cleverly written and conspicuously researched, *The White Buffalo* was a commercial production targeting a specific audience in a particular era, written almost a century after Hickok was murdered in Deadwood and Crazy Horse was killed at Camp Robinson in Nebraska.[28]

"A Crazy Blue Fire"

Jerome Charyn had already written fourteen novels and a book of short stories before he turned to Hickok with *Darlin' Bill: A Love Story of the Wild West* in 1980. By the age of eighty he had published fifty-one novels and works of nonfiction. Critics called him "a contemporary American Balzac." *Darlin' Bill* found Hickok on a Civil War spying mission in Galveston, Texas, when he saved precocious twelve-year-old Salome "Sally" Blackburn from a Yankee rapist. Sally, who narrated the story, was married off by her mother to a New York fugitive masquerading as the headmaster of a girls' school. After the war, she found a "craziness" in Kansas caused by "the Ten-Cent Romance. They were books you could fold and put inside your pockets. They were all about this character Wild Bill. *Wild Bill, the Indian Slayer.* Kansans were terrified of any Indian who walked. . . . People were scared to death. That's how come they adored Wild Bill."[29]

Sally and Wild Bill reconnected in Hays City and Abilene. The Civil War cloaked the Kansas towns like a blood-soaked shroud, and Hickok had trouble with ex-Confederate "Texians" and a tribe of murderous, razor-wielding orphans transported from Chicago. Sally despised her husband, who was pursued by Pinkerton agents and rode with the Klan. She loved Hickok, ran a hotel in Abilene, and told fortunes. As in *The White Buffalo*, Hickok's increasing blindness drove the story. His complaint was thought to be moon blindness, but whatever it was, it was driving him mad. When a monstrous groaning was heard in the city, the Abilene *Star* created a panic by reporting a series of alleged assaults by a ghoul or a werewolf. Sally found Hickok hiding in a barn, his eyes "bleeding that horrible milk. The blue irises had gone way into his skull, and it was hard to believe the irises would ever come back again." Hickok believed his ailment was recurrent "snow blindness," but Sally suspected "bat fever" or worse. Hickok wouldn't consult an eye surgeon, however. "What if the surgeon talked? The Texians would love to hear how Hickok has blind fits. They'd dog my tracks until that pain bit me. . . ."[30]

The Texians, however, already had a plan to eliminate Wild Bill. They recruited Archibald Aloysius Blackburn, an educated free black man from Boston who had been kidnapped and enslaved by Sally's father, then later sent to prison. Embittered, he became another "two-gun man," called the Black Wild Bill. The Texians goaded him into a fight with Hickok, which Sally tried to prevent because she considered "Archie" her brother. She inadvertently had revealed Hickok's eye troubles to Archie, so he thought he had a chance. Charyn's description of the gunfight, through Sally's eyes, was a rare realistic account of a "walkdown" in Hickok literature:

> The guns spit a crazy blue fire. The doors shattered behind Bill. Archie walked in a slow circle and shot five times. The balls didn't touch Bill. Archie's eyes seemed to go out of his head. He'd dance and fire, dance and fire, and the balls would break wood and glass. Hickok only pulled once. The ball ripped into Archie's spangled shirt and the spangles went gray with smoke and a red ink burst out everywhere. . . . Archie kept on walking in a circle that got shorter and shorter until he dropped.[31]

When Hickok met Agnes Lake, Sally thought the romance was just another consequence of the Hickok mythology. "How did she get so stuck on Bill? She must have read about him in the Ten-Cent Romance. Is that why she stopped in Abilene? To meet the Slayer?" Sally found out that the dime-novel romances drew people with a local origin to Bill. When she bought *Hickok, Marshal of Abilene*, she found the story was current and the ink still wet on the dime novel printed in New York. She figured out that the author was Jorrid Ferguson, the editor of the Abilene *Star*, who had been denouncing Hickok in the newspaper while turning him into a hero in the dime novels. "Where's the harm?" he said, miserable as hell. "Everybody enjoys seeing his name in print. Hate him or love him, it comes to the same thing. . . . I've swindled

Wild Bill all these years, living off those novels. . . . But the truth of it is, miss Sally, there isn't much fat in writing novels. Bookmen lie and cheat. I didn't clear a hundred dollars from *Marshal of Abilene*, counting paper and ink."[32]

That conversation revealed how the Hickok legend was created. Hickok became a swindled commodity with hard-luck scribblers panning for literary gold, but not finding much that glittered in the silty stream. The writers gambled with the time and paper it took to manufacture stories, just as Hickok gambled with cards and made a half-hearted effort to find gold in Deadwood. And that was where he wound up in Charyn's novel, as in life. Sally went after Darlin' Bill. She wanted to care for him, have his child. When she found him, starving and nearly blind, in Deadwood, she bankrolled him and read him the dime novels that Ferguson had written. Wild Bill befriended John "Broken Nose Jack" McCall, who murdered him and ended the story, a dime novel that could never be written.

Loren D. Estleman told Hickok's story by way of McCall's trial. Writing a crime and courtroom novel came naturally to Estleman, who had been a crime and community reporter for Michigan newspapers for six years. Estleman's first novel came out in 1976. In 1981, *Aces and Eights* was published, followed by some two dozen Westerns. Estleman generally followed the transcripts and the biographical and newspaper accounts of McCall's trial and execution, but he admitted to "enlarging upon historical fact" when it suited him. He likely drew on Connelley and earlier sources to put the blame for Hickok's murder on Deadwood men who allegedly paid McCall to kill Hickok. The case turned against McCall when the prosecution proved Hickok was going blind, thus undermining McCall's claim that Hickok saw his killer's reflection in a shot glass and tried to draw on him first. All the publicity and press interest in the trial of one killer accused of killing another caused the prosecutor to wonder: "What sort of man had Hickok been that he could exercise such influence over the lives of others months after his own was finished?" It was a question writers continued to explore.[33]

The Idea, Not the Fact

The most important work of fiction yet written about Hickok was inspired in part by what Pete Dexter called "the most celebrated bar fight in South Philadelphia," which took place in 1981. A few days earlier, the Philadelphia *Daily News* had published Dexter's column about a community trying to stop drug dealing. Dexter told the sad story of a young man who had died. The man's mother and brother took exception to the column, which claimed that he used drugs. Dexter agreed to meet family members at the brother's local tavern to discuss what he had already written, but he would not retract the story. Assailants mauled Dexter when he got there. The battered writer managed to find his friend Randall "Tex" Cobb, a prominent heavyweight boxing contender. Cobb and a few others returned to the bar with Dexter only to be met by some two dozen bat- and crowbar-wielding adversaries. Dexter was hospitalized with a broken back and head injuries. Cobb sustained a broken arm. While recuperating, Dexter began writing fiction, which came naturally to him because he knew how to tell a story. His second novel, *Deadwood*, was published in 1986. Stories like this have made Dexter a legendary rough-and-tumble journalist as well as a much-admired writer whose third novel, *Paris Trout*, won the National Book Award.[34]

Dexter graduated from the University of South Dakota in 1969. He was hired as a reporter for the *South Florida Sun-Sentinel* and then the Palm Beach *Post*, which he quit in 1972. In 1974 David Lawrence, the publisher of the Philadelphia *Daily News*, found Dexter working at a gas station and offered him a job. "He was a stunning talent, but something of a loose cannon," Lawrence, later the publisher of the Miami *Herald*, recalled. Dexter soon was writing hard-hitting street columns for the Philadelphia paper, building a national readership before signing on to write columns for the Sacramento *Bee* in 1986. His brash, street-pounding personal journalism was once a mainstay of big city newspapers. A collection of Dexter's columns was published in 2007, and several of his pieces were included in an anthology of the best columns ever written.[35]

What brought Dexter to the topic of Deadwood and Hickok? A youth spent in South Dakota would be one qualification. Another was that he was "very comfortable writing about violence since I understand a lot about it." Like Hickok, Dexter was a self-invention. He had attracted both followers and controversy. Also like Hickok, he was quotable, full of badinage and banter, a good interview subject for journalists who admired his colorful anecdotes and vivid prose. Perhaps what attracted Dexter to Deadwood was a story line featuring the kind of lonely characters and tragic or amusing situations he had been writing about in his nine-hundred-word columns. A chrestomathy of journalistic Dexterisms might reveal the germination of the text.

For example, one of Dexter's most famous columns, "Head in a Box," appeared in the Philadelphia *Daily News* in 1982. The column described a parking meter repairman who found a head in a paper sack in Camden, New

Jersey. Soon, the head was lost in a maze of bureaucracy, and at the end of the column it was on its way to a government office in Newark. Early in the novel *Deadwood*, a Mexican rode into town with an Indian's head he turned in for a municipal reward. A few pages later Boone May, a deputy sheriff and Deadwood stage guard, tried to claim the reward on a wanted gunfighter and stage robber, Frank Towles, whose head he carried in a bag. May ran into a Jersey-esque adventure in bureaucracy himself as he attempted to collect. Sheriff Seth Bullock told May the reward wasn't good in Dakota Territory and he should take the head to Cheyenne, the equivalent bureaucracy. Camden became Deadwood. Newark became Cheyenne.[36]

Although Hickok was the most celebrated character in *Deadwood*, Dexter shifted attention to Charlie Utter, Hickok's friend, moral compass, and conscience, who lived on until 1912. Western film and fiction usually gives the hero or antihero a sidekick. Dexter put the sidekick at the center of the story and expanded Hickok's afterlife, the better to explain the hero while hanging in suspension the possibility that the sidekick is the more interesting character. In an editorial note, Dexter said that the "large events and settings" of the novel were real and the characters, with a single exception, were "also real, and were in Deadwood at the time these events occurred." This seems to mean that many characters corresponded to real and legendary personages if one is not too particular about dates. The novel had five parts, and Wild Bill was shot at the end of the first part on page 149 of a 365-page book.

Dexter used metafiction for comic effect. Early in the novel Utter reflected on changes that had come over Hickok after their arrival in Deadwood. He recalled that, soon after the Coe shooting in Abilene, a reporter from Philadelphia had described the incident for Hickok in fanciful terms. The reporter, who exaggerated the scope of the walkdown and claimed Hickok had shot multiple Coes and deputies, asked Hickok, "How do you sustain your courage in the face of death's odds?": "Bill never blinked. He said, 'When you know in your heart the bullet hasn't been made with your name on it, there is no tremble in your hand at the weight of a Colt.' The reporter took it down word for word—Bill had to say it twice for him—and then got drunk four nights straight and then he got on the stage east and went home to Philadelphia. Bill said later he was a good reporter. . . ."[37]

As to the identity of this gullible, bibulous Philadelphia reporter, Dexter, the hard-drinking Philadelphia columnist, offered a clue when he told a New York *Times* interviewer that he started out in journalism as "a careful writer but a careless reporter. Reporting is a talent but it's also just a matter of rolling up your sleeves. . . . That wasn't what I wanted to do." The Philadelphia reporter who came to Abilene didn't want to do it either. but, unlike Dexter, he continued reporting. He was just another legend builder following in the footsteps of George Ward Nichols, the careless reporter who didn't want to take the time to get the facts straight about Hickok. Wild Bill may have thought the writer a "good reporter," but the results were the same: more fantasy. Dexter knew the difference between fact and fiction, and he strove to get the facts right even when the facts might get him killed, as they almost did in Philadelphia. The "Philadelphia reporter" and his ilk, like Nichols, turned Hickok into a fictional character with deleterious consequences long before Dexter wrote his carefully researched novel.[38]

Hickok, in the novel, distrusted language and writers because meaning was so malleable and potentially vexing to privacy and celebrity so inimical to truth. His concern about the veracity of memory was prophetic. "I wish there was a general reluctance to bring my name into things. . . . The trouble is accuracy. You can't explain what you did to anybody, especially a reporter, because things don't come out the same in words. And the words you give them, they get it wrong. I tremble to think what the writers do after a body dies."[39]

Hickok was a laconic, death-haunted shadow of his imagined self, suffering from syphilis, cataracts, regret, and alcoholism. "Something had told him there was an issue to be settled in the Black Hills, maybe between him and God. . . ." Utter acted as Hickok's protector when he could, but Wild Bill had become too much of an embittered loner for Charlie to reach him. Hickok sensed a reckoning: "You don't wind up in a place like this for no reason." Soon there was a conspiracy to kill him.[40]

The novel's popularity owed a lot to its black humor and humble wit, much in evidence in the following scene: A new cemetery had been built on Mount Moriah in 1879, and Utter and several companions were ineptly exhuming Hickok's body for reburial. "Charlie looked then and Bill was almost vertical in the corner, leaning against the wall of dirt. His clothes were decomposed, scarcely clothes at all. His color was bad, and the cross in his cheek where Jack McCall's ball exited had opened and the skin had rolled back on itself. Even so, Charlie had seen him looking worse."[41]

Even in death Hickok was on the way to immortality, his body petrified like a statue, "perfect and hard, hidden like a diamond three years in the dark." In life, Hickok was neither perfect nor petrified. His West was real, not the dime-novel West of unblemished heroes. He mattered in the novel because he was flawed, pliable, human, and inscrutable. Sheriff Bullock affirmed that no one knew what Hickok was really like, "but that's where popularity lay, in the idea, not the fact." He mattered, too, because Utter and Agnes Lake loved him in spite of himself. Dexter's novel contributed to a revival of interest in Hickok, Western fiction, and film, taking Wild Bill to a new level, a postmodern presence. Washington *Post* critic Dennis Drabelle said that *Deadwood* "may be the best Western ever written." Drabelle was correct.[42]

A Publishing Shake-Up

By the 1990s, hardback Westerns, including books such as *Deadwood*, once the reliable standard for the genre, were no longer selling well as publishers adapted to several market trends. Readers wanted longer, better-researched books and less of the formulaic writing found in the shorter novels that comprised Western series. Some of this had to do with the economics of the publishing business. As book prices rose, readers balked at paying for fewer pages. Publishers could make more money by publishing a few longer, higher-priced books by top authors than by putting out a lot of books by category writers with limited sales potential. Libraries facing tighter budgets also cut back on hardback and paperback Western purchases.

Demographic changes were also affecting publishing strategies. Men had been the primary audience for Western fiction, while up to 70 percent of all book buyers were women. Western lines were discontinued or repackaged as "frontier," historical, or regional fiction to attract more female readers. Titles introduced more women, Native American, Latino, and African American characters who were more than foils or background scenery for the traditional white male six-gun hero. Some publishers and writers resisted what they saw as revisionism and political correctness, promising instead to stick to the successful formulas of earlier years or looking for ways to combine Westerns with fantasy, horror, and science fiction themes. Hickok endured the shake-up and emerged as a marketable character in both traditional and new genre-mashing Western fiction.[43]

The prolific fantasy writer Richard Matheson published *The Memoirs of Wild Bill Hickok* in 1996. Matheson admitted the novel might be considered fantasy despite the copious literature imagining Hickok as a frontier hero. His take, however, portrayed Hickok as no hero but a drunk, coward, clown, whoremonger, and con man who couldn't even convince his wife he was a fraud. "I want you to know the truth about me," he protested. "So you won't think you're married to some—*fiction*." Agnes preferred the fiction. She blamed exaggerations about his heroism on yellow journalism—a term that didn't come into use until 1897—but still insisted that, even if he hadn't killed hundreds, he certainly killed seven men at Rock Creek and was a Civil War hero.[44]

Matheson's rise in the fantasy genre began soon after his graduation from the University of Missouri School of Journalism in 1949. In the 1950s and 1960s he wrote eighty short stories and eight novels, many adapted for television, especially Rod Serling's *The Twilight Zone*, and cinema. Matheson's Western stories were collected in 1994. He dedicated *The Memoirs of Wild Bill Hickok* to Steven Spielberg, Serling, and other celebrated imaginers. By giving Hickok a first-person voice, Matheson unburdened the legendary character of the cloak of celebrity, revealing him as both victim and collaborator in his own deception. The book was a primer on fantasy written by a twentieth-century master with the subject on stage commenting on nineteenth-century deceivers.[45]

Matheson used the literary device of a found manuscript to frame his story. It was the same device he used to tell the story of Marshal Clay Halser, a Hickok doppelganger, in *Journal of the Gun Years*. Some readers complained that the apocryphal *Memoirs* was a rip-off of *Journal*, but the two novels really worked in tandem as genre-bending sendups of the classic Western. Halser even appeared in *Memoirs* as he and Hickok discussed the "interesting parallels" in their careers. "We are victims of notoriety," said Hickok. "No longer men but figments of imagination." Both figments were shot dead soon after their meeting. Hickok's story began in Deadwood in 1877. Frank Leslie, real-life publisher of *Frank Leslie's Illustrated Newspaper*, had edited Halser's journal for publication and was in Deadwood to write about Hickok's murder when he was visited by Agnes Hickok. She offered Leslie a box containing a manuscript written by Hickok even though it was potentially damaging to his reputation. Leslie was cautious: "I had a specific image of Hickok. Did I want to risk it?" Although suspecting the manuscript might be a hoax, he verified some of its contents and published it in 1878.[46]

The fictional Hickok wrote with eloquence unrevealed in his actual correspondence and quotations in newspapers and magazines. He claimed he had been "obliged to conceal my reading and education from the general public, feeling that, in their eyes, it besmirched my image as the deadliest killer of blah ad infinitum." He said that Nichols "expected, even probably yearned for, a more rough-hewn manner of speech, so I began to drop the bandbox image and feed him more the lingo he was looking for." He hoped, in his memoirs, "to correct the misapprehension that I have been and am an uneducated clod with little to recommend me in the intellect department." Matheson's *Memoirs* were similar in form to *Wild Bill's First Trail*, the dime novel written in Hickok's first-person voice. Matheson's Hickok was a modernist voice probing the psychology of his harsh upbringing and apotheosis as "some manner of icon, a two-gun god." This gave the sophisticated reader of pulp fiction a pass as well, like admitting a fondness for professional wrestling. If it's all an act, one's taste can't be sullied by joining in the fun.[47]

Hickok's deception intensified following his dalliance with Sarah Shull, resulting in the shooting of McCanles "more by reflex than design" after McCanles discharged a double-barreled shotgun in Hickok's direction. Hailed as a hero, Hickok joined the Missouri Militia and picked off Confederate soldiers as a sharpshooter. His first real battle experience almost got him killed when he tried to pull his pistol out from his waistband and blew a hole through his trousers. This gag worked in fiction because so little was known of his Civil War service.[48]

His "memoirs" became an ironic commentary on an embellished version of Hickok's interview with a pompous, dissembling Nichols, "that lord of liars, that emperor of exaggeration." Matheson had General Sherman telling Hickok that Nichols was a fraud, "no more a colonel than my horse." Rather than the dramatic walkdown described by Nichols, the Tutt showdown featured Hickok and Tutt firing wildly at one another without effect, a terrified Hickok frantically trying to find more ammunition in his carpet bag and then killing his adversary with a lucky shot. Hickok murdered Coe by shooting him from an alley, then panicked and shot Williams and wounded two bystanders. Humiliated by his stage appearances, Hickok all but drank himself to death before finally bluffing some bullies in Deadwood and being murdered by McCall. Leslie thought Hickok welcomed his own demise. It was an odd book for a writer who said he didn't want to demean his subject. But Hickok's heroism had been so overblown in film and fiction that a comical send-up was overdue, especially with revisionist Western films around like *Dances with Wolves* (1990), *Buffalo Girls* (1995), *Wild Bill* (1995), and *Dead Man* (1995). [49]

Hickok came riding into the new century with Judd Cole's eight-book Wild Bill series, launched in 1999 with *Wild Bill: Dead Man's Hand* and concluding with *Wild Bill: Gun Law* in 2001. Judd Cole was a nom de plume for John Ames, author of eighty-three novels and a nonfiction book on Deadwood. The Wild Bill books stuck to the traditional Western formulas—gunfights, swindlers, homesteaders, Indian attacks, treachery and vengeance, pursuit and justice, along with plenty of saloons, saddle leather, gals, and gamblers.

Ames wrote for pulp magazines and newspapers before turning to historical fiction and Western book series.[50]

Wild Bill: Dead Man's Hand introduced Hickok as a heroic figure in the dime-novel and pulp tradition. Ames laced the fictional concoction with a shot of history and a dash of romance, keeping the characters and the story as credible as necessary. He gave Hickok an amanuensis in the person of Joshua Robinson. The nineteen-year-old from Philadelphia represented the New York *Herald* as a bureau chief reporting news from the Wild West. His dispatches would be transmitted nationally by the newly formed Associated Press. Robinson was the East Coast tenderfoot, a ploy used liberally by most Western writers. Robinson initially saw Hickok through the lens of the dime novels he had read. His first story was an account of a Hickok shooting in Denver, a "dispatch about a dispatching." Hickok was hired as an agent by Civil War spymaster Allan Pinkerton to protect Professor Vogel, the German inventor of an air conditioning machine ("Ze artificial cooling of za air") that could help doctors mitigate fevers. A competitor who sold natural ice wanted Hickok and the inventor eliminated. A jealous Calamity Jane, Sioux warriors, and gunsels trying to collect a bounty on Hickok's head complicated the picture. By the end of the story, Robinson's dispatches were making Hickok a hero in the East and in Europe. Introducing a Pinkerton Agency detective to the series was a throwback to the dime novels. The real Pinkerton and his ghostwriters also published potboilers featuring detectives, probably to drum up business.[51]

Wild Bill: The Kinkaid County War was another paean to the gunman. Word had gotten around about the McCanles gunfight. Everyone knew Hickok's background as spy, scout, and tracker. He was Hickok the law-and-order man as well as Hickok the killer, with a body count of at least forty so far. Hickok's tracking and shooting skills were supernatural. Hickok again was working for Pinkerton to settle a range war in Wyoming, and Robinson made sure the *Herald* got the story. Dime novels were even praised by Hickok, who told Robinson: "You're a damn good scribbler. . . . Better than Ned Buntline, and that jasper made me famous. . . ."[52]

Wild Bill: Bleeding Kansas dropped the duo into a railroad war involving competing routes across Kansas to corner the cattle shipping market. Pinkerton asked Hickok to stop two men hired by the Santa Fe Railroad to murder surveyors, workers, and soldiers protecting the Kansas-Pacific Railroad near Abilene. Hickok figured out that the killers were 'Bama Jones, credited with more than a thousand kills—an entire regiment!—as a Confederate army sniper, and Ansel Logan, a former trick shot artist. 'Bama was armed with a Big Fifty Sharps buffalo gun, deadly at fifteen hundred yards and firing seven-hundred-grain slugs. Logan shot Wild Bill in the chest, but Robinson saved him with some improvised surgery. Wild Bill killed Logan in a shootout and later blew up 'Bama with a land mine. The stories had some twists. Robinson started out covering the West, but his full-time beat became Hickok to boost newspaper circulation. Robinson had his first kill, saving Wild Bill by blasting a bounty hunter with the Lefaucheux six-shot pinfire revolver Hickok trained him to use. In a later shootout with 'Bama and Ansel, Robinson opened up with a Winchester repeating rifle. Each novel drew upon Hickok's well-thumbed biographies with additional invention. He was a Civil War hero, for example, but fought against Jeb Stuart, spied on Stonewall Jackson, and worked with George McClellan and Pinkerton, all in Virginia. The real Hickok was never there.[53]

In *Wild Bill: Yuma Bustout*, Pinkerton sent Hickok into Mexico to rescue the governor's wife and her sister from cutthroats who escaped from the Yuma Territorial Prison. Wild Bill killed ten men, half of them Mexican soldiers, recovered some stolen silver and the kidnapped women, and thwarted a murder-for-hire scheme. *Wild Bill: Santa Fe Death Trap* brought the weary "national icon" to New Mexico. Hickok recovered a solid-gold church bell stolen by the bandit El Lobo Flaco and his hireling Frank Tutt, who was trying to avenge his brother by killing Hickok. When Frank murdered Hickok's mentor, a U.S. marshal, Hickok became a deputy marshal to exact his own revenge. There was an ancient curse involving the bell; Calamity Jane, a battalion of army camels, and a Gatling gun also appeared. Wild Bill lifted the curse, slaughtered another ten men, including another Tutt, and Robinson killed a few himself and got the story.[54]

Wild Bill: Black Hills Hellhole brought Robinson and Hickok to Deadwood to investigate the killing of three Pinkerton agents sent to a gold mine owned by a consortium of European bankers. The agents were looking into suspicious robberies of gold ore at the mine, ostensibly guarded by the Regulators, recalcitrant ex-Confederate Klansmen who murdered Sioux at the Copper Mountain Reservation. Among the Regulators was Keith "Boomer" Morgan, a munitions expert immortalized as the Grim Reaper in Gray for his war crimes. Hickok and Robinson infiltrated the mine and broke up a plot to steal the gold, blame the Sioux, and smelt the ore at Devil's Tower.[55]

Although *Wild Bill: Point Rider* began with Hickok killing two men in Texas, the body count in this novel about a cattle drive was comparatively low. Robinson realized that Pinkerton "had become a master at a fairly new

American creation some called 'promotion,' others 'hucksterism.'" Pinkerton promoted his agency by encouraging Robinson to dramatize Hickok's heroics. Hickok took Pinkerton's commission because he felt trapped. Robinson's stories made Hickok a fearsome adversary, deterring young gunfighters. If word got out that Hickok was turning down commissions, newspapers would suggest that he was losing his fast draw.[56]

With *Wild Bill: Gun Law*, a year had passed since Hickok and Robinson met. The Overland Stage and Freight Company wanted them to stop a former agent and a gang that rode with Quantrill's Confederate raiders from robbing secret gold shipments from the Black Hills to the national mint in Denver. Hickok drove the stage, killed another half-dozen men, saved the gold, and headed for Deadwood to fulfill Calamity's prophecy that he would die in the No. 10 Saloon. Robinson was recalled to New York, his name to be on his newspaper's masthead. Hickok assured Robinson that the young journalist would write books "that will make the American West practically talk to the reader, it'll seem so alive."[57]

Several themes stood out in these titles. Most of the bad guys were former Confederates, who made use of trickery, bombs, explosive arrows fired from a crossbow, and Gatling guns. Wild Bill and his "Yankee" friends were never far from the Civil War. Desperate situations prompted the recall of battle memories and learned lessons to save the day in the postwar West. Women were sometimes treacherous but always powerless to resist Wild Bill's machismo. He, in turn, feared nothing except Calamity Jane, who relentlessly pursued him, extricating him from danger so she could have him. Wild Bill lived by an ironic code, "The Code of Hickok," which prohibited backshooting (but allowed shooting a killer on sight), deserting a partner (but also remaining "a one-man outfit, loyal to nothing but the harsh code of gun law"), and disrespecting women (they were to be protected). Despite his panache, Hickok was "a lonely, haunted man who had whipped his fear but never quite his despair." He also was a patriot "who sense[d] that democracy's fate hangs in the balance—and his life is committed . . . to the cause of freedom." That freedom required, in the absence of authority, "the harshest and most final law in the West: gun law," as well as a staggering body count.[58]

Wearing Out Like the Wild West

Matt Braun's *Hickok & Cody* imagined the famous pair solving a New York crime after cutthroats abducted two children from a mansion and murdered their parents. The drugged children were sent west on an orphan train to be sold as laborers, but Hickok and Cody rescued them in Nebraska and returned them to New York. The plainsmen discovered that the murderers had been hired by the children's uncle, who coveted the family fortune. Hickok was taciturn, saturnine, and vulgar in contrast to the smoother Cody, and the comical byplay between them and the hero-worshiping orphans animated the 2001 tale.[59]

Bill Brooks began a three-book Law for Hire series with *Protecting Hickok* in 2003. Hickok, half blind, broke, and addicted to alcohol, gambling, opium, and the occult, as well as haunted by the ghost of Williams and longing for death, was wearing out like the Wild West. The Abilene marshal had shot Phil Coe, and Coe's lover had hired a crazed, drug-addled preacher with a brain tumor, the former Civil War sniper and rogue Secret Service agent Paris Bass, to kill Hickok. Bass located Hickok's favorite prostitute, Squirrel Tooth Alice, in Abilene, and before shooting her saw a letter from Hickok posted from Cheyenne. Agnes Hickok, taking Charlie Utter into her confidence, retained a Pinkerton detective, Teddy Blue, to protect her husband. While tracking Hickok to Cheyenne, Blue took up with Kathleen Bonney, the mother of the future Billy the Kid, whom he defended in court. Blue saved Wild Bill from Bass, but not from Jack McCall. This novel had both sexualized violence and mystical pretentions, going off the rails when Utter "thought Bill looked a lot like what Charley imagined Jesus looked like, and it was as if it *was* Jesus sitting across from him instead of Bill—Bill/Jesus admonishing him with an accusing look of betrayal in those sad, sad eyes."[60]

Randy Lee Eickhoff took a more ethereal approach in *And Not to Yield: A Novel of the Life and Times of Wild Bill Hickok* in 2004. Eickhoff had worked as a crime and sports writer for the Lincoln *Star* in Nebraska before becoming a scholar of classics and theology. He translated the *Odyssey* and *Beowulf*, lectured on Dante, wrote twenty-nine books (including several Westerns), and taught at the University of Texas, El Paso. Like Matheson's *Memoirs of Wild Bill Hickok*, Eickhoff's *And Not to Yield* was told in Hickok's voice. But unlike Matheson, Eickhoff imagined Hickok, who was born in a place called Homer, growing up with mythology and stepping into a mythological world pulsing with creatures emerging from the author's library and lecture notes. The 466-page tome started with an epigraph from *The Odyssey*. *Sir Gawain and the Green Knight* showed up on page 3, and by page 80 a young Hickok was communing with the Archangel Gabriel, who gave Hickok a prophetic commission to take his gunfighting skills to the dark side and stand up to bullies. During the Civil War, Ezekiel arrived by chariot while a wounded Hickok was in a stream-of-consciousness delirium, followed by Charlemagne and Orlando. In his reverie, Hickok was spirited off to Camelot where he played Lancelot to a sultry Guinevere.[61]

All this time- and literary-book travel was disorienting to the fictional Hickok and likely baffled readers innocent of the classics. When Eickhoff returned to the well-worn trail trod by the biographers, he told a familiar story peopled by Buffalo Bill, the Custers, Nichols, Tutt, Susannah Moore, McCall, and Agnes Hickok. Agnes at least snapped Wild Bill back to reality when she told him, "You are not Odysseus. You look more like Falstaff, staggering around, proclaiming your honor." When lucid, Hickok talked too much and sounded more like a professor than a paladin. He thought in essays: "Memory is the country of the usable past when one is aware of misinterpretation of experiences, leaving man in his age with an imperfect view of his life and the momentary importance of his actions. . . ." But this Hickok was born knowing, however imperfectly, that it was "for those who came after that I had been sent for and it was for them that I would fight" even though he would "be banished in order for civilization to continue to grow."[62]

Also appearing in 2004 was *East of the Border.* Johnny D. Boggs worked as a sports writer for the Dallas *Times Herald* and the Fort Worth *Star Telegram* before writing more than fifty Westerns. Boggs called *East of the Border* "bogus truth" in that it blended what passed for fact with fiction as he imagined what happened during 1873 and 1874 when Hickok joined Cody and Texas Jack Omohundro on their stage tour of Eastern cities. Boggs consulted biographies, autobiographies, memoirs, and even a doctoral dissertation to develop his story. He included excerpts from newspaper accounts in the cities where the trio performed.[63]

Hickok, as Boggs imagined him, was a reluctant celebrity, an awful actor, a mean drunk and brawler, and a querulous companion albeit with occasional displays of charity, and wounded pride. Hickok objected to the troupe's pimping the "animated dime-novel" version of the West: "We're making fools of ourselves. We're making fools of what we done out West." Hickok, Cody, and Omohundro were being promoted as "Links between Civilization and Savagery" in an advertisement in the Terra Haute, Indiana, *Express*, promising "A Tribe of Wild Indians." This must have resonated in 1873 when the frontier was still being pushed back, yet there was an odd presentism to Boggs's account of the tour, as if an outlaw roadhouse band had worked its way through the heartland determined to indulge its partisans by trashing hotel rooms and hired halls and instigating riots. Boggs had the merry touch of the sports writer enjoying the game when it was most absurd. One of his cleverest lines came when Buffalo Bill confronted an actor from a rival company trying to impersonate Hickok at a Manhattan theater: "My name's William F. Cody, and I know Wild Bill Hickok. Wild Bill is a friend of mine. You, sir, are no Wild Bill Hickok." This anachronism anticipated Sen. Lloyd Bentsen's campaign rejoinder to Sen. Dan Quayle when he invoked John F. Kennedy on October 5, 1988, during a televised vice presidential debate. [64]

Voice of an Angel

When McCall shot Wild Bill in Max McCoy's 2006 novel *A Breed Apart*, the dying Hickok heard singing, "voices in perfect harmony, and above them all was the voice of an angel." The celestial chorus preceded the story of Hickok's life in the Civil War years beginning with the Rock Creek shooting and concluding with the Tutt killing in Springfield. Hickok's murder served as a preface, and the angel harkened back to the novel's epigraph taken from the hymn "Suffield" in *The Missouri Harmony*. Late in the novel, Hickok attended church with Susannah Moore, the daughter of a Millerite preacher, and thought she had the voice of an angel. Hickok, meanwhile, was called the angel of death "with hell in both hands." This more ambitious novel attempted to show a tragic side of Wild Bill, who aspired to live a moral life despite two classic Western showdowns.[65]

McCoy's Hickok was pithy, melancholic, and ironic, a man hardened by the bookended killings of McCanles and Tutt and the violence in between. He ended up a loveless drunkard, a hunted man, a half-blind gunfighter, a compromised idealist, a hero to others but not to himself. McCoy was a police reporter for the Pittsburg, Kansas, *Morning Star* and an investigative reporter for the Joplin, Missouri, *Globe*. He gave Hickok an oracular voice, partial to odd soliloquies: "There must still be some traffic on this meager artery," he said, for he had fallen at last into the habit of talking to himself. "By and by a rider or a wagon must pass, and then I will engage the travelers in some little conversation. Perhaps they will stop for water, for the stream here is sweet. Then my loneliness will be ended for a time, and perhaps even I may glean some bit of intelligence that will reveal my location in these rough hills."[66]

Joe R. Lansdale plumbed a congruent gunfighter creation myth in his 2015 novel *Paradise Sky*. His nominal subject was Nat Love, the African American cowboy who published his memoirs in 1907 under the title *The Life* and *Adventures of Nat Love, Better Known in the Cattle Country as "Deadwood Dick,"* although there were at least five other claimants to the title. Deadwood Dick, Edward Wheeler's dime-novel creation, first appeared in print in 1877. Lansdale's novel was narrated by the former slave, who would become Nat Love. The real Love, according to his own memoir, loved the West, fought Indians, knew Cody, James, and Billy the Kid, settled in Denver, and worked as a sleeping-car porter, courier, and security guard. He died in 1921.[67]

His fictional friendship with Hickok in *Paradise Sky* was part of the "mythology-building tradition of all great western story tellers of the time," according to Lansdale. Love fled from a mob led by a former Confederate who wanted to lynch Nat for ogling his slatternly wife. Love was befriended and named by another ex-soldier, a former preacher who gave him a Colt .45 Peacemaker, a LeMat revolver, and a rapid-fire Winchester rifle, teaching Love how to use them with alacrity and accuracy. He also taught him the classics and made him his heir. Nat soon held forth with irony and droll understatement in the Mark Twain manner. Love found his way to Deadwood, where he helped Hickok even the odds in a gunfight and gained his trust. Hickok and Love were both misfits in Deadwood, and targets. Because Hickok accepted Love as a friend regardless of his race or reputation, Love gained self-confidence. When Wild Bill was murdered, Love was diminished. "Bill had faith in you and that's good enough for me," said Charlie Utter. Love then became "Deadwood Dick," like Hickok a more fictional hero than sometime-lawman and perpetual drifter.[68]

Lansdale told an interviewer that his story redressed a missing part of Western history. "Since Nat was someone that sort of represented the black experience in the West—and wrote a kind of combined autobiography and dime novel at the same time—I took his lead but mixed in other characters to invent my own Nat Love, using his name to represent that experience for a lot of blacks in the West." Casting Hickok as a moral character in this drama gave Wild Bill a contemporary spin as a man who rose above racism. The friendship was plausible given Hickok's family background as abolitionists in Illinois and his antislavery militia experiences in Kansas.[69]

5. ✵ Box Office Bill: Hickok in the Movies

> To be Wild Bill Hickok must have been a joyless enterprise.
> —Roger Ebert, 1995

ickok was an even better fit for the movies than he was for literary fiction. He was a ready-made myth, a creation of the press, the dime-novel industry, Wild West shows, and a few stage plays. The public knew who he was and what he looked like, his stature, vesture, and accoutrements. His protean character rendered him adaptable for a multiplicity of roles, and his inflated biographies promised that there was always more to learn—certainly the absence of facts left an immense capacity for invention. He was destined to have a long afterlife on the big screen.

History, especially Hickok history, was a casualty in cinema, however. Alleged facts, like vagrant bullets in a walkdown gunfight, missed the target but hit something unintended. History, like the innocent bystander in the doorway of the saloon, took a bullet in the chest, spun, and started to bleed. The riderless horse, a perennial symbol in Western movies, bolted and galloped away with the script, taking history along for the ride. Biography, like the bad guy holding a rifle on the roof, tumbled into the trough. "Once the first word of dialogue is written, it is a work of fiction," said historian Paul Andrew Hutton. "Thus every Western film, just like every Western novel is fiction, not history, entertainment, not fact." The best historical Westerns "get at the heart of why we remain so fascinated with the West and why that story still resonates today." What drives that story is violence as spectacle, solution and retribution. Historian Michael Bellesiles even gave Western movies credit for introducing "glorified violence." The point, he concluded, is not that the "public came to believe that the Western was an accurate portrayal of reality, but more that historians did." If so, we have yet another spanner tossed into the memory works, confounding the ways we engage the past.[1]

The first known silent-era movie depiction of Hickok occurred in 1913 in a two-reeler titled *The Pioneer Peacemaker*, which was based on stories told by

Harry Young, who may have been the bartender in the saloon where Hickok was shot. The next was *In the Days of '75 and '76, or The Thrilling Lives of Wild Bill and Calamity Jane* in 1915. Both films established the pattern of myth superseding fact. William S. Hart's *Wild Bill Hickok* followed in 1923. Hart, the famous Western actor who played Hickok, was almost sixty years old at the time. The dime-novel-influenced story, written by Hart and J. G. Hawks, involved Hickok, with failing eyesight, trying to retire to the card tables in Dodge City after the Civil War. At Custer's behest, Hickok took up his guns and joined forces with other lawmen to restore order. Hickok had small roles in *The Iron Horse* (1924), *The Last Frontier* (1926), *Aces and Eights* (1936), and *Custer's Last Stand* (1936). In *The World Changes* (1933) he was played by Charles Middleton, famous for his role as Emperor Ming the Merciless in the *Flash Gordon* serials.[2]

Gary Cooper gave Wild Bill his box office breakthrough in Cecil B. De Mille's 1936 epic Western *The Plainsman*, based on stories by Frank Wilstach and Courtney Ryley Cooper. Both had been newspaper reporters and theatrical publicists. The film, packed with grand American themes, began with the Civil War ending and Lincoln and his cabinet extolling the coming destiny of the West. Discharged soldiers could work the new lands, and the reunited nation could look forward to unlimited prosperity, a welcome message for New Deal audiences. Lincoln proclaimed what had to be done for the nation to achieve its manifest destiny: "The Frontier must be made safe!" The film audience might have heard that as another call to make a world made safe for democracy with a new war on the way. Up on the screen, though, "safe" meant stepping up the Indian wars.

Hickok appeared in uniform, mustered out of the army in 1865 at Leavenworth, and on his way to Hays City. He was already Wild Bill, slayer of "the whole McDaniels gang," the familiar McCanles incident transferred to the screen. Despite sketchy claims that the Depression-era film was based on historical events, most of it was bogus, although the sets and costumes looked good. Hutton called this "*The Plainsman* syndrome" in Western cinema—getting the details right but the story wrong. A projected marriage between Hickok and Calamity Jane in the initial script was just one incident with no basis in fact. After hearing protests from Hickok's family, DeMille canceled the wedding, while Calamity remained in the film as a persistent love interest pursuing the misogynist Wild Bill.[3]

The film ignored the historical timeline. Almost immediately the Sioux and Cheyenne were on the warpath, Hickok and Buffalo Bill with about fifty men were defending an ammunition train against an attack by a thousand Indians, and Custer and his command were slain at the Little Bighorn. Hickok took care of the gunrunners in Deadwood, but Jack McCall shot him anyway just as the cavalry arrived. Cooper played Hickok as self-effacingly virile—but not crazy wild—and convincingly moral. A stirring message at the end of the film celebrated a restored nation, "molded to last." Wild Bill Hickok, American hero.[4]

Bill Elliott played Hickok in a fifteen-episode adventure serial produced by Columbia in 1938. Called *The Great Adventures of Wild Bill Hickok*, the series was based on Miles's newspaper serial from 1928. Hickok was appointed U.S. marshal to restore order in Abilene, which had been taken over by the Phantom Raiders. Elliott, born Gordon Nance, grew up in Missouri and moved to California to become a cowboy actor. He appeared in his first Western in 1927 and by 1938 was called Bill Elliott, and then Wild Bill. Next came B-movie roles as Hickok in such films as *Beyond the Sacramento* (1940), *Hands across the Rockies* (1941), *King of Dodge City* (1941), and *Prairie Gunsmoke* (1942). He played the title character in sixteen *Red Ryder* films, had his own radio show, starred as a film detective, pitched Viceroy cigarettes, and died from lung cancer in 1965.

Most of Elliott's Hickok films were about one hour in length. Hickok sporadically was hired as a lawman, but he typically interrupted his peaceful, wandering life only to thwart criminals, seek revenge, or defend himself when attacked. In *Beyond the Sacramento*, he broke into a corrupt publisher's print shop during the night and reset the next day's front page to reveal the newsman's swindles. In *King of Dodge City*, he started a run on a crooked bank. When such tactics didn't work, Hickok resorted to conventional gunfights.[5]

Frontier Scout, another 1938 film, was the first Western film telecast on the experimental television station W2XBS in New York, on Sunday, April 21, 1940, from 3:30 P.M. to 4:30 P.M. Ten years after its theatrical debut, the film was shown January 21, 1948, on WEWS, a pioneer station in Cleveland, Ohio. Wild Bill was off to a fast start on television in the 1940s. *Frontier Scout* starred George Houston as Hickok, a casting choice *Variety* said would mean nothing to the youthful B-Western movie theater audience, which had a lot of Wild Bill actors to choose from. Houston had performed with a strong tenor voice in operas and Broadway musicals. He won some bit parts in the movies before being cast as Hickok. He had sought singing roles but only got to croon a few bars of "Oh Susanna" in *Frontier Scout*.[6]

Hickok had a comic sidekick, Whiney Roberts, played by Al St. John. The chemistry between them gave the film some humor. The story began with

Hickok racing though Confederate lines to report an imminent attack to a worried General Grant. The Federals were "outnumbered ten to one with two more regiments on the way." Grant sent Hickok back through Rebel lines with a message ordering Gen. Philip Sheridan to attack a weak spot in the lines "to end the war." The message got through, and Hickok won the war. The history in this scenario was addled. Hickok was never in Virginia with Sheridan and Grant, who never faced a Confederate attack at such a disadvantage in 1865. Stock footage of Civil War movie action was mixed up with Wild West scenes shot in California. The story involved Hickok wooing the sister of one of his army buddies, who unwittingly went into partnership with a Texas cattle rustler. Hickok, appointed a deputy U.S. marshal, recovered the cattle, rounded up the corrupt partner and his gang, and won the girl, but then was sent off on another assignment. The transition from Civil War to Wild West was seamless.[7]

A Singing Gunfighter

With anxiety about war with fascists rising, the famous lawman got mixed up in another 1940 film, *Young Bill Hickok*, featuring a secret agent plotting to acquire California for a "foreign power" during the Civil War. The agent, Nicholas Tower, played by John Miljan, met in San Francisco in 1864 with a cabal of conspirators, promising to bring "order out of, let us say, your democratic chaos." They really wanted to intercept shipments of gold to the Federal forces in the East while cutting off lines of communication between California and the Atlantic Coast. The conspirators hired a brigand named Morrell whose Overland Raiders attacked the Russell, Majors, and Waddell lines hauling the gold and other supplies.

Veteran Western screenplay writers Norton S. Parker and Olive Cooper skimmed the Connelley biography and made use of the Rock Creek story in creating their script for *Young Bill Hickok*. Connelley claimed McCanles "had developed a band of devoted followers—wild and reckless men, many of them voluntary outlaws." According to Connelley, McCanles attempted to join forces with Dr. Albert Morral, a Confederate sympathizer who owned land on an Overland stage route near Palmetto, now Marysville, Kansas. Morral, who might have been the inspiration for "Morrell" in the film, later served in a South Carolina cavalry company during the Civil War. This "band," if it existed, might have been the ten desperadoes who supposedly attacked Hickok at Rock Creek Station, according to what Hickok allegedly told Nichols.[8]

Young Bill Hickok, freely conflating earlier stories, placed Hickok, incongruously played by Roy Rogers, at an Overland station to protect the stagecoach and Pony Express from attacks by Morrell (Morral? McCanles?) and his band. He fought them off just as his sidekick Gabby Whitaker, played by George "Gabby" Hayes, arrived with his niece Calamity Jane. Earlier in 1940, Rogers had played Cody in *Young Buffalo Bill* with Hayes again playing Gabby Whitaker and Joseph Kane again directing. Audiences had begun to see Rogers playing himself, along with Gabby, in the late 1930s, and by the 1940s he was the "King of the Cowboys," one of the most recognizable Western stars in cinema and, later, television. Rogers, playing Hickok, sang cowboy ballads to his love interest, Louise Mason. The real Hickok was not the fellow to sing "When the Shadows Fall across the Rockies" or "A Cowboy Wedding." Singer-actor Howard Keel portrayed Hickok in the 1953 Western musical film *Calamity Jane* starring Doris Day. About the only thing Keel and Hickok had in common was that they both grew up in Illinois. A stage musical based on the movie was first performed in 1961 and broadcast on the CBS network in 1963. It was still being performed in 2018 in Australia in "a spare production with a Brechtian streak." Each revival kept the faux romance story in the public eye.[9]

In *Young Bill Hickok*, Louise was the daughter of a Confederate officer but still loved the Yankee Hickok, the sentimental romance of reunion theme that saturated Civil War film and fiction. There was a secret plan to have Gabby and Calamity move gold east while Wild Bill led a decoy party to draw off Tower and Morrell, but Louise blabbed the plan, and the villains temporarily seized the gold. Wild Bill got it back, foiled the plot, and won the girl. There was a wedding as one war ended, the curtain descended, and the 1940 theater audience exited into the gathering storm. With World War II underway, Hickok was an established presence in cinema, a rowdy fighting man right for the times.

The 1941 film *Wild Bill Hickok Rides*, the same film Joseph Rosa remembered seeing as a boy, put Hickok on the side of homesteaders in the Powder River Basin, Montana, as they were pitted against Chicago swindler Harry Farrel and his henchmen who tried to jump their land claims, drive them out, take over the town, and open a casino. Bill's friend Ned Nolan, the owner of the largest ranch in the valley, was framed on a murder charge and lynched. Hickok, played by Bruce Cabot, rallied the homesteaders to fight back, thereby settling scores with Farrel. Cabot had roles in more than one hundred films, including the 1933 classic *King Kong*, before making the leap to Wild Bill. In 1947, *Wild Bill Hickok Rides* was playing at the Palace Theater in Jersey City, New Jersey, when police arrived to apprehend three youths who had escaped from an Ohio reformatory. After a police sergeant spotted the fugitives entering the theater, some thirty officers and detectives quietly took seats during the afternoon performance "without interrupting Wild Bill Hickok's ride," according to the New York *Times*. When the lights came up, the fugitives were accosted and told to surrender.[10]

A decade passed before Hickok was again much of a screen presence. He reappeared briefly in 1950 in *Dallas* with Blayde "Reb" Hollister, played by Gary Cooper, a former Confederate tracking the brothers who murdered his family and took his land in Georgia. In Dallas, Hollister found a friend in Hickok, who was about to depart on a theatrical tour, leaving the incompetent Yankee Martin Weatherby to police the town as U.S. marshal. Hickok didn't think much of Weatherby's chances. "We had a war down here and you'll find men in high offices who are thieves and cutthroats. You'll find others who are branded outlaws that are only fighting for what's their own. There's those known as bad men and those as are bad men. You better learn to tell the difference." Hickok was played by Reed Hadley, who had appeared with Bill Elliott in *The Great Adventures of Wild Bill Hickok*. Wanted by the law, Hollister faked his death with Hickok's help and changed identities with Weatherby so he could take on the killers and bring peace to the town. Hollister's friendship with Hickok, who fought for the North, began the reconciliation necessary to unify the West.[11]

Wild Bill Goes Rogue

If the lawman Hickok formula was wearing thin by 1953, Hollywood had a solution: turn Wild Bill into a bad guy. *Jack McCall, Desperado* was a deceptive title because Hickok was the desperado and McCall the hero. The switch would not have worked well if Hickok had been an unblemished Western hero. He was enough of a libertine, however, to succumb plausibly to lawlessness. Still, it was asking a lot to open a movie with the virtuous McCall facing off against duplicitous Deadwood marshal Hickok and then being tried for murder. McCall told his tale at his trial in a flashback. Written by David Chandler, the story was a Civil War Western, a popular fusion in 1950s cinema. Although a wealthy Southerner brought up on a plantation, McCall had served with Sergeant Hickok in the Union Army. McCall had been falsely accused and convicted of spying for the Confederates when the army unit neared his home. He managed to escape and immediately returned home, pursued by Hickok, who killed Jack's parents and took over the plantation with a McCall family accomplice. After the war, Wild Bill ran guns to the Sioux, precipitated a massacre, and attempted to cheat the Indians out of their tribal lands in order to control the goldfields. McCall trailed Hickok to Deadwood, where he cleared his name and killed Wild Bill before being acquitted of Hickok's murder. Hickok was played by George Kennedy, and the better-known George Montgomery starred as McCall.[12]

In 1956, Hickok was cast as a crooked sheriff who swindled the cavalry, ran guns to the Indians, and got mixed up in a land-buying conspiracy. *I Killed Wild Bill Hickok* was written and produced by Johnny Carpenter, a B-movie star who played a former Confederate soldier in his own film. His character, Johnny "Rebel" Savage, had held an entire company of Union soldiers at bay, so he was not intimidated by Hickok. Savage shot the sheriff in an awkward walkdown by dropping to his knees and firing a rifle at his belly. Hickok walked away, spun several times and fell dead in the street. Hickok was played by Tom Brown, a former child star who modeled Buster Brown shoes and had small parts in many films and television programs. The low-budget movie flopped.[13]

Film audiences had gone wild in 1975 over Steven Spielberg's *Jaws*, as attested to by ticket sales. That Halloween and the next, American kids squirmed into shark suits and rang doorbells. Sightings of nonexistent sharks closed beaches. In 1976, producer Dino De Laurentis brought out *King Kong*, then *The White Buffalo* and *Orca* in 1977. Animals were going rogue all over. Audiences and critics finally balked. Richard Sale wrote the screenplay for *The White Buffalo* based on his provocative 1975 novel. The movie was directed by J. Lee Thompson, who cast his frequent star actor, the veteran tough guy Charles Bronson, as Hickok. Bronson was almost twenty years older than Hickok would have been in 1874, which enhanced the story's elegiac quality. With the taciturn Bronson on the screen paired with aging temptress Kim Novak as Poker Jenny, Hickok was a long way from Rogers or Cooper. It didn't help that in his first appearance in *The White Buffalo* Bronson was wearing sunglasses that might have been mistaken for Ray-Bans. According to legend, the real Wild Bill wore dark glasses in Cheyenne in 1874 or 1875 and coiled his flowing locks to escape attention, although the opposite effect might have resulted.[14]

Special effects immediately took over the movie as the spectral white buffalo, which was actually was a full-sized mechanical puppet, rampaged through Hickok's nocturnal visions and destroyed Crazy Horse's Oglala village, reappearing intermittently until the final bloodbath. The cast included veteran character actors Will Sampson as Crazy Horse, Jack Warden as Charlie Zane, Slim Pickens as the stagecoach driver, and John Carradine as Amos Briggs, an undertaker with an untoward fondness for bodies. The novel's *Moby-Dick*-sized ambitions gave way to the film's dime-novel provenance, but that wasn't enough to save it from box office implosion and critical ridicule.[15]

Oedipal Issues

The 1995 film *Wild Bill* was unremittingly barbaric, so much so that it bordered on parody. Hickok shot, slashed, choked, pummeled, stomped, butted, bit, or decanted at least three dozen men in ninety-four minutes of blood-splattered cinema marked by feral violence. An accurate death count was impossible due to the oscillating camera and tumbling bodies, although by the end of the film twenty-two men appeared to have been sufficiently riddled with bullets or concussed never to rise again. Hickok was so rapid on the draw and accurate with his multidirectional firing that the whooping barroom bystanders had no fear of being ventilated in the crossfire. "Instead of diving out of windows and running for the door, as you or I would do if a gunfight broke out, they line up around the room and look on eagerly, just as if they are movie extras happy to be in the shot," film critic Roger Ebert gleefully noted.[16]

The film was scripted and directed by Walter Hill, who was inspired to bring Hickok to the screen after he saw Thomas Babe's play *Fathers and Sons* in Los Angeles in 1980. Babe had been writing plays since 1974 based on American history, heroes, and national mythology. *Fathers and Sons* was first performed in New York in 1979 with Richard Chamberlain in the role of Hickok. The play, according to Babe, "was originally written as an evocation of the murders at Kent State and Jackson [State in Mississippi] in May, 1970. No shred of the first play remains but the gestus, which was the remorseless and violent injury that the generations inflicted on themselves and each other."[17]

The play connected this Vietnam-era theme to an imagined relationship a century earlier between Hickok and McCall, revealed to be Hickok's illegitimate son by Susannah Moore. "I made up everything about him. I chose lurid," Babe told a New York *Times* critic. "That he would drown cats, sleep with his mother, put on a dress was a portrait of nihilism. He was someone Wild Bill would not want as a son." Babe's ahistorical approach was based on the belief that facts can impede narrative, and by including an excerpt from Connelley's biography in the published preface to the script, and a likely bogus 1881 newspaper article alleging that Hickok had a son, Babe winked at unreliable documentation and moved on. "You have a problem with things that are heavily documented because you can get into a contest with people who have more information," said Babe. "But with things that live more in the shadows, you have more room to say what might have been in a way that's closer to a psychological truth."[18]

Such slighting of history had no appeal for Rosa, who called the plot "preposterous and macabre." He deemed *Fathers and Sons* historically "worthless, but it indicates that Hickok continues to fascinate audiences and motivate sometimes weird interpretations of his character." Illuminating the shadowlands of history and myth for theatrical effect is firmly grounded in literary tradition. McCall's Oedipal issues might owe something to Sophocles, who Babe perhaps had in mind with his dark tale of McCall's madness, Hickok's blindness, and apotheosis. Rosa's historical Hickok is buried on a plateau above Deadwood Gulch. Babe's mythic Hickok never died, which appealed to Hill, who had directed *The Long Riders* in 1980 and *Geronimo: An American Legend* in 1993 and wanted to make a film about Hickok.[19]

"I was interested that Wild Bill was in love with the thing that finally killed him, his own legend," Hill told the New York *Times*. "He was this kind of expansive American personality, a historical artifact." He had optioned *Fathers and Sons* and developed a screenplay when he was contacted by producers Richard and Lili Zanuck, who were shopping around a screenplay written by Pete Dexter that was based on his novel *Deadwood*. Lili Zanuck said they were drawn to the creation of the celebrity culture in a Western context, a logical extension into the history of the culture that was defining the era. "Figures like Wild Bill were like rock stars. They had sex appeal." The project moved forward with a script credited to Hill that combined ideas from both *Deadwood* and *Fathers and Sons*. Critic Jamie Diamond thought it unusual that Hill "turned not to the historical record but to two literary sources to shape his story." Yet the film's peculiar provenance is another example of the Hickok myth feeding on itself rather than seeking a historical corrective. What suspect history does seep into the film is only a device to revisit Hickok's career in flashbacks. A script based on "hearsay and fiction" and the appearance of Calamity Jane, played by Ellen Barkin, as a love interest showed the film's debt to "Hollywood historians," according to Rosa; Rosa nevertheless thought the director's focus on Hickok's character "at least suggests that Hill was more concerned with the real Hickok than most of his predecessors," rather damning Hill with faint praise.[20]

Hickok's late period was the ostensible conceit in *Wild Bill*, the lonely lion in winter wearied by the afflictions of fame. Weakened by venereal disease, his eyesight failing, Hickok alternated between opium-fueled reverie and prickly ructions that followed transgressions of the Western code. "Shouldn't touch another man's hat," said Wild Bill before destroying a saloon. "I never apologize." Jeff Bridges, at forty-five, inhabited the Hickok role as snugly as Hickok wore his own legend. Charlie Prince, an English dandy played by the venerable John Hurt, doubled as Wild Bill's companion and conscience and commented on the Hickok myth in a portentous voiceover narrative. "The theatre of Bill's life," intoned Prince, "had come to demand that he walk up the center of a street rather than use the boardwalk. He had discovered that being Wild Bill was a profession in its own right." Therein lay the tragedy, because the hero must die, and with each death "we're all the less. It drags down morale. People get anxious, depressed. They drink more, fight more, causing more killings 'til the general uncertainty destroys whatever useful or good remains."[21]

Reviewer Michael Wilmington thought Hill couldn't decide "whether to celebrate or spoof the legends, evoke the past or send it up." The modernist dissonance, however, sustained a false dichotomy. The past evoked was an imagined reality filtered through more than a century of dime novels, movies, television, stagecraft, folklore, and general media hogwash. Thus, the film wound up treating history "with both precision and whimsy." The more it looked like the public conception of a Western set with all the proper homage, the more self-referential and whimsical—even idiotic—it became. Wild Bill and Calamity made love in a deserted saloon accompanied by the "Battle Hymn of the Republic." When Will Plummer, a crippled victim of one of Wild Bill's shootouts, showed up in a wheelchair to settle the score, Bill took a seat on a chair in the street so it was a fair fight, maybe the genre's first "rolldown." The fatal blast from Hickok's guns threw Plummer backward. Plummer was played by Bruce Dern, the actor who specialized in playing crazed Western gunmen and infamously pistol-whipped an unarmed John Wayne in *The Cowboys* in 1972. When Wild Bill's own spawn stalked his father in *Wild Bill* to "kill the legend," the audience knew that the real-life McCall committed no patricide when he murdered Hickok in Deadwood, and that he bolstered the legend rather than destroying it. In Babe's play, Bill and Jack shot each other, a statement about generational implosion in 1975 rather than what had happened a century earlier. It's a better ending.[22]

Influential British film historian Philip French liked *Wild Bill*, "a dark, complex picture—fierce, elegant, self-conscious, not a little mysterious." He thought the film reflected "the mood of a post–Cold War America where the enemy is no longer defined and the righteous hero has no obvious place to exert himself." That Wild Bill might be a tempting analogy for the 1990s to some—America as a chancred, half-blind gunfighter firing wildly in all directions as he staggered from brothel to card table while stalked by a mad assassin. Nevertheless, the film was a commercial bomb, losing almost $28 million, and a critical disappointment. The film's impact, however, would be evident in the television series *Deadwood*.[23]

Moon-Blind

Hickok returned to the screen during the summer of 2017 after a long absence, a season when facts were contested, Confederate monuments removed, and national memory a fugitive pursued by a political posse. The air crackled with invective, deceit, dishonesty, protests, threats, and violence amid promises to build walls, drain swamps, and make America great again even as rising waters flooded Texas, Florida, and Puerto Rico and the moon eclipsed the sun. Wild Bill, a compromised redeemer with moon blindness, was a welcome distraction to these disgruntlements and fit right in as a bloviating celebrity.

The opening scene of the eponymous *Hickok*, a low-budget film directed by Timothy Woodward Jr., placed Wild Bill in the midst of a Civil War skirmish. When a Union detachment was pinned down by Confederates improbably firing a Gatling gun, Wild Bill rashly rode into action with his unaimed revolvers blasting in opposite directions. Invulnerable to the overwhelming firepower confronting him, six barrels revolving around a central shaft, up to six hundred rounds per minute coming at him, he nevertheless quieted the Confederates with a remarkable display of pistolry. Never mind that Gatling guns were seldom used in the war, especially in small-unit engagements—they were used mainly by Union forces during the Petersburg Campaign in Virginia. The Confederates did have a few Williams Guns, one-pound rapid-fire cannons operated by a hand crank, but no Gatling guns. In the fall of 1864, Confederate general Sterling Price may have had a Williams Gun when he led some twelve thousand men and young boys constituting the Army of Missouri out of Arkansas on a futile invasion of Illinois. Turned back near St. Louis, the Confederates reversed course and followed the Missouri River westward in an attempt to recapture the state until they were repulsed at the Battle of Westport, Missouri, and driven back to Arkansas. Hickok was scouting in the area at the time and might plausibly have seen action against

Price's Confederates, but if so, the film had the wrong gun in the opening frames. Right away, viewers were in for some hand-cranked action with history riddled in the crossfire.[24]

Michael Lanahan's screenplay bolted from the Civil War to Abilene, which had recently been overrun by rowdy ex-Confederates from Texas, Missouri, and Arkansas. There, Hickok agreed to clean up the cattle town. Hickok was played by the Australian actor Luke Hemsworth. He looked nothing like the more conventional interpretations of Hickok drawn from photographs and dime-novel illustrations. His Hickok was more buoyant than the austere Hickok captured by Keith Carradine in *Deadwood*. Lanahan made free use of conflicting accounts and competing legends. Given the opening scene and the subsequent violence, it was evident that the Civil War was still going on in Abilene. George Knox, the city's beleaguered mayor, played with insouciant restraint by a hoary Kris Kristofferson, handed Hickok a marshal's badge and approved his order to disarm the drunken hedonists who were inclined to shoot Yankee lawmen and one another, warning that taking away their guns would not be popular. The real Hickok did try to enforce the city ordinance banning firearms, which merely reiterated an 1868 Kansas law prohibiting former Confederates, drunks, and vagrants from carrying any deadly weapon.[25]

Hickok's principal adversary in the film was saloon owner Phil *Poe*, played by country music star Trace Adkins, whose presence, along with Kristofferson's, gave the film a Nashville ambiance. The real Hickok did shoot Phil *Coe*, one-time owner of the Bull's Head Tavern in Abilene. Changing just the first letter of Coe's last name was a tip of the Stetson to make believe, reminding viewers that this wasn't history but amusement-park reality playing off history. Writers could only get away with this if the audience already had some familiarity with Hickok, but it would have taken experts to get the joke.

The real Hickok also had animus with former Confederate Ben Thompson, Coe's partner in running the Bull's Head. Some sources say Hickok and Thompson quarreled over a prostitute named Jessie Hazell. Some sources say Coe, not Thompson, shared a mistress with Hickok. The film introduced the character Mattie Lyles, played by Cameron Richardson, as the femme fatale. She was engaged to Poe/Coe/Thompson, who discovered that Mattie and Hickok had a history. In fact, they had even had a son who was obsessed with guns and probably well on his way to upstaging his father once he discovered his paternity. In addition to his dalliance with Mattie, Hickok was also shaking down Poe/Coe/Thompson for a share of the profits, so the publican had ample motive for putting a bounty on Hickok's life.[26]

Looking for a hired gun to get rid of Hickok, the real-life Thompson may have turned to John Wesley Hardin, the eighteen-year-old Texan already on his way to becoming one of the West's most notorious killers. Hardin allegedly told Thompson that if he wanted Hickok dead, he should kill him himself. In his memoirs, Hardin told how he had rebuffed, by some fast-draw trickery, Hickok's demand that he surrender his guns in Abilene. Hickok, he claimed, liked his spunk, and they became friends. Hardin spurned Poe, signed on as Hickok's deputy, and added firepower to several shootouts. Assessments of the real-life Hardin ranged from homicidal maniac to psychotic killer, although Bob Dylan wrote a song portraying Hardin (or "Harding") as a Robin Hood character. The real Hardin became a lawyer and met his end, like Hickok, by being shot to death from behind in a saloon. With considerable understatement, Rosa noted in 1993 that "Hardin's present reputation is not good." The film may have offered some slight improvement.[27]

The marshal and his new deputy easily aerated killers stupid enough to take on the two fastest guns in the West, but Hardin and Poe suspected that Hickok was "moon-blind," an ancient disease most commonly associated with horses and once thought to occur with phases of the moon. Wild Bill had consulted Doc Rivers, played tongue-in-cheek by the ubiquitous Bruce Dern, about his eye problem: "Whenever I look into a light of any kind, it's edged with halos, bright as January sun dogs." He learned he would be totally blind in five years. The real Hickok probably did suffer from eye problems, which may have contributed to his accidental shooting of Williams in Abilene. As to the cause, one theory was that a stage footlight exploded while he was performing with Buffalo Bill in the Rochester Opera House in 1874. Rosa, with his characteristic thoroughness, spent months searching for medical records and consulting with archivists, ophthalmologists, and opticians in the United States and England. Hickok's eye problems were attributed to syphilis, glaucoma, gonorrhea, granular conjunctivitis, trachoma, ophthalmia, arthritis, overexposure to the sun, or some combination of the above. It would be hard to disagree with one of the physicians Rosa consulted who concluded, "I can't help but feel that there was definitely something about Wild Bill's eyes that bothered him. . . ."[28]

Hickok swore Rivers to secrecy about his medical condition—how much bravado would be sacrificed when word got out that the West's most famous gunfighter was moon-blind? And, of course, it did, as Hickok learned when he found Hardin reading a newspaper announcing Hickok's handicap, replete with the nickname "Prince of Pistoleers" given him by journalists and dime novelists. His cover blown, Hickok put Mattie and his son on a train to Wichita where he told Mattie to find Wyatt Earp, "a good man. He'll take care of you." Hickok shot Poe at close range in a dark room and faded away, "done running" even when the audience knew he wasn't.[29]

This was a middling Western all too familiar, safely within the Hickok canon, and so not overly concerned with fact. The post–Civil War tensions were given a closer look than usual, but not with much development. Hickok was just another war veteran having difficulties adjusting to civilian life. Every character was a stereotype or rip-off from other Westerns. When decoupled from killing, whiskey, women, and gambling, *Hickok* was left without much of a story. Or, as Mattie told her husband-to-be, the four things Hickok cared about were "shootin', gamblin', drinkin', and you can guess the last." That may be the truest biography of Wild Bill's ungilded life: a moon-blind plot about aimless wandering while looking to make enough money.

6. ✸ Fancied Up Rooster: Hickok
in Radio and Television

> He seems, in fact, fictional: a man who lived out his life as though
> anticipating his future glorification in a television serial.
> —Richard O'Connor, 1959

Wild Bill made a few appearances on *The Lone Ranger* radio series in the 1940s. In "The Lone Ranger Meets Calamity Jane," broadcast April 10, 1944, Hickok and Calamity were secretly wed in Deadwood. The two legends struggled to accommodate their celebrity marriage. Hickok, whose skills were waning, acknowledged Calamity's increasing fame and recommended her to Custer for scouting duties. Only after Jack McCall murdered Hickok did Calamity acknowledge she was Mrs. Bill Hickok. The episode highlighted the limitations of Hickok's story for radio. If audiences expected him to get shot in every episode, there wasn't much of a story line for writers to work with. Nor was a Calamity Jane romance likely to compete with Roy Rogers and Dale Evans. Hickok needed a sidekick and a new image if he was going to continue to be a media commodity.

He got the makeover he needed in one of the longest-running radio Westerns, *The Adventures of Wild Bill Hickok,* broadcast several times a week on the Mutual Radio Network from 1951 to 1956. The program was unusual in that it made a simultaneous transition to the new medium of television. Television syndication began in 1951 and continued, first on CBS and then on ABC, until 1958 for 113 episodes. Combined with reruns, that long run made Hickok an icon of the 1950s. Guy Madison played Hickok as a U.S. marshal, and gravelly voiced Andy Devine played his deputy marshal, sidekick, and jocose foil, Jingles P. Jones. Jingles made all the difference to the show's success. The series was developed by producer William Broidy, who had obtained the rights at a time when Madison's career was at a low point. The former lifeguard and telephone lineman had come out of the navy after World War II to star in a few unmemorable films for RKO Pictures. The better-known Devine was offered the sidekick role and partial ownership of the show after singer-actor

Burl Ives turned it down. It took about nine months for the show to get going. In a memoir about his father, Dennis Devine recalled Madison as "pleasant, uncomplicated, and vulnerable" while lacking much sophistication or charisma. He didn't need much, and young audiences loved him.[1]

The stories followed the pattern established by dime novels, comic books, movies, and radio Westerns. Wild Bill and Jingles, clad in fringed buckskin jackets, galloped desultorily around the West on their horses Buckshot and Joker, dispensing justice in compressed twenty-five-minute adventures, rarely acting in any kind of official capacity as law enforcement officers. The episodes were made for about $12,000 each and shot in two and a half days. Devine helped Broidy obtain sponsorship of the series, which was bought by the Kellogg Company. The stars pitched Corn Pops, later called Sugar Pops, to eager young listeners and viewers, who could write in to receive badges and buttons along with a "Special Offer, Pardner" to get an "Authentic Colt" six-shooter like the one held by Wild Bill on the box. The six-shooter was made of blue plastic and came without bullets. After all, the sponsor insisted that Wild Bill was to stay out of saloons and never kill anyone.[2]

Whenever possible, at Kellogg's behest, story lines were to portray Hickok outwitting outlaws rather than resorting to violence, even further detaching the program from history and dime-novel mayhem. Although there wasn't much actual history in the series, it did at least remind the Baby Boom generation that the country had a past, however distorted and manipulated by the advertising-driven scripts. Advertisers were targeting this growing prepubescent audience, which in turn was being conditioned to see popular history as a form of entertainment and support for an American narrative of triumphal expansion. The first television episode, "Behind Southern Lines," established how Wild Bill and Jingles met when Hickok, disguised as a Confederate general while on a spying mission, tried to reach Union lines, presumably during the Battle of Westport. "Behind Southern Lines" and a subsequent episode were combined and released as a feature film under that name in 1952.[3]

As a syndicated series, the program appeared at different times on different stations. Around New York City, *The Adventures of Wild Bill Hickok* was seen on WNBC-TV at 5:00 p.m. on Friday, September 11, 1953. The next day Wild Bill appeared on WOR-TV at 5:30 p.m. At 7:00 p.m. Saturday, the episode "Mexican Gun Running" was broadcast on WABD DuMont. In 1954, *The Adventures of Wild Bill Hickok* gained the coveted 6:00 p.m. spot on the NBC station opposite the fifteen-minute CBS evening news program. Choices on early television were limited. For some viewers, Wild Bill and Jingles were the best option, especially with episode titles such as "The Monster in the Lake," "The Gorilla of Owl Hoot Mesa," and "Masquerade at Moccasin Flats."[4]

Guy Madison became a hero to children, and he seemed genuinely to like them. "They're wonderful—perfect little ladies and gentlemen. . . . When I meet them . . . the kids are courteous, say 'Thank you' for my autograph or for a picture, ask me to wave at them or say 'Hello' next time I'm on TV."[5]

Television was still a relatively new medium in January 1954 when Madison was interviewed. The producers and advertisers planned to turn those youthful fans into consumers. The economy was expanding, and media boosterism had moved "from fearful amazement between roughly 1946 and 1948 to wondrous superlatives" between 1953 and 1957. Gross revenues in the advertising industry expanded by 75 percent during the 1950s, and television was fueling much of the growth. By 1953 already two-thirds of American households owned a television set. "We're going into the merchandising line next—Wild Bill Hickok shirts, belts, jackets—then rodeos, and all the personal appearances the people will take," said Madison. Fans could purchase a "Wild Bill Hickok Western Action Figure" with "poseable arms and legs" and "2 accessories" from the Excel Toy Company, along with a *Wild Bill Hickok's The Cavalry and the Indians* board game and a "Wild Bill Hickok and Jingles" lunchbox and coloring book, and they could trade Picture Puzzle Bubble Gum cards featuring Hickok. The timing was right because Wild Bill had just received an endorsement from an American president.[6]

"Read Your Westerns"

Dwight D. Eisenhower had been asked to accept the Anti-Defamation League of B'nai B'rith's Democratic Legacy Award for his contributions to the advancement of civil rights. The award was a ploy to get Eisenhower to actually do something about civil rights, which had not been high on his administration's agenda. The invitation to accept the award at the League's fortieth anniversary celebration in Washington on November 23, 1953, came with an expectation that the president would make a few remarks. That interested the television networks, which in turn girded the president's staff. The event was billed as *Dinner with the President*, a documentary-style extravaganza complete with stage entertainment and a VIP guest list. CBS offered live coverage, and NBC, ABC, and DuMont carried a kinescope for later viewing. About thirty-eight million viewers watched the speech, and another twenty million people heard it on radio.

Never known as a great speaker, Eisenhower alarmed his speechwriters by tossing aside the remarks they had written for him. In doing so, the president brought the mythic Hickok into the crossfire of politics. Eisenhower was eager to temper Sen. Joseph McCarthy's attacks on alleged communist influence in government, education, and media and went off script to indict McCarthyism without directly mentioning the senator and his followers.

In part, he said,

> I was raised in a little town of which most of you have never heard, but in the West it's a famous place! It's called Abilene, Kansas. We had as marshal for a long time, a man named Wild Bill Hickok. If you don't know him, read your Westerns more. Now that town had a code, and I was raised as a boy to prize that code.
>
> It was: meet anyone face to face with whom you disagree. You could not sneak up on him from behind, or do any damage to him, without suffering the penalty of an outraged citizenry. If you met him face to face and took the same risks he did, you could get away with almost anything, as long as the bullet was in the front.
>
> And today . . . you live after all by that same code in your ideals and in the respect you give to certain qualities. In this country, if someone dislikes you, or accuses you, he must come up in front. He cannot hide behind the shadow. He cannot assassinate you or your character from behind, without suffering the penalties an outraged citizenry will impose.
> . . . I would not want to sit down this evening without urging one thing:
>
> If we are going to continue to be proud that we are Americans, there must be no weakening of the code by which we have lived; by the right [*sic*] to meet your accuser face to face. . . .[7]

But the Abilene that Eisenhower knew as a boy had changed from the days when Hickok served as the cattle town's lawman. Born in Denison, Texas, in 1890, the future president lived in Abilene from 1891 until he left for West Point in 1911. He had an early fascination with Hickok and other Western gunfighters based on his reading and tales told by old timers who remembered, or thought they remembered, Hickok's exploits from 1871. As boys, Eisenhower and his brother Edgar acted out Western gunfights, competing for the prime role of Wild Bill. Eisenhower returned home for vacations while he was at the military academy and made occasional visits afterward. He spoke often about his hometown, most memorably in that 1953 television address when he invoked Hickok's legacy. Eisenhower perhaps was inspired by Hickok in facing down the Wehrmacht and the Cold War Red Army, and—in his own way and in his own good time—McCarthy. Not surprisingly, Eisenhower's favorite film was the allegorical 1952 classic *High Noon*, a treatise on the Hollywood blacklist whether he realized it or not. Maybe it also reminded him of D-Day. Ironically, the code didn't protect Eisenhower's hero Hickok when he was shot from behind in Deadwood, nor did it protect Eisenhower's successor when he was shot from behind in Dallas a decade later.[8]

Eisenhower loved Western novels, films, and television shows, although their reliability as sources of historical truth may have eluded him. One can't fault Eisenhower for not knowing much about his hero because the first reliable biography of Wild Bill Hickok wasn't published until more than a decade after Eisenhower's speech. The Hickok that Eisenhower conjured had been a marshal in Abilene for less than a year, not "a long time." While Hickok was often remembered as a lawman, he lost at least one election in his career and was discharged or resigned from other law enforcement posts. Eisenhower and most of his audience may not have known that Hickok had been raised by abolitionists or that he supported the Free State cause in Kansas, fought for the Union, and was a loyal Republican, but Eisenhower's predecessor surely did. Harry Truman's parents and grandparents in Missouri had suffered at the hands of pro-Union Kansas guerrillas and considered William Quantrill a protector. Truman recounted how Federal soldiers drove his family out of the county and half-starved them at a settlement camp.

Despite his border-state baggage, Hickok aligned more with the larger myth of the West than with the code Eisenhower invoked. Such codes, where they existed, were based on tradition. The idea that the West even had a code was popularized by Zane Grey in *Code of the West*, a novel published in 1934. The code was a mutable set of high-minded platitudes in many of his more than seventy Westerns novels as well as in the works of his many contemporaries. Grey was Eisenhower's favorite Western writer, and he was reading *West of the Pecos* on March 28, 1969, the day he died. A stack of Grey novels was at his bedside. Hickok still turns up as Eisenhower's simplified Western hero wielding his gun and his code. When the travel editor for the Los Angeles *Times* visited Abilene just before the D-Day anniversary celebrations in 2019, she learned that residents still like Ike in the quiet town where Wild Bill was said to have killed an astounding "50 miscreants."[9]

Western codes evolved from the earlier sportsman's codes that aspiring upper-middle American gentlemen adapted from European aristocracy to separate themselves from commercial hunting and fishing interests and the bumpkin's indifference to mannerly killing. Such codes failed to deter the high-minded gentlemen from firing on buffalo from trains when it suited them, nor did the cowboy or the lawman always follow the rules when the prey became human. Western codes became a legacy of the movies, popular fiction, and early radio. Western historian Ramon F. Adams summarized the codes in a 1969 book, *The Cowman and His Code of Ethics*. The essence of the codes was that they were unwritten. If you had to ask, in other words, you weren't to be trusted. Chief among them were loyalty, friendship, honesty, and, especially, privacy—which meant not asking too many questions. "Where you from, stranger?" might be an invitation to a hasty dismissal. Also of importance was the so-called "rattlesnake code." You always warned before you struck, and you never shot an unarmed man. Movie audiences learned to identify which gunmen were on the side of law, order, and fair play and which were not. "According to the mythic code the bad man would crouch behind a rock, rub dirt on the barrel of this rifle so that the glint won't betray him, and shoot a man in the back. The good man will face his enemy and make sure his enemy is facing him. He will call out to warn him before he draws and fires. These are the rules of the game," said Jenni Calder, a British literary historian.[10]

Western codes received a lot of attention during the Eisenhower administration. As broadcast historian Erik Barnouw pointed out, "an administration that had begun with the Eisenhower advice, 'Read your westerns more,' had achieved a stampede of westerns" in the 1950s. Most of the popular Western shows early in the decade, broadcast in black and white befitting the unambiguous, anodyne characters, were aimed at young viewers. The Lone Ranger, Hopalong Cassidy ("the highest Badge of Honor a person can wear is Honesty"), Roy Rogers, and Gene Autry ("a cowboy always tells the truth") had fan clubs and codes associated with their shows, and *The Adventures of Wild Bill Hickok* was no exception. Each "Deputy Marshal" agreed to follow the show's Code of Conduct Certificate posted on the back of the Kellogg's Sugar Pops cereal box.[11]

About the time *The Adventures of Wild Bill Hickok* was finishing television production in 1958, the Hickok character turned up in an episode of the short-lived Sunday afternoon radio series *Frontier Gentleman*, written by the London-born Western writer-producer Antony Ellis. The CBS series starred New Yorker John Dehner, a former broadcast journalist, as Jeremy Brian Kendall, a *Times of London* reporter who traveled the American West writing stories about colorful characters who would interest British readers. This narrative device of having a British reporter tell a story accurately reflected the British interest in the American West, with the added feature that the decorous Kendall, a former cavalry officer, wielded a gun and a knife as well as a pen, an early spin on participatory journalism.

British interest in the West had increased throughout the reign of Queen Victoria, who enjoyed stories of the American frontier and paintings of Western landscapes. Some aristocratic travelers came from Britain to establish utopian colonies, attracted by publicity promising easy fortunes to be made in ranching, mining, and farming. All of this did catch the attention of the *Times of London*. A reporter not unlike the fictional Kendall dispatched a long story making life on the range sound like an outing on Clapham Common in London. In the radio episode "Aces and Eights," broadcast on April 20, 1958, the frontier gentleman found his way to Deadwood and met McCall, who disparaged Hickok, and Calamity Jane, who adored him. Kendall was playing cards with Hickok when Wild Bill was murdered, and he prevented Calamity from hacking McCall with a meat cleaver. Just another day at the office for the gentlemanly reporter.[12]

Dehner appeared as Hickok in a July 26, 1954, radio episode of *Gunsmoke*. Dodge City marshal Matt Dillon, played by William Conrad, was accused of murdering Lou Price, the partner of Red Samples, a local rancher who wanted Dillon out of town so he could control gambling interests. Hickok arrived from Abilene to arrest Dillon and take his old friend to Hays City for trial. Hickok and the suspended marshal got Jim Huggins, a witness bribed by Samples, drunk and coaxed the truth out of him: Samples killed Price and paid Huggins to implicate Dillon. To help along the extralegal procedures, Hickok deputized the suspended Dillon, who outdrew the rancher in the saloon. The radio play was adapted for the television series episode "Matt for Murder" broadcast on September 13, 1958, with James Arness as Matt Dillon and Robert J. Wilke as Hickok.

Jack Cassidy appeared as Hickok in a television episode of *Bronco* that aired on March 19, 1962. The series was broadcast on ABC from 1958 to 1962. The teleplay was based loosely on author and screenwriter Steve Frazee's story, "One Evening in Abilene." Bronco was a former Confederate officer leading a cattle drive to Abilene, where Hickok was marshal. A woman and her father, Confederate sympathizers, were returning to Abilene with the body of her fiancé, who she said Hickok killed. She tricked a young ex-Confederate gunfighter into taking on Hickok, despite Bronco's objections that Hickok was too fast.[13]

One of the signature CBS programs of the early television era was *You Are There*, a holdover from radio. The series ran from 1953 to 1957. The idea of the show was to blend history and news by using CBS network journalists to interview historical figures as if news events were in real time. *The Great Adventure*, a historical anthology that drew on the earlier concept, ran for twenty-six hourlong episodes during the 1963–64 season. "Wild Bill Hickok—The Legend and the Man" starred Lloyd Bridges as Hickok. McCanles, Tutt, McCall, and other adversaries made appearances as the aging Wild Bill struggled with his eyesight problems. The episode was scheduled for broadcast on November 22, 1963, but was preempted by coverage of the Kennedy assassination. Wild Bill's television assassination had to wait until January 3, 1964.

"A Calamity Called Jane" on television's *Death Valley Days* highlighted the supposed romantic interest between Hickok and Canary. *Death Valley Days* had been a radio program from 1930 to 1945 and resumed as a television anthology series in 1952, continuing for eighteen years. Ronald Reagan acted in the series and hosted it in 1964 and 1965 before running for governor of California. Rhodes Reason played Hickok in the December 29, 1966, episode, with Fay Spain as a cackling, boozy Calamity. Against Wild Bill's advice, Charlie Utter recruited Calamity to join their Wild West show on its way to Deadwood, where writers like Ned Buntline had built up interest in Hickok. "They're gonna be writing about him one day," Utter told Calamity, with heavy irony. "Wild Bill Hickok. That name's gonna be up there with Buffalo Bill, Custer, with all of 'em." Calamity fell in love with Wild Bill, who wanted no part of her ("She's trouble"). Stephen Lord's script turned Hickok into a buckskin-clad moralist who found Calamity unladylike and crude. When she bought a dress and tried to impress him, Hickok found her inauthentic. "Sometimes we can't change what we are, Calamity," he said. Irate, she called Hickok a "fancied up rooster," denounced men, and stalked off to get drunk, only to rush back to the saloon when she heard a shot. Hickok had been murdered, his aces and eights plainly visible in his dead man's hand, the grief-stricken Calamity sprawled across his bleeding corpse. "Another true story of the Old West," the announcer dissembled at the conclusion, the story being a jumble of feminism, pop psychology, and transposed characters and timelines, more 1960s than 1870s.

In fact, television was changing. So-called "adult Westerns" had begun crowding out programs like *Wild Bill Hickok*, which were aimed at young people. The new lineup had brushed aside "its juvenile predecessors, as its car, cigarette, and beer sponsors swept aside the cereals, toys, and candy bars." With new programs such as *Bat Masterson*, *Have Gun, Will Travel*, and *Wyatt Earp*, the TV Western hero "took his first cautious steps out of the 'West' and into the shadows," according to journalist Tom Englehardt. This didn't happen quickly, and, well into the mid-1960s, television remained "an ideological wagon train, circling constantly to ensure that it was the least haunted of entertainment forms," yet "even out there in the safety of the 'western' frontier, the story was being transformed almost imperceptibly into something less triumphantly American." The audience was receptive to the narrative because, as David Foster Wallace pointed out in a now-famous essay in 1990, television was "an incredible gauge of the generic. If we want to know what American normality is—i.e., what Americans want to regard as normal—we can trust television. For television's whole raison is reflecting what people want to see." Just where Wild Bill would fit in was still to be determined, however, and aside from television reruns, the occasional movie, and a few cameo appearances, he all but disappeared from the small screen for twenty-five years.[14]

The Young Riders, a Western series set in the Nebraska Territory before the Civil War, imagined the adventures of "Jimmy" Hickok, "Billy" Cody and other high-spirited horseback delivery boys—and a girl in disguise—as Pony Express recruits. None was supposed to be older than eighteen. Hickok had nightmares about confrontations between his parents in Illinois, and the unpleasant memories seemed to be driving him to become a gunfighter. "Full of demons, ain't you? Got to learn control," advised Teaspoon Hunter, a former Texas Ranger played by Anthony Zerbe. The series ran from 1989 to 1992 on the ABC network. Josh Brolin starred as the hotheaded Hickok who was learning to be a gunfighter. The riders were based at Sweetwater Station, where they were mothered by Emma Shannon, played by Melissa Leo.

Plots involved the usual assortment of bad guys, and it wasn't always clear how the lads had time to deliver the mail. The second episode of the first season, "Gunfighter," was broadcast on September 21, 1989, and was a fairly typical learning experience. Hickok accidently muddied a hired gunfighter, Longley, who demanded an apology, which the reckless lad declined to offer. Emma begged Hickok to apologize rather than confront Longley, who was rumored to have killed more than one hundred men. "Once you take that path, there's no turning back," she warned. She tried to bribe Longley not to kill Hickok by giving him a family heirloom watch. Longley shot an older gunfighter who wanted to get out of the killing business and raise his son. The boy, looking for a hero, begged Hickok to avenge his father. The riders knew Longley had an accomplice who fired surreptitiously from a window. Hickok reluctantly rode off to apologize to Longley and retrieve the watch for Emma, but Longley wanted satisfaction. The teenage riders followed and shot the accomplice while Hickok fatally shot Longley. Although Hickok had tried to avoid bloodshed, he had to fight, and there was no retreat. The series appealed to a young audience. As a study of the callow Hickok, however, it was hardly an advance over *Young Bill Hickok*.

Legend, a series that lasted four months on the troubled United Paramount Network in 1995, mixed the horse opera formula with science fiction to spoof Western mythology in the tradition of *The Wild Wild West*, which ran on CBS from 1965 to 1969. What made *Legend* different was its richer parody of self-invention along with its jumbled steampunk anachronisms. Richard Dean Anderson, also an executive producer, played struggling dime novelist and former San Francisco *Chronicle* reporter Ernest Pratt, who competed with real life dime novelist Ned Buntline in inventing the Wild West. Pratt learned that his fictional hero, Nicodemus Legend, was being impersonated in Sheridan, Colorado, by Janos Bartok, a rogue scientific genius likely inspired by Nikola Tesla. Pratt continued the ruse by taking on the identity of Legend, who served as a cavalryman in the Michigan Brigade under Custer during the Civil War, to live up to his character's Code of the West. His deception was not difficult because Pratt wrote his dime novels in the first person, causing the same sort of confusion of identity that contributed to Hickok's growing mythology at the hands of Chris Forrest (actually William Osborne Stoddard), Buntline (Edward Judson), and other potboiler scribblers. Bartok added credibility to the decidedly unheroic Pratt by actually inventing some of the fantastic devices only imagined by Pratt in the dime novels.[15]

"The Life, Death, and Life of Wild Bill Hickok," an episode broadcast on May 16, 1995, sent up the whole dime-novel industry and the mythology of the West. Hickok, played by William Russ and marked for death, came to see Pratt in Sheridan, another victim of Buntline's imagination. Buntline knew of Pratt's scam and made Pratt's problems worse by boosting the Legend mystique, thereby leaving him as vulnerable to toxic celebrity as was Hickok. Wild Bill told Pratt that he had been hired by the Santa Fe Railroad to bring in McCall's gang, and he wanted Legend's help. But Hickok's arrival brought danger. A young man claiming to have been the bellman at the hotel in Springfield the day Hickok shot Tutt touted Hickok's prowess with a gun. A kid challenged Hickok to a gunfight in the street because he, too, wanted to be a dime-novel hero. Hickok fired and missed, revealing his failing eyesight.

Hickok knew his time was running out. "What's a man to do when he can't do what he does anymore?" asked Wild Bill.

First he needed glasses, and then he wanted to retire, so Bartok gave him an eye exam, proper spectacles, and a lecture about technology. Bartok believed lone gunfighters were being rendered obsolete by science. His whimsical inventions included airships, wings, drones, lightning-bolt transmitters, bulletproof vests, radio, and all-terrain vehicles, anticipating the tools of future warfare. Some of this wizardry was used to repel McCall and his gang when they came into Sheridan to fight Hickok. Legend and Bartok gave pursuit in their airship, zapping the gang with lightning bolts and extricating the outgunned Hickok from a tight spot in a parody of a Blackhawk helicopter rescue. Legend was captured and argued with McCall about fair play and technology. "Whatever happened to the Code of the West?" asked Legend. "The Code of the West! Another of these stupid lies you writers put in your dime novels," replied McCall. "Writers don't know anything about the West."

Wild Bill rescued Legend, McCall escaped, and surviving gang members were rounded up and taken to Deadwood for trial. As in history, though, Wild Bill was shot by McCall—but he didn't quite "meet his end." As an empty coffin was lowered into the earth, Legend, Bartok, and an unscathed Wild Bill, still wearing his bulletproof vest, watched from a distance. "I guess you could sell a few novels telling what really happened here," said Wild Bill, who was heading for a California retirement. While survival myths have not often been part of Wild Bill mythology, at least the gimmick was a twist on an old story. But Legend preferred the more tragic ending because readers, and history, demanded it. "Print the legend," in other words. Plus, it took care of Buntline. "Poor old Ned," said Legend. "We seem to have killed off his golden goose. Too bad." Too bad for poor old Legend as well. The series was canceled.

The television Western, so popular in the 1950s, was by 1996 "as dead as if it had been gunned down on the streets of Dodge," according to New York *Times* cultural reporter and film critic Caryn James. The 1950s Westerns, she said, had appeared during an era with shared moral assumptions and more willingness to accept platitudes about the West as a landscape of American values. Television series had offered "cozy communities" and a "comforting sense of family," an innocence that had been lost at century's end. Television and movie Westerns that had once rejuvenated each other and shared the same audiences had moved apart as television demographics shifted and advertisers responded. Minority audiences expected more diversity. Younger viewers disdained the formulaic "adult westerns" and nostalgic horse operas watched by their parents, while the film industry turned to revisionist Westerns. Attempts to appeal to these new audiences on television had not been too successful, however—and Hickok had not appealed to them either.[16]

The White Rose

But Hickok was ready to make a comeback, and television had the sprawl to give storytellers room to take on some bigger issues. One of the most imaginative Hickok television appearances, a made-for-cable production, came out just in time for the millennium. *Purgatory* fit the millennial mood by mixing exhausted twentieth-century Western movie and television themes with metaphysical questions right out of Dante. The pop theology worked well because the mythical American West is the land of second chances, an American purgatory.

The film had its debut on the TNT network on January 10, 1999. Written by long-time Sam Peckinpah collaborator Gordon T. Dawson and directed by German television veteran Uli Gellen, the story began in Sweetwater, a generic Western town near the Mexican border, in 1886. The loathsome Blackjack Britton, played by Eric Roberts, and his huge gang planned to rob the bank. Sonny Miller, a kid obsessed with dime-novel Westerns, begged his uncle, the sadistic Cavin Guthrie, to let him ride along. The kid, played by Brad Rowe, started showing off and attracting attention, so Guthrie made him wait outside the bank. A stage arrived, and Sonny met Dolly Sloan, the "Harlot with a Heart," who told him that dime novels didn't get the story right. The robbery went bad, and Dolly was shot and died in Sonny's arms. The gang escaped by riding into a fogbank during a storm and passing through a tunnel that opened onto a broad green valley.

They came to a town called Refuge, where they were welcomed by a friendly sheriff played by the actor-playwright Sam Shepard, famous for his own Western dramas. The sheriff offered them free drinks and lodging, while only lightly admonishing them about cursing. Blackjack played along, but soon he was scheming to loot the town, which he thought was full of cowards or members of a pacifist religious sect summoned to regular worship by the doomsday bell tolling in a church belfry. Any acts of aggression by the gang provoked an ominous Indian gatekeeper, a silent Chiron the Boatman figure who watched the town from what appeared to be a cemetery gate, to summon storms and bring down lethal bolts of lightning. Miscreants were hauled off to the abyss.

Sonny pursued an attractive young woman named Rose, played by Amelia Heinle. As tensions between gang members and townspeople increased, Sonny, absorbed in his dime novels, recognized that the sheriff was Wild Bill Hickok, late of Deadwood, and dead for almost a decade. The storekeeper was Jesse James, played by John David Souther. Doc Holliday, played by Randy Quaid, was the town doctor (although the real Holliday was a dentist), and Hickok's deputy was Billy the Kid, played by Donnie Wahlberg. All the gunfighters were dead as they would have been in real life in 1886, except for Holliday, who died of consumption in 1887, a minor gaffe in the script.

When Sonny confronted Holliday with his suspicions, the doctor warned Sonny that his life was in jeopardy. "A few bad choices, a man can lose his soul." The arrival of Dolly Slone in a stagecoach made it evident to Sonny that everyone in this literal ghost town must be dead except the gang. The stage driver, played by R. G. Armstrong, one of the most recognizable Western character actors for half a century, alerted Hickok that "come noon Sunday, you're going home," and gave him a white rose, symbolic of innocence, pacifism, and—in some contexts—cowardice.

Sonny found out the gang was going to destroy the town and take Rose to Mexico. Rose wouldn't escape with Sonny because she had murdered her father, a molester, and been the first woman hanged in the Arizona Territory. She had to remain in Refuge. When Sonny urged the townspeople to fight the gang, he learned that if they resorted to violence they would be consigned to Hell. The only other way out of Refuge was to avoid violence and debauchery for ten years. "Refuge is where the marginally good are gleaned from the hopelessly wicked," James explained. The longer they stayed in Refuge, the meeker they became, however. "I don't reckon I have it in me anymore," said Hickok, who was to leave Refuge in a matter of hours if he refrained from violence. Sonny wouldn't have it, and told the gunfighters, "And to think some of you used to be my heroes." After a severe beating by Blackjack, Sonny pledged to fight the gang alone. Hickok realized that because Sonny was willing to die to save Rose "with no thought to himself," he had made the right moral choice. Wild Bill, in contrast, understood that in life he had thought only of himself. He threw down the white rose and retrieved his guns, ready to fight, then lined up with Billy, Jesse, Doc, and Sonny for a classic Western walkdown.

A sanguinary battle ensued with everyone firing wildly and hundreds of rounds of ammunition discharged. The gang was slaughtered and Sonny, mortally wounded, shot his uncle, leaving only Blackjack to square off against Hickok, who nailed him with a fancy spin move, leaving the dying Blackjack unredeemed. "I guess I'm one of you, now," said Blackjack. "I don't think so," said Hickok, administering the coup de grâce. Blackjack and Cavin were carted off by the Indian and dumped, screaming, into Hell. Hickok, James, Holliday, and Billy followed the Indian, assuming that they, too, were going directly to Hell. The film ended, however, as the justified gunfighters boarded a stagecoach to Heaven after the driver told them, "The Creator may be tough, but He ain't blind." Meaning, apparently, that this very old-school deity liked a good gunfight if the bullets flew for a good reason. Sonny stayed behind with Rose, wearing the sheriff's star Hickok had given him. He had learned that his dime novels didn't always get the true story, and he resolved to be a different kind of hero, one motivated by love.

That Hickok was in such bad company in the first place meant that he was a killer and an outlaw, not a lawman. Purgatory was open to the "marginally good" but not the "hopelessly wicked." Billy the Kid got a chance, but Blackjack Britton went straight to Hell. For this to work as a moral premise, Hickok had to be more or less on both sides of the law, worthy to wear the star in purgatory but headed for perdition for dastardly crimes unless he kept his guns locked away. When he was confronted with an unredeemable evil, however, homicide was justifiable as long as it was done selflessly and in the interest of love. Hickok, only minutes away from earning his way out of purgatory, took the greatest risk. Holliday—not yet dead in 1886—shouldn't even have been in Refuge yet. It's weird morality and weirder theology for Hickok and company to earn a pass to Paradise courtesy of a bunch of cutthroats. The counterrituals turn the traditional Western on its head. This turn-of-the-century Western put a marginally good Hickok in a house of mirrors, a white rose clenched in his teeth, guns blazing, glass shattering, the audience lost in the fog of its own purgatory as the church bell rang in the new era.

Living without Laws

Hickok's next major appearance in 2004 attracted wide attention and solidly revived the Western genre on cable television. The creation of David Milch, *Deadwood* used nine writers and seven directors to develop a dozen episodes in its initial season. Walter Hill, director of the 1995 film *Wild Bill*, directed the first episode of the original HBO series. The episode introduced Hickok as a character played by Keith Carradine, who had a brief role as Buffalo Bill in *Wild Bill*. Milch was a writer and producer for several urban crime dramas before he approached HBO with an idea for a series to be set in ancient Rome that was rejected because a similar series already was in production. HBO liked his alternative idea for a series to be set in Deadwood, beginning with Hickok's arrival in 1876. Hickok was murdered in the fourth episode of the first season and buried in the fifth.[17]

Hickok's character was central to the series, Milch said, because Hickok was a primitive "used by American society virtually from his adolescence as an instrument of order whose organized principle was not justice but force." By the time he reached Deadwood with Charlie Utter and Calamity Jane, Hickok "had lived past his utility to the culture except as a caricature and he wasn't good at that. . . . That soul could not live in the modernity that was in the process of generating itself." Heroes were out of fashion. "In his essence, [Hickok] represented all of the capacities that we kind of associate with the American character," Milch said. Hickok was polite and patient, and he loved children. He was courtly and kind, but he tolerated no impudence and was quick to violence. He was effective "because he had no illusion about the process." If threatened, he would take preemptive action without undue reflection. Such a man was useful in the face of disorder, such as civil war or Indian attack, but would self-destruct with time on his hands. Milch's larger theme, questioned more fully in subsequent seasons and a 2019 movie, was the establishment of law and order, "specifically, how does order develop without law? It isn't just a matter of brute force. Even brute force can only be used by somebody with an idea of order. How does chaos evolve into order?"[18]

Deadwood interested Milch because it was "a completely illegal city, a town that existed without legal authority and which went through a maelstrom of turmoil before its citizens learned to impose some kind of order on themselves." Some critics saw Milch's emphasis on Deadwood's greed and disorder as a critique of the reckless capitalism and moral relativism of the 1990s or even Hollywood excess, which read too much into the series. Others fixated on the American tropes of fresh starts and second chances, gender, race, American empire, and addiction—everyone in *Deadwood* was addicted to something, to the point of farce.

A libertarian reading of the series by Paul A. Cantor drew on economic and political philosophy, seeing in Hickok's preemptive violence an example of the natural condition of mankind that might have been taken from Thomas Hobbes's *Leviathan*. For Hobbes, there could be no order without law, while Milch speculated that a degree of order without law might be possible. According to Cantor, *Deadwood* exemplified the Western at its best. "Such is the remarkable result when Thomas Hobbes, John Locke, and Jean-Jacques

Rousseau meet Wild Bill Hickok and Calamity Jane on the American frontier," he wrote. Hickok's fatalism, "blindness," dissipation, and weariness with celebrity aligned well with Deadwood's illegality, corruption, gold rush excess, gambling, and prostitution. The troubled Hickok had no interest in taming Deadwood or even staking a mining claim. He spent his last days gambling and died with cards in his hands. Milch achieved financial and critical success from *Deadwood*—the series averaged 4.5 million viewers each week during its first season, HBO's second most successful debut. Ironically, he gambled away a fortune within a decade after the series ended.[19]

Hickok first appeared in the initial episode recumbent in the back of a wagon. "I wanted Hickok to look like he was lying in state from the first we saw him because it seemed to me he was kind of living into a premature death right from the first," Milch explained. "He kind of went out there to die." Hickok became friendly with former Montana sheriff Seth Bullock, played by Timothy Olyphant. Bullock, who was a decade younger than Hickok, was also a recent arrival in Deadwood along with Sol Star, his partner in a hardware business. Vice lord Al Swearengen, played with diabolical panache by Ian McShane, didn't want them in town, especially after Bullock was appointed Deadwood's first sheriff. Bullock and Hickok rescued a child whose Norwegian pioneer family had been slaughtered by road agents likely in league with Swearengen and jointly shot the hireling who tried to blame Indians for the attack. Hickok also shot a would-be assassin before he was finally murdered by McCall, played by character actor Garret Dillahunt. Hickok was played elegiacally by Carradine, who was able to craft a more credible interpretation of Wild Bill than other actors have managed. Among the many curiosities in the film, Carradine's father John had played the ex-Confederate gambler Hatfield in John Ford's classic *Stagecoach* in 1939. Hatfield drew the "dead man's hand" and was therefore doomed. Carradines keep turning up in Hickok filmography. In creating the role, Keith Carradine, who at fifty-five was playing the thirty-nine-year-old Hickok, acknowledged the need to establish Hickok's presence and bearing. "These gunfighters, they were the rock stars of the era and they had a great sense of theatricality about them," he said. The swagger he gave Hickok, however, was physically understated and emotionally economical, the very opposite of the real Hickok's own bungled interpretation of himself on stage.[20]

Milch said he regretted the necessity to eject Hickok from the series so early and had considered having Hickok reappear as a specter or illusion. Instead, he challenged characters to live into Hickok's legacy as the series moved from disorder to order. Ultimately, a well-imagined Deadwood itself was the star of the series, not Carradine, McShane, or Olyphant. Milch said he used the available sources to develop the series with historical accuracy, but he knew when to let the research go. "The most important part is to forget it and allow it to become an imaginative reality. The truths of storytelling are not the truths of reportage," he insisted. The events, he said, "have to come alive in the imagination of the viewer." Much of the appeal of the series had to do with its crossing the barbed-wire boundaries of the conventional Western genre. This "generic instability," according to journalist and media scholar Wendy Witherspoon, mirrored *Deadwood*'s theme of living without laws.[21]

A study in contrasts, journalist-turned-army-staff-officer George Ward Nichols founded the College of Music of Cincinnati in 1878. His firsthand account of the March to the Sea had helped make William Tecumseh Sherman famous. After the Civil War, he transformed Hickok into an enduring symbol of the Wild West. *Courtesy Archives and Rare Books Library, University of Cincinnati.*

THE FAREWELL.

"The Farewell." Colonel Nichols takes his leave from Wild Bill soon after he met the army scout in Springfield, Missouri. The image implicitly connects Hickok to the Civil War and suggests the trust placed in him by senior officers. Their intense expressions give the interview a gravitas undermined by the tall-tale content of the article that would make Hickok famous. Harper's New Monthly Magazine *34, February 1867. Courtesy of HathiTrust, https:// babel.hathitrust.org/cgi/pt?id=uc1.b000541577&view=1up&seq=295.*

HARPER'S
NEW MONTHLY MAGAZINE.

No. CCI.—FEBRUARY, 1867.—Vol. XXXIV.

WILD BILL.

In its first Hickok illustration, *Harper's* depicts a knight of the West, armed and stylishly attired. He is a deadly gentleman. Harper's New Monthly Magazine *34, February 1867.*

THE STRUGGLE FOR LIFE.

In the same issue that showed Hickok on the cover in gentlemanly pose and attire, we see the deadly Hickok in action. He will overcome five assailants in hand-to-hand combat, two of them already down. Harper's New Monthly Magazine *34, February 1867.*

The buckskins contrast to another common image of Hickok—the frontier dandy, a fashion plate among pistoleers. Though clad in wilderness fashion, he remains armed, boots apparently polished enough that light from the long exposure required of the camera technology of the time could reflect off them. *Courtesy of Kansas Historical Society. Image cropped at edges.*

Hickok is photographed in fashionable attire. With the fur hat, he is linked to the American frontier. The suitcoat and tie signify a gentleman. *Courtesy of Kansas Historical Society. Image cropped at edges.*

Wyoming, Utah, Nevada, Arizona, New Mexico, and Colorado.

He knew Denver when it was but a miner's camp; Leavenworth and Omaha when they were only military posts; North Platte where to-day stands his elegant home, when there was not a habitation near, save the tepee of the Indian; and Salt Lake, when it was but the unindicated locale of the present splendid capital of the now Mormon State. He has fought back the Indians step by step over spots where now are grand centers of population and wealth, as witness, the Queen City of the West; or, as it really is, the matchless metropolis of the Rocky Mountains and Plains—Denver, the Beautiful!

Appointed chief of scouts to the superb Fifth Cavalry, promoted to brigade and then division chief of scouts, Buffalo Bill won the hearts of the officers and men by his daring dash, his skill, his sturdy manhood, and his true nobility of nature.

Sent to guard and guide the advance of the Kansas Pacific Railway through a land of peril, he there made, for a second time, a claim to the name he now bears as "Buffalo Bill," for as a lad, on account of his prowess in bringing down the big game, Wild Bill had christened him "Buffalo Billy, the Boy Hunter."

The second claim to the name was when he killed, in one season, four thousand three hundred and sixty-two buffaloes, for the sustenance of the army of workers on the great iron highway.

This seeming slaughter was not mere destruction or "sport," but in the line of duty, and not a beast was felled which was not required for food. No person more than Cody disapproved the senseless destruction of the herd by so-called "sportsmen," and he clearly foresaw the early extinction of the noble game.

During his services as army scout, Buffalo Bill made some of the most remarkable rides on record, and through an unknown country, filled with hostile Indians. Chosen by General Sheridan as chief guide and hunter of the Grand Duke Alexis hunt, Buffalo Bill arranged all to the satisfaction of his commander and all concerned, getting old Spotted Tail and his village to camp near, so that the Russian Prince could see what the American Indian was, in his wild state. Calling Buffalo Bill aside, General Sheridan said:

"Now, Cody, I leave all to you; and remember the Grand Duke would not dare go home without killing a 'buffalo.'"

"General, I know where the herds are, but if they give us the slip, there is a sick buffalo over in the canyon near, and he can get him, for he won't know the difference," was Buffalo Bill's jovial reply.

Giving the Grand Duke his trained buffalo horse to ride, and explaining to him just what to do and what not to do, they started on the hunt and found a small band of buffalo.

The Grand Duke brought down his game and immediately suggested that they should go to camp and drink a bottle of champagne.

"Do you intend to open a bottle of champagne for every buffalo you kill, duke?" asked Cody, innocently.

"Yes, certainly, Guide Cody!"

"Then come quick; I have got a big herd over here just waiting for you to kill them," Buffalo Bill assured.

Whether the Grand Duke cared to keep to his resolve I need not say, but he certainly won a name as a daring hunter and expert buffalo-killer, and so pleased was he with his guide and director that he took a valuable pin from his scarf and presented it to him, while upon his return to Russia he sent other presents, among them a gift from the emperor himself, which is now one of Cody's most precious treasures.

Having met Buffalo Bill in the West when on a hunting expedition, Mr. James Gordon Bennett of the New York *Herald* invited him to visit the East, and, soon after, urged by Colonel E. Z. C. Judson—Ned Buntline—to come, the famous scout decided to do so.

When he started for New York he carried letters of indorsement as to his career from Generals Sherman, Sheridan, the lamented Custer, Nelson A. Miles, now commanding the Department of the East, Crook, Terry, E. A. Carr, Merritt, Royall, and others.

The papers of New York teemed with mention of his deeds and personal character-

istics, and he became quite the lion of the hour—a fact that was seized upon by Ned Buntline to make an actor of him, there then being upon the stage a play called "Buffalo Bill," in which Jack Studley was playing the leading *role*.

After much persuasion Cody consented, and sending West for Wild Bill and Texas Jack, then famed as scouts and frontiersmen, to join him, they opened in Chicago in the "Scouts of the Border." If he ever repeated a word of the lines Buffalo Bill says that he does not remember, and when he and his two pards faced the audience it took all of Bunt-

BUFFALO BILL.

line's pleading, praying, scolding and profanity to keep them from stampeding and taking the first train for the Far West, never to go East any more.

But, they got through, and had a most fashionable audience, the receipts being over three thousand dollars for the week.

Speaking of the play, Ned Buntline stated that he had written it in *four* hours; whereupon the papers wanted to know what he was doing *all that time!*

Still, it was a real melo-drama—a play, as a play of marked merit—and Ned Buntline's genius as a literary man none will dispute, as his scores of novels attest.

Buntline's play served as a means to an end, for it made a powerful impersonator of

Buffalo Bill, and if he was criticised by some, the critics did not fail to recognize the fact that he was depicting scenes through which he had passed, life which he had known, impersonating no fictitious characters, but simply acting Buffalo Bill.

Taking up the man as a hero whose life, deeds and character were wholly real, the writer of this sketch, his "Pard on Plaza and Plain" for many years, found in Buffalo Bill such a fruitful fund for the pen of the romancer that he has written story after story, with the demands ever growing from the increasing host who now enthusiastically admire the man and are eager to read of deeds and adventures in which Buffalo Bill was chief actor.

Other writers have followed in the same fields—Leon Lewis, Major Sam Hall, Major John M. Burke, and the star of army novelists, Captain Charles King; while poems were written of and to the great plainsman, in this country and abroad, until to-day hundreds of novels and scores of biographies or biographic sketches are to be found the world over.

As an instance: a naval officer told me that, while he was stationed in China several years ago, he met a book-agent there selling the *Life* of Buffalo Bill and the Bible!

As his fame grew, Buffalo Bill was sought after by publishers for sketches for their literary papers, and finding that he also possessed genius as a story-teller, he received very large sums for his novels, numbers of which were published by Messrs. Beadle and Adams of the BANNER WEEKLY, of New York—so many, indeed, that this publishing firm have a series of "Buffalo Bill Novels" both from the scout's own pen and from the pens of other authors named, the great scout being the central figure or title character.

Telling his story in an interesting, modest, direct way, with no flourish of words or tawdry sentiment, Buffalo Bill is as entertaining as a writer as he is as a conversationalist.

Having made a success in all his undertakings from messenger boy on the Overland, bullwhacker, trapper, hunter, wagon-master, stage-driver, Pony Express rider, soldier, guide, scout and, Indian-fighter, down to actor and author, and after making a considerable fortune, too, in his work, it occurred to Buffalo Bill to interpret in realistic life the true scenes and incidents of the Wild West.

The idea of producing before the public in an arena the veritable wild scenes, Indian battles, scouts and soldiers on an Indian trail, redskin villages, their dances, Overland stage travel, attacks on settlers, and all else the pioneers of the West knew so well, was considered an impossibility; but with money and brains to back him, Buffalo Bill won a new triumph, as the "greatest showman on earth," making Barnum himself take off his hat to him!

After several successful tours in this country, he chartered a steamship, and, with Mr. Nate Salsbury as his partner, sailed for Europe, where he conquered instant success, being received by the queen, and the Prince of Wales, and was introduced into all the famous clubs, and became the guest of many of England's most prominent men.

Presented by the Queen and the Prince and Princess of Wales with costly gifts, Buffalo Bill commanded the same respect and admiration from the crowned heads of Germany, Austria, Italy, the Pope of Rome, the President of the French Republic, the rulers of Spain, Portugal, Belgium, Sweden, and the Sultan of Turkey.

Mr. Nate Salsbury shared everywhere in these honors, and deservedly so, for it was his efficient management of the tour which carried the Border Life of the New World into the Capitals of the Old World.

Unspoilt by flattery, modest, unassuming, true as steel to his old friends, to-day he stands for what is noblest in manhood—a representative and typical American.

Long may he live!

NEXT DIME LIBRARY, NUMBER 883.

The Man from Mexico in New York;
OR, TURNING DOWN
THE SHYLOCK PAWNBROKER.
BY HAROLD PAYNE.

Prolific dime-novel author Col. Prentiss Ingraham discovered camaraderie in the mission of the "three Bills." This account takes place in a Rocky Mountain mining camp. "Breadbox Bill" tells Hickok and Cody, "Well, this coffin is to have an occupant to-night, gentlemen, and the man is alive and in good health who is to fill it." Beadle's Dime Library, *September 18, 1895. Courtesy of Nickels and Dimes, Northern Illinois University Libraries.*

Buffalo Bill's Story by Special Contract!

BEADLE'S

Dime New York Library

Copyrighted, 1891, by Beadle and Adams.   ENTERED AS SECOND CLASS MATTER AT THE NEW YORK, N. Y., POST OFFICE.   February 21, 1894.

No. 800.   Published Every Wednesday.   Beadle & Adams, Publishers, 98 WILLIAM STREET, NEW YORK.   Ten Cents a Copy. $5.00 a Year.   Vol. LXII.

WILD BILL, THE DEAD-CENTER SHOT.

BY "BUFFALO BILL,"—(GEN. WM. F. CODY.)

"HOLD ON, BLACK JACK! I KNOW YOU AND HAVE YOU COVERED!" CRIED WILD BILL.

Mere accuracy was not enough for a dime-novel gunman. He needed to be a "dead-shot," which in the case of the Hickok myth meant pistol prowess so great that he could shoot a coin at incredible distances, splitting the bullet on the edge. Hickok stands openly while three or four desperadoes cringe behind a tree and barrels. Beadle's Dime Library, *February 21, 1894. Courtesy of Nickels and Dimes, Northern Illinois University Libraries.*

A ROMANCE OF BUFFALO BILL'S OLD PARD.

BEADLE'S

Dime New York Library

COPYRIGHTED IN 1881, BY BEADLE & ADAMS.

ENTERED AT THE POST OFFICE AT NEW YORK, N.Y., AT SECOND CLASS MAIL RATES.

Vol. XIII. Published Every Week. *Beadle & Adams, Publishers,* 98 WILLIAM STREET, N. Y., January 11, 1882. Ten Cents a Copy. $5.00 a Year. No. 168

WILD BILL, THE PISTOL DEAD SHOT;
Or, DAGGER DON'S DOUBLE.

BY COLONEL PRENTISS INGRAHAM,

AUTHOR OF "MERLE, THE MUTINEER," "MONTEZUMA, THE MERCILESS," "FREELANCE, THE BUCCANEER," "THE DARE DEVIL," "THE CRETAN ROVER," "THE PIRATE PRINCE," ETC., ETC.

"WALL, PARD STRANGER YER HEV STRUCK IT RICH," CRIED ONE OF THE COWBOYS. "THREE WITH THER TOES TURNED UP, AN' TWO IN A DURNED UNHEALTHY GRIP," SAID ANOTHER.

Beadle and Adams was among the leading publishers of dime novels, introducing the short sensations in 1860. In this January 11, 1882, edition, the heroic Hickok is overcoming four-to-one odds against Indians—two down and two doomed. Beadle's Dime Library, *January 11, 1882. Courtesy of Nickels and Dimes, Northern Illinois University Libraries.*

"PISTOLS ARE TRUMPS!"

BEADLE'S
Dime New York Library

COPYRIGHTED IN 1882, BY BEADLE & ADAMS.

ENTERED AT THE POST OFFICE AT NEW YORK, N. Y., AT SECOND CLASS MAIL RATES.

Vol. XIV. | Published Every Week. | Beadle & Adams, Publishers, 98 WILLIAM STREET, N. Y., March 1, 1882. | Ten Cents a Copy. $5.00 a Year. | No. 175

Wild Bill's Trump Card; or, The Indian Heiress.

A Romance of Thrilling Adventure, Founded Upon Real Incidents in the Life of J. B. Hikok—"Wild Bill "—and Companion Story to "Wild Bill, the Pistol Dead-Shot; or, Dagger Don's Double."

BY MAJOR DANGERFIELD BURR,

AUTHOR OF "VELVET FACE," "CAPTAIN CRIMSON," "DASHING DANDY," "BUFFALO BILL, THE BUCKSKIN KING," ETC., ETC.

"HOLD! PISTOLS ARE TRUMPS IN THIS GAME OF DEVILTRY, AND WILD BILL PLAYS THEM!"

Hickok rescues the Indian maiden, a take on the old theme of the knight saving the lady in distress, and in contrast to the more common theme in dime novels in which "savages" were slain. The cover claim is "founded upon real incidents" but was in fact fictional, much akin to modern-day "reality TV." Beadle's Dime Library, *March 1, 1882. Courtesy of Nickels and Dimes, Northern Illinois University Libraries.*

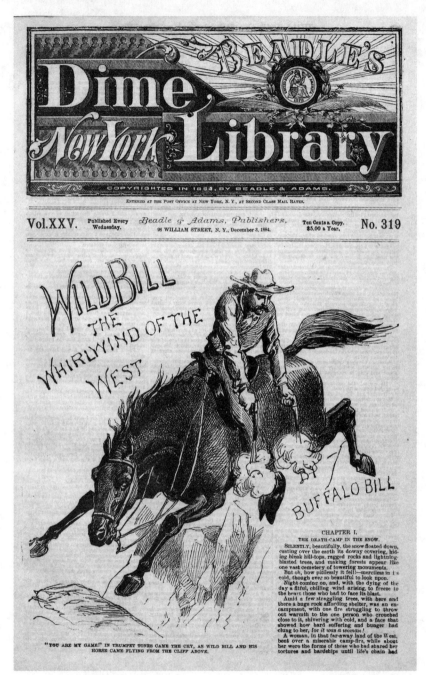

Vol. XXV.   Published Every Wednesday.   *Beadle & Adams, Publishers,*   98 WILLIAM STREET, N. Y., December 3, 1884.   Ten Cents a Copy. $5.00 a Year,   No. 319

CHAPTER I.

THE DEATH-CAMP IN THE SNOW.

SILENTLY, beautifully, the snow floated down, casting over the earth its downy covering, hiding bleak hill-tops, ragged rocks and lightning-blasted trees, and making forests appear like one vast cemetery of towering monuments.

But oh, how pitilessly it fell!—merciless in its cold, though ever so beautiful to look upon.

Night coming on, and, with the dying of the day a fitful, chilling wind arising, to freeze to the heart those who had to face its blast.

Amid a few straggling trees, with here and there a huge rock affording shelter, was an encampment, with one fire struggling to throw out warmth to the one person who crouched close to it, shivering with cold, and a face that showed how hard suffering and hunger had clung to her, for *it was a woman!*

A woman, in that far-away land of the West, bent over a miserable camp-fire, while about her were the forms of those who had shared her tortures and hardships until life's chain had

"YOU ARE MY GAME!" IN TRUMPET TONES CAME THE CRY, AS WILD BILL AND HIS HORSE CAME FLYING FROM THE CLIFF ABOVE.

Dime novels were among the creators of the gunslinger myth. At times the feats of these gallant gunslingers were only slightly less than miraculous. Here, "the Whirlwind of the West" leaps from a cliff on horseback, firing at the unseen nemeses of justice. Beadle's Dime Library, *December 3, 1884. Courtesy of Nickels and Dimes, Northern Illinois University Libraries.*

Hickok's phenomenal shooting ability was part of his myth. Not only was he a fast-draw pistoleer, but he also could spot an assailant in a looking glass and fire over his shoulder with accuracy. Unfortunately, he saw no reflection before Jack McCall shot him from behind. In *Wild Bill*, actor Jeff Bridges portrayed Hickok as a man struggling with the afflictions of fame. *Photofest.*

Radio and television's Wild Bill Hickok was portrayed by actor Guy Madison. He tried hard to please his young fans, and the show's sponsor, Sugar Pops, gave them a code of conduct certificate on each box of cereal they purchased. *Photofest.*

Actor-playwright Sam Shepard affirmed that Hickok had a good side in *Purgatory*. He kept his passport to Heaven by some righteous shooting when confronted by evil. "The Creator may be tough, but He ain't blind." *Photofest*.

Actor Keith Carradine defined the Hickok character for a new generation in *Deadwood*. For series creator David Milch, Hickok was effective because he had "no illusion about the process" of violence. But he had lived past his time. *Photofest*.

7. ❀ Scribes and Tourists: The Hickok Hunters in Deadwood

> We seemed to have strayed into a bizarre and unnatural place, a
> kind of madhouse.
>
> —Fraser Harrison, 1994

Deadwood attracted journalists from the first gold strikes, and like Tomb-stone, Arizona, Deadwood had a great name for the coming entertainment era. Early reports based on facts as elusive as gold dust soon gave way to the fantasies of tourists searching for a town they imagined. Deadwood remains vital to the Hickok myth, what philosopher Pierre Nora called a "lieu de mémoire," a place where recollection is concentrated and decoded. Other Hickok sites would include the Mendota Museum and Historical Society in Mendota, Illinois, in front of which a life-size bronze sculpture of Hickok was erected in 2008. Nine miles away in Troy Grove in 1929, the state of Illinois placed a stone marker with a plaque that says, in part, that Hickok "contributed largely in making the West a safe place for women and children." Some Troy Grove residents resent Mendota's claim jumping, pointing out that Hickok only visited the larger of the two towns once.[1]

These competing monuments are not likely to draw crowds. Sooner or later, anyone fascinated by Wild Bill will make a pilgrimage to the South Dakota city to find him. Hickok's story is remembered most often because of what happened last, in Deadwood. Visitors know the irresistible images, aphorisms, and anecdotes. Aces and eights. The dead man's hand. Always have your back to the wall when you play cards. Journalists light the way because they still recognize Deadwood as a great story. Given the nation's penchant for guns and violence, the cultural air continues to inflate Hickok's legacy. Each new Hickok novel, film, and television series brings new fans to Deadwood. These "Hickok hunters," scribes and tourists, keep Hickok alive in public memory.

The first and most celebrated writer spent a few days with Hickok and was among the first journalists to visit the scene of his shooting. Just twenty years old, Leander P. Richardson already had the biggest story of his life, and his own story became part of it. That story illustrated how the journalism of the time spread the news from west to east with unexpected consequences. Richardson was born in Cincinnati on February 28, 1856, the son of journalist Albert D. Richardson, who later reported the Civil War for the New York *Tribune*. By the age of sixteen, Leander was writing for the Chicago *Inter-Ocean*. In 1876 he traveled to the West to gather information for a book. He planned to see some of the places his father had visited when writing *Beyond the Mississippi*, a travel narrative published in 1867. Leander had interest from his father's publisher and an agreement to send stories to the Springfield, Massachusetts, *Republican*, which was underwriting some of his travels.

In Cheyenne, Richardson made contact with A. C. Snyder, the Associated Press agent for the territory. Richardson intended to discredit what he believed were fantastic newspaper stories circulating about prodigious riches in the Black Hills gold fields. Especially in Cheyenne, he claimed, the newspapers promoted the gold rush and ignored its attendant dangers in order to sell advertising. Local business interests were competing with other railroad towns to establish Cheyenne as the most favorable supply center for the Black Hills. Snyder warned Richardson about the possibility of Indian attacks and asked him to leave word for the Associated Press in the event he was killed. This preposterous request took the form of a note in a book that might be discovered were Richardson to be slain. Snyder may have been trying to protect Richardson by frightening him off the trip to the Black Hills. Just weeks earlier, Mark Kellogg, a brash Associated Press correspondent, had died with Custer at the Little Bighorn, becoming the wire service's first martyr. Undeterred, Richardson reached Fort Laramie and departed with seven men aboard a large freight wagon on July 22. The young reporter and his party were heading northeast through country contested by hostile tribes. He was also on his way toward his encounter with Hickok. On July 27, 1876, however, news of Richardson's death was reported on the front page of the New York *Times*, transmitted by Snyder.[2]

A YOUNG JOURNALIST KILLED

L. P. RICHARDSON, SON OF THE LATE A. D. RICHARDSON, KILLED BY INDIANS—THE BODY RIDDLED WITH RIFLE BALLS—HOW IT WAS IDENTIFIED.

CHEYENNE, JULY 26.—The following was received by mail to-day, with the enclosure mentioned:

FORT LARAMIE, July 24

A.C. Snyder, Agent Associated Press, Cheyenne:

This memorandum I found on a dead body—scalped, and having about twenty bullet holes in it—about one hundred miles north of Fort Laramie yesterday. I buried the body, and send this to you on account of a note made in the memorandum-book. If you know any friends of the deceased let them know and send them this book.

JOHN MARSH, of Deadwood

The book belongs to L.P. Richardson, correspondent of the *Springfield (Mass.) Republican*, who made a note therein which reads: "If anything important send to A.C. Snyder, Associated Press, Cheyenne."

The story was bogus, and Marsh was a party to the hoax. Marsh had arrived in Deadwood along with Richardson on July 30. When Richardson's wagon driver returned to Cheyenne on August 8, he told the Cheyenne *Daily Leader* he had last seen Hickok, Marsh, and Richardson boozing in Deadwood. The *Leader* started calling the young prankster "Puttyhead" after being taken in, along with the *Times*, by the claim that Richardson had been killed by Indians. Although Richardson's opportunistic stunt had given a national audience the blood and violence it expected from a Western adventure, Snyder had been duped into moving a false story magnifying the Indian threat between Wyoming and the Black Hills. On the other hand, some newspaper editors in the Wyoming Territory were writing sensational stories about just that sort of violence to pressure the federal authorities and the military to clear Indians out of the region.[3]

Snyder came of age at a time when news transmission was accelerating. Stories developed quickly, and they could be distributed nationally by wire. Obscure places like Deadwood and deadly doings like Hickok's murder could suddenly appear in newspapers hundreds of miles away without context or relevance. There was no assurance that haste would lead to accuracy. Snyder was born in 1844, the year telegraphic communications began in the United States. His experience with the U.S. Military Telegraph Corps led to employment with the Western Union Telegraph Company in Philadelphia. He moved to Cheyenne in the early 1870s. Western Union had gained monopoly control of the telegraph industry, in part because of its alliance with the Associated Press. Given exclusive access to telegraph lines, the AP could franchise its news product throughout the country. Snyder both managed Western Union's Cheyenne office for fourteen years and served as the AP agent. Such arrangements had led to a Senate investigation two years earlier. Newspapers feared losing wire access to news reports if they criticized Western Union or the AP, both linked politically to the Republican Party.[4]

Richardson's droll account of his journey, which appeared the next year in *Scribner's Monthly*, was flecked with ironic understatement certain to indulge Eastern readers wishing to experience Western adventures from the comfort of a drawing room easy chair. "The prospect of riding three hundred miles on a springless wagon was not inviting," he caviled, while complaining of sand-gnats that wriggled down the neck "in a most annoying fashion." Meals had more to do with bacon-grease and dust than food the scribe was used to eating. One "melancholy meal of raw ham and hard-tack" was washed down by creek water "as thick as molasses, and so white with alkali as to resemble cream. A pailful of this delectable beverage was set inside the roofless hut, and seven or eight prickly pears, pounded to a pulp, were put in to 'settle' it for our morning meal." Stormy nights were spent writhing in blankets sodden with pools of water accumulated during a chilling rain.[5]

"A Cowardly, Skulking Crew"

Richardson's first impression of Deadwood on a Sunday afternoon was not favorable. "Taken as a whole, I never in my life saw so many hardened and brutal men together, although of course there were a few better faces among them," Richardson wrote. "Every alternate house was a gambling saloon, and each of them was carrying on a brisk business." Charlie Utter introduced him to Hickok, "the greatest scout in the West." Hickok, unlike most scouts the twenty-year-old claimed to have met, was singularly courteous, circumspect, strong, and self-reliant, with a voice "low and musical," an intelligent countenance, and hair "blonde, and falling in long ringlets upon his broad shoulders." Asked to give evidence of his shooting prowess the next day, Hickok put two bullets through a tin can Richardson tossed fifteen feet into the air. The following morning, Richardson learned that Hickok had been shot dead by a "dastardly assassin." He rushed to the saloon with Utter, and later was present at Hickok's funeral and burial. "And so ended the life of 'Wild Bill,'—a man whose supreme physical courage had endeared him to nearly all with whom he came in contact, and made his name a terror to every Indian west of the Missouri."[6]

Richardson's epitaph for Wild Bill appeared in *Scribner's Monthly* a decade after George Ward Nichols introduced Hickok to a national audience. Each writer had imagined a fictional character who could never have existed outside the pages of a dime novel. Richardson's interest in theatrical writing served him well later when he became a New York drama critic, and he also wrote plays, books, and dime novels. He also was the European correspondent for the Boston *Herald*, edited the *Rocky Mountain News* in Denver, the New York *Enquirer*, the *Dramatic News*, the New York *Review* and a trade publication. He founded the New York *Morning Telegraph* and wrote for the New York *Times*.[7]

Richardson never tired of talking about his interview with Hickok, and at least once changed his story. Because Hickok was only thirty-nine when he died, people who claimed to have known Hickok were numerous well into the twentieth century. Their recollections conflicted with one another or proved to be fabrications. In 1894, Richardson alleged he had read in Charles Dana's New York *Sun* an article with the headline "How Wild Bill Died," copied from the Denver *Republican*. The author, a man identified only as Adler, said he had witnessed Hickok's death. Richardson disputed Adler's account and wrote a long letter to the New York *Sun* offering his own recollections of Wild Bill and Deadwood. The information in the letter was at odds with what Richardson had written for *Scribner's*. In the earlier story, Hickok is the "fashionable dandy" and Utter is barely mentioned. In the letter, Utter emerges as the dandy, described much as Hickok was described in the *Scribner's* article. In his final days, Wild Bill seems often to have been in a stupor, during which he endured "the fierce tongue lashings of his dudesque little partner." When awake, Hickok drank, gambled, told tall tales around the campfires, calmly observed gunfights, stabbings, fisticuffs, and a lynching, and, if other articles written by Richardson are to be believed, went to the theater.[8]

Neither the letter Richardson wrote to the New York *Sun* in 1894 nor the issue in which it was published have been found. Instead, a reprint of the *Sun* article appeared in the *Weekly Press*, a New Zealand newspaper, on February 17, 1894. Just why the article showed up in New Zealand is unexplained, but the paper did publish occasional articles about Hickok, and it was not uncommon for papers to lift stories from other newspapers. Portions of the article were published in the Georgetown, Colorado, *Courier* in 1937 and were also included in Agnes Wright Spring's *Colorado Charlie, Wild Bill's Pard*, published in 1968. The entire letter, titled "Last Days of a Plainsman," was published in *True West* in 1965, and portions appear in Joseph Rosa's *They Called Him Wild Bill*.[9]

In his reply, Richardson called Adler's article "a fairy tale" and said it was "late in the day to plaster the mud of a falsehood over the memory of this fallen giant of the frontier." Fantasy can be detected, he said, because good liars are usually "shy about going into details. It is in little places that a fraudulent armor is fatally defective." In contrast, Richardson's letter was full of details, but they were at odds with, or omitted from, what he had written previously. In his account, Hickok, too, was dishonest. "I love truth," wrote Richardson, "but I do not yearn to obtrude my preferences so far away from home. They were great stories that Wild Bill told, and as his other hearers knew nothing about them, and I did'nt [*sic*] contradict him, he had a very fair margin for the play of his imagination." The detail with which he padded most of the letter had less to do with refuting Adler than with affirming his veracity in describing the last days of Hickok's life. "I know all about them, because I was there."[10]

Richardson's opinion of the "hardened" and "brutal" men in Deadwood, as described in his 1876 article, had hardened as well. "It was probably by all odds the toughest outfit ever brought together in one community. . . . [A]ll the other choice spots of the West poured the most effulgent of their star criminal citizens into Deadwood Gulch, and of the 14,000 or so inhabitants in August, 1876, about 10,000 would have started out large beads of cold, apprehensive sweat upon the stone walls of any penitentiary in the world. They were a cowardly, skulking crew at that."

Overflowing with "elements of disorder," Deadwood at the time was "rapidly coming to the point where some sort of government was necessary. At such times on the frontier there is always a struggle and usually a hand-to-hand combat between the lawless and the orderly classes. Wild Bill had been Marshal in other and similar places, and people began to talk of him for Marshal of Deadwood." The story continued with the conspiracy of gambling interests paying Jack McCall to murder Hickok. Hickok had been warned of the coming assassination and had stood his ground rather than leave town, according to Richardson. Utter gave Richardson a strand of Hickok's hair "as glossy as spun glass and as soft as down . . . a touch of roughness where the life blood of a brave, great-hearted American man gushed out as the assassin's bullet burst through his brain."[11]

This kind of prose owes a good deal to the dime novel, not surprising because Richardson had drawn upon his Black Hills adventures and other travels to write *Captain Kate: The Heroine of Deadwood Gulch* two years after writing the New York *Sun* letter. A few years earlier he had written *The Road Agents: A Tale of Black Hills Life*. In significant ways, Richardson, first on the scene, established the tone for Hickok remembrance as the story erupted and the lava spread across the media landscape.[12]

An Unmerited Reputation

Black Hills boosterism found its champion in journalist and judge Horatio Nelson Maguire. He also arrived in Deadwood during the summer of 1876 and may have had some contact with Richardson. Maguire was born in Kentucky in 1837 and grew up in northwestern Ohio. By the age of about seventeen he was working as a typesetter with the Detroit *Free Press*, then became an itinerant journalist on newspapers in Chicago, St. Louis, Memphis, New Orleans, Denver, and San Francisco. In Oregon he worked as editor and publisher of the Portland *Daily Morning News*. He stayed until his wanderlust took him to the Idaho Territory, where he published the *Golden Age* in Lewiston. In 1865 he took a job with the *Montana Post* in Virginia City, then became co-owner and coeditor of the *Rocky Mountain Gazette* in Helena, and later founded the Helena *News-Letter* in the Montana Territory. In 1869 he founded the first newspaper to be published in Bozeman. He wrote for national publications, including *Harper's Weekly* and New York *Saturday Journal*, a Beadle and Adams publication. He edited the Pioche, Nevada, *Daily Record* before returning to Bozeman in 1873 to practice law and serve for two years as probate judge.[13]

Bored in Bozeman, Maguire headed for the Black Hills, where he joined a Deadwood law firm, but before long he was publishing and editing the *Black Hills Pick and Plow*, the *Black Hills Central News*, and the *Black Hills Journal*. He turned his initial impressions of Deadwood and the Black Hills into material for several books, alternating between publicity and moral outrage. Although "John" B. Hickok had been shot dead by Jack McCall, allegedly at the behest of those interests who didn't want Hickok in Deadwood, "personal altercations seldom occurred," he wrote. Deadwood seemed to have risen unblemished from the earth as the "Genius of Progress waved her wand and a city of several thousand was in existence." Maguire attributed stories that the Black Hills were plagued with violence to Hickok. "The great notoriety 'Wild Bill' had acquired by his adventurous career as a scout in the civil war, and in many desperate *rencontres* on the frontiers . . . caused his murder to be noticed and commented upon by all the newspapers of the country, resulting in giving the Black Hills an unmerited reputation for lawlessness."[14]

In other words, it was Wild Bill's murder that energized the entire American press to tarnish the reputation of an otherwise sublime gold rush mining camp swarming with gamblers, gunfighters, and harlots. The American press, however, had more compelling news to report in 1876—including Custer and the Little Bighorn, a presidential election, and the Centennial International Exposition. Maguire's principal discovery in Deadwood was Calamity Jane and her "remarkable career of ruin, disgrace and recklessness." He first saw her outside of Deadwood riding a "bucking cayuse," which she spurred "on up the gulch, over ditches and through reservoirs and mudholes, at each leap of the fractious animal giving as good an imitation of a Sioux war-whoop as a feminite [*sic*] voice is capable of." Biographer James D. McLaird found that dime novelist Edward Wheeler drew upon Maguire's brief account of the buckskin-clad hellion to turn her into a raven-haired heroine and a national celebrity.[15]

Maguire blamed Indian troubles in the West on government corruption abetted by party newspapers and a mercenary press. Nevertheless, he extolled the virtues of Deadwood, the Black Hills, and the West, predicting a tide of emigration from the East. The civilizing aspects of this tide, he claimed, "will halo the whole with moral beauty and intellectual splendor." The economy was strong, and by the spring of 1877, he noted, Deadwood property was increasing in value, and the business district was marked by "fire-proof business houses, excellent hotels, and many elegant private residences." His optimism was premature, however. Deadwood was gutted by fire in 1879.[16]

An unnamed reporter for the Chicago *Times* arrived in May 1877 and found mud. Problems with streets "back in the states" bore no comparison to Deadwood's morass, the reporter explained. "[Y]ou would be speechless could you stand upon any of Deadwood's boulevards and see the spectacle presented at this time. Mud? The main street is bottomless. . . ." The daily stagecoach from Sidney, Nebraska, was pulled by "six horses so completely covered with mud that their color could not be determined." Passengers were discharged and found themselves "swimming along on foot. Pedestrianism is attended with great danger, for the few miserable structures called sidewalks are inches deep in slippery mud, and every step throws up a shower as from some huge atomizer."[17]

None of this deterred "hundreds of pilgrims en route on foot and in private vehicles." No rooms could be found in any hotel or boardinghouse, and building construction was continuous. "Every thing here is purely marvelous," wrote the reporter, "and so different from the accustomed sights of more ancient parts that the new arrival stands and gazes in utter astonishment." Gambling drew crowds, undeterred by the potential for the kind of violence that befell Hickok the previous year. "They bet, win and lose with the utmost nonchalance, and

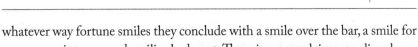

whatever way fortune smiles they conclude with a smile over the bar, a smile for every acquaintance, and smilingly depart. There is no rowdyism, no disorder—peace and happiness prevails." This sort of delusion probably encouraged even more would-be Wild Bills to seek their fortune in the goldfields, only to lose their vests and return-ticket fare in the blissful saloons.[18]

Fred Ellsworth Sutton, born in 1860, turned up in Deadwood in 1926 to write a story about the town's fiftieth-anniversary festivities for the Dallas *Morning News*. Sutton reported that "much has been done to make that wonderful little city appear as it did fifty years ago." The "entire male population" of Deadwood had formed a Whiskers Club and pledged to remain unshorn for four months. Deadwood was "a very thriving little city, but nevertheless, its past still lives vividly and never again will this country see a town like it." Sutton said things were not so sanguine when he visited Deadwood in August 1876, and "found it to be one of the world's wildest mining camps." He claimed to have known the hard-drinking Calamity, "an uncommonly good looking woman." He recounted the improbable heroics cited in her autobiography and elsewhere. Just as Sutton arrived, Hickok was shot, and the West lost its greatest gunfighter, according to the article. At the time of Sutton's return, Deadwood had been transformed into a "beautiful and prosperous city, filled with happy people, who in retrospect look back to those terrible days when Deadwood was the capital of the Black Hills."[19]

Sutton's accuracy would be questioned after he and journalist A. B. Mac-Donald collaborated to write *Hands Up! Stories of the Six-Gun Fighters of the Old Wild West*, published in 1927. MacDonald, who had been a circus press agent and a Kansas City *Star* reporter, transcribed Sutton's tall tales, which placed him all over the West in the presence of legendary outlaws at critical moments. He claimed to have been friends with Hickok even though he was only sixteen at the time of Hickok's death. MacDonald won a Pulitzer Prize for reporting in 1931 and should have known better than to take Sutton's stories at face value.[20]

A Modern Sodom

In 1938, a reporter for the Boston *Evening Transcript* found a town eager to preserve its Wild West image, one that its former "sheriff" would find congenial. "Many easterners revel in Deadwood. Some aver that Broadway could learn a lot from this city. Sheriff Hickok has long since passed to his reward, but the prevailing western atmosphere attests to the fact that Deadwood is a misnomer for that 'wide open' spot. The east has no counterpart for it. There is still a west and this is its final stand."

The article was cited by the reform-minded Edward L. Senn, publisher of the Deadwood *Daily Telegram* and the state temperance newspaper, *Senn's Forum*, published in Sioux Falls, South Dakota. The *Transcript* writer, Senn said, was being too circumspect. Deadwood was indeed wide open, a "modern Sodom," worse than New York's bawdy Broadway, and its "notorious wicked-ness." Laws were ignored, he said, and the city's saloons "tolerate drunkenness, and on special occasions are bedlams of howling, drunken mobs, nearly half of them women." The chamber of commerce cared naught for its reputation in the East, and brazenly circulated the *Transcript* story in its publicity, according to Senn.[21]

Michael Watkins, a writer for the *Times of London*, visited Deadwood during a tour of the American West in 1982. He found Hickok and Calamity Jane "persons of such lasting notoriety that one's travels through the American Old West become inextricably involved with a sense of history." Watkins reprised for British readers the story of the gold rush, the founding of Deadwood, and Wild Bill's death.

> By 1876 Deadwood was a suburb of Sodom and Gomorrah, with imperative need for law enforcement. With 32 known notches on his gunbelt, Wild Bill Hickok became marshal, the question of his services being pensionable remaining in hypothesis due to a .45 caliber bullet becoming lodged in his skull soon after he was sworn in. . . . Calamity Jane, believed to "carry a torch" for him, cradled Wild Bill's head in her arms. The *Black Hills Pioneer* edition June 8, 1876, takes up the story: "The dirty rat," she screamed. "I'll get him." Which, of course, she did.[22]

Practically none of this is true. Hickok was shot on August 2, so the paper hardly could have had the story before it happened. The *Black Hills Pioneer* was founded on June 8, 1876. The story Watkins saw was first published on August 5, 1876. He probably saw a reprint for tourists. Hickok was not the marshal. Calamity Jane did not "get" McCall. As for the thirty-two deaths attributed to Hickok, Joseph Rosa cited "seven known victims and several probables." The gun notches were more nonsense. Watkins noted Deadwood's "nostalgically seedy aspect," a town in which time stopped about 1880. Visiting the graves of Wild Bill and Calamity Jane in Mount Moriah Cemetery, and observing the town below, Watkins concluded that Deadwood "still draws together the threads of the old West. Tourism has come, but has not defiled the spirit of that age."[23]

Not everyone who came to Deadwood found that it evoked the mystique of Hickok and the Old West. Travel writer Bill Bryson, an expatriate American living in England, visited Deadwood for a few hours in spring 1988. He included impressions of Deadwood in *The Lost Continent: Travels in Small-Town America*, the report of a bemused fourteen-thousand-mile road trip to rediscover the country of his youth. The Deadwood he saw on a Sunday morning "lived up to its first syllable. . . . Today the town makes a living by taking large sums of money off tourists and giving them in return some crappy little trinket to take home and put on their mantelpiece." Most stores were "souvenir emporia, and several were even open," although coffee shops and restaurants were closed. He was the only customer in the Gold Nugget Trading Post, "a large room where nothing but souvenirs were sold—moccasins, beaded Indian bags, arrowheads, nuggets of fool's gold, Indian dolls." He saw the "same stuff at identical prices in "The World Famous Prospectors Gift Shop." Finding no sign of what was once the "liveliest and most famous town in the West," he headed for Mount Rushmore and the Badlands. Bryson, maybe homesick for England, did not think much of the rest of South Dakota either, a "flat and empty" state he called "the world's first drive-through sensory deprivation chamber," like driving over "an infinite sheet of sandpaper." He had been seeking a mythic America and found only a lost continent, good for laughs. Bryson's take on South Dakota—that it was empty and dry—had it wrong. He thought that landscape existed in comparison to the Appalachians or the Yellowstone. Its allure was the openness, the absence for the most part of the garish tourist traps he found in Deadwood, the lack of refrigerator magnets and coffee cup souvenirs. Its highway markets tended toward gasoline and coffee. The desert went on forever and was ideal ground for cacti that prick the foreigner.[24]

Poet Kathleen Norris moved from New York City to her family home in Lemmon, South Dakota, in the early 1980s, and wrote about living in a silent, stark, and windy landscape that functioned as an American province dependent on external interests, tourism, and gambling. In her 2001 contemplative reflections, *Dakota: A Spiritual Geography*, she dated the region's "mystique" to 1876 and the legacy of Custer, Hickok and Deadwood. "Nearly every storefront along the main street in Deadwood now houses a casino. . . ." The region's appeal was "apparently inexhaustible in Europe, judging from the number of starstruck Europeans" who passed through Lemmon every summer on their way to the Black Hills and beyond.[25]

A Mania for Memory

As if to prove her point, the French philosopher-journalist Bernard-Henri Lévy passed restlessly through South Dakota while writing his 2006 book *American Vertigo: Traveling America in the Footsteps of Tocqueville.* Lévy pondered "the derangement of the mechanisms of memorialization," which he found in such South Dakota attractions as the Corn Palace in Mitchell, as well as in Black Hills spectacles such as the World's Largest Petrified Wood Park and Museum in Lemmon, the Mammoth Site Museum in Hot Springs, and pliosaurus relics collected in Deadwood. He thought such roadside attractions along with halls of fame and faux historical tourist sites cultivated a kind of pathological memory, what philosopher Frederick Nietzsche called "antiquarian history"—a mania for collecting and remembering just about anything, however worthless, and thereby trivializing memory and history. Lévy thought it best to consign some memory to oblivion rather than becoming obsessed with a largely meaningless past and losing the America of Enlightenment ideals. He did not mention a visit to the No. 10 Saloon or the Gold Nugget Trading Post, but he surely tossed Wild Bill into the ash heap of history as well.[26]

One of those starstruck visitors, journalist Fraser Harrison, grew up in Liverpool, England, watching television and movie Westerns.

> Americans do not realize the degree to which the Wild West penetrated British culture when I was growing up in the 1940s and 1950s. To my generation of children, who played cowboys and Indians in our suburban back gardens, imitating American movies and television shows, the Wild West was more real to us and imaginatively closer to hand than any equivalent from our own history. As far as I was concerned, no other scenario possessed the same charismatic glamor as the American West of the nineteenth century, especially when represented by the frontier town with its bank, general stores, saloon and dance hall, its sheriff's office and the dusty street where the hero was destined to face the last shootout with the last surviving guy in a black hat.[27]

Harrison shared his love of Westerns with his father, who fought in World War II but rarely spoke of it. Nor was it much discussed in school. "I taught myself more about Geronimo than I learned at school about Hitler's generals, and I could not have told you the year of D-Day, though it was the year of my birth." This historical silence existed because his parents' generation wanted to move on. Watching Westerns with his father helped them come to terms with the past. "The bloodshed and sudden death that usually went unmentioned could be brought into our sitting room, and contemplated with relative tranquility. We were able to witness battles that were safely removed to a distant time and place, fought between mythological enemies in a war that had become a storybook convention. . . ." Such exterior memory provided by media technology alters cognition of actual events. Like millions of others, Harrison was remembering an imagined West that never existed, a shared memory with his father of another war that was very real.

After graduating from Cambridge, Harrison wrote for the *Times of London* and *The Independent*. A 1992 family visit to South Dakota led to his becoming obsessed with Deadwood's history, which inspired his BBC Radio 3 documentary *Black Hills, Dakota*, broadcast in 1994. Harrison was shocked to find that Deadwood had become "a town-sized casino, a cowboy Vegas," as the result of legalized gambling introduced in 1989. "We seemed to have strayed into a bizarre and unnatural place, a kind of madhouse. . . . It slowly dawned on us that every business on the street was a gambling hall . . . redesigned to look like gold-rush saloons. . . ." The town's confused identity revealed itself to Harrison when he observed the new gold rush tourists, mainly retired couples "who wandered like zombies from casino to casino bearing their shiny quarters in little plastic buckets. . . . Gone were the grizzled prospectors of '76, the prostitutes, and gun-slinging cardsharps—the cast of HBO's *Deadwood*—and in their place were these innocuous oldsters. . . . There was a laughable and touching discrepancy between Deadwood's actual customers and the blood-curdling atmosphere conjured up. . . ."[28]

Deadwood was billed as a family attraction, a virtuous simulacrum of a historic place, presided over by its "patron saint . . . who came to town in July 1876 and did the place the inestimable kindness of getting himself shot in the back of the head while playing poker." Hickok revealed the contradictions in Deadwood's self-image.

> Standing by the road at the entrance to the city is a large construction made of pink and cream sandstone blocks, an elaborate affair with recessed pillars and decorative brickwork, enclosing an area resembling the side of a small truck. This serves as the frame for a bas-relief bust, cleverly sculpted in pink brick, of a man with flowing locks, droopy moustache, bow tie, and ten gallon hat. "Welcome to Deadwood,"

the sign reads, and below, as if anybody could doubt the identity of its subject, are the words, "Resting Place of Wild Bill Hickok."

Duped into believing they were embarking on an educational experience, visitors rolled past the Hickok statue into a sanitized, postmodern faux-brothel inspired by a television series raw with foul language, oozing muck, violence, and debauchery. A glossy brochure showed a picture of Hickok's "death chair" and invited visitors to sit on it. In other words, "tourists are encouraged to believe that they are doing something far more adventurous than simply gambling in a kind of Vegas in a cowboy costume; they are visiting history."[29]

Harrison concluded that Hickok's importance to Deadwood could be found in his innocence. Hickok came to Deadwood to make money and then return to his wife. He even had written her a letter promising domestic bliss. Although his reputation got him murdered, Deadwood honored Hickok as a victim, not a killer. "McCall, the motiveless drunk, is the psychopath, while Hickok, 'slayer of a hundred men,' is canonized as the saint of Deadwood." That left Hickok "at once the incarnation of the Wild West and its sacrificial victim." He died "to save Deadwood's sins," and his death is reenacted four times a day each summer. Hickok lived on in "the never-never land of 'legend,' where there is no right or wrong, only tall tales and colorful characters." Each would-be gambler who arrived in Deadwood with a pot of quarters was free to draw upon Hickok's legend. It was a win-win situation for the tourists—"not losers, they're wild, like Bill."[30]

Returning to Deadwood in 2011, Harrison found that the town had "toned down its old emphasis on murder, hanging, and prostitution; at any rate there were fewer nooses and brothel tableaux to be seen." Its new probity had done nothing to discourage tourism. Two million visitors were drawn to Deadwood each year. Even Mount Moriah Cemetery presented a quiet dignity to as many as one hundred thousand annual visitors. The graves of Wild Bill and Calamity Jane were "immured behind a forbidding cast-iron and mesh fence, which resembled a jail cell and placed an impassable division between his plot and hers." He had at last been granted a reprieve from Calamity Jane.[31]

Harrison again returned to South Dakota, having received a fellowship to write in Yankton, on the Missouri River, for seven weeks in 2013. On Third Street he found the courthouse where McCall had been convicted. Harrison had written earlier that McCall may have committed the "first modern homicide on what you might call the Andy Warhol principle: McCall, an unknown murderer, murdered a famous murderer because he wanted to be famous himself, as a murderer." In 1968, American artist Warhol famously remarked, "In the future everybody will be world famous for fifteen minutes."[32]

Yankton's local history "was an echo of the city's own creation myths, and, as with all myths, it invoked paradoxes." While residents of Wild West towns affirmed their heroic origins, "these same historically minded citizens would have no patience with such behavior in their own time. I am certain that a brothel catering to drunken riverboat sailors would not be tolerated on Levee Street today, not even a mock one to match the territorial capitol replica." A woman told Harrison that a residue of "bad blood" from up the river, presumably a legacy of the steamboat era, continued to contaminate the city. History, in other words, was fine as long as it could be viewed from a safe distance in time or space.[33]

The first thing that Denver *Post* correspondent Emilie Rusch did when she came to Deadwood in the spring of 2015 was hike up Mount Moriah to find Seth Bullock's grave. She felt she knew Deadwood's first sheriff because she'd spent the winter watching the HBO series for the first time. Local officials told her people had been coming on similar pilgrimages since 2004. The city, rebuilt after the great fire of 1879, was a living simulacrum of the original. A century later, the last brothel closed, but she could find a door to another brothel stored in the Adams Museum, bursting with artifacts. Deadwood "oozes history" because the visitor walked in the footsteps of the past. Here walked Bullock. There walked Al Swearengen. There died Hickok. Deadwood was a ghost town, which is to say that Bullock's ghost prowled the hotel he built. "His presence was everywhere, in the odd pitch of a second-floor corridor, the grand skylights, the mustachioed bust in the lobby." She found Hickok's grave piled with tributes: playing cards, bottles of whiskey, cigarettes, coins, even pinecones and rocks. Placing a single penny on Hickok's grave made her feel like she was honoring a friend, "my serial gambling, murdered TV friend." Deadwood was a virtual community existing simultaneously in the past and the present. Like so many visitors before her, Rusch had indulged in what travel journalist Robert Sullivan called "an American style of contemplating history . . . to stand where before stood someone else."[34]

Another was Chandra Lahiri, a travel writer for the Omani newspaper the Muscat *Daily*. Lahiri reported from Deadwood on June 20, 2018, toward the end of a one-month journey across the Great Plains. He had arrived anxiously, feeling he was the "only non-white in the whole of South Dakota," but was greeted with "benevolent indifference" and soon was enjoying himself. He found Deadwood a "hugely atmospheric" town, built on "pure, unadulterated, unabashed greed and venality." Although worried about the town's reputation for debauchery, he felt prepared after watching *Deadwood*. He visited the major tourist spots, such as the No. 10 Saloon, noted the aces and eights story, and found nothing quite as authentic as a hotel room once occupied by actor John Wayne. A closer look at the town, "a baby Las Vegas, but with a history," revealed it to be prospering from gambling and tourism, although no longer the sin city he anticipated. A paid ticket gained him admission to a "trial" of McCall during which he was called to the stage to testify as a "witness" to Hickok's assassination. A jury composed mostly of six-year-olds ("disreputable minor miners") acquitted McCall. Lahiri walked back to his hotel room imagining the ghosts of 1876 and prepared to transmit his story from the imaginary Wild West to the Middle East.[35]

Into the Future

Visitors to Deadwood have continued to find the city appealing two decades into the twenty-first century. The city's $7 million annual budget for historic preservation is an investment intended to keep Deadwood looking like the virtual Wild West town the tourists have imagined. Kevin Kuchenbecker, the city's historic preservation manager and spokesman, sees historical ambiance as Deadwood's real gold mine. "It's been legendary from the beginning," he told a reporter in 2019. "Deadwood was the last of the American West in so many ways. Then with legendary figures Wild Bill Hickok and Calamity Jane, Deadwood promoted its history early on. . . . [W]e've been promoting Deadwood's history for well over a century and keeping those myths, legends and realities alive. It's the romanticism of the American West, which is still alive here in Deadwood. People come here to witness that."

Asked to predict what might be ahead for nurturing the Hickok myth in Deadwood, Kuchenbecker said the next thirty years would see improvement in the brick-and-mortar "building stock," such as museums, hotels, and saloons, and the stories they tell. "[S]ome of these stories will be more technologically advanced in the interpretation and presentation of our past. I mean, can't you see a hologram of Wild Bill walking down Main Street?" Those who prefer not to await the hologram can make a virtual trek to Deadwood by entering *Deadwood 1876*, a historical role-play "sim," or simulation, through *Second Life*, an online virtual world. Visitors, called avatars, can costume themselves in a long prairie dress and bonnet, a gambler's ruffled shirt and vest, or a prospector's ensemble complete with red suspenders, boots, pick, and mining pan.

Suitably attired, the avatar can enter a virtual library portal, key questions in a chat box, and "ask the librarian what sort of outfit a prostitute would have worn, or where to find information on panning for gold," according to author and journalist Marilyn Johnson, who wrote a lively book about digital-age librarians. Johnson pointed out that Deadwood has had an actual library for more than a century where the resident librarian offers an information "goldmine, the history of a town that relies on history for its identity." Either way, said Johnson, the librarian's job is "to create order out of the confusion of the past, even as she enables us to blast into the future."[36]

The twenty-first-century saloon of the Wild West is a raucous information brothel that the historian has no choice but to frequent if a bet is to be placed on the historical cards she or he has been dealt. The relevance to Wild Bill is that historians of such dodgy characters and the journalists who write about them are faced with the dilemma that Johnson sees for librarians in the Information Age. "Who," she asked, "can we trust?" The answer: no one. Visitors need to get a seat with their back to the wall, keep a chary eye on the room in front of them—which is full of characters besotted with a frothy brew of tall tales, dazzling images, glib impressions, and, yes, holograms—cut the cards, ante up, hedge their bets with a loaded six-shooter, and leave town in a hurry with their winnings. They can either blast into the information future or, like Hickok, be blasted back into the confusion of the past.[37]

8. ✻ Conclusions: The Last Remaining Home

> Lawlessness, like wilderness, is attractive, and we conceive the last remaining home of both to be the West.
>
> —Wallace Stegner, 1995

The Civil War

The memory of the Civil War is at the heart of Wild Bill Hickok's story. An estimated three million veterans survived the Civil War and remembered it for the rest of their lives, some living well into the twentieth century. Millions of civilians were touched by the war, which shaped the context for Western expansion. In 1870, some thirty-five thousand soldiers remained in uniform, most stationed on the frontiers. Eager to cultivate favorable publicity to support its postwar mission, the army celebrated "earlier conventions of individual heroism, by figuring the heroic scout as an intrepid individual rather than part of a sophisticated war machine . . . ," according to cultural historian Joy S. Kasson. Sheridan, the commander of the Military District of the Missouri after 1869, thought Wild West shows and similar spectacles "made the army look good at a time when its social and political purpose was highly contested." That support extended to the dime novels and stage productions featuring former scouts Hickok and Bill Cody, as well as to the journalism that fueled them. George Ward Nichols was still an active-duty officer when he wrote the article that made Hickok famous, as was Custer when he wrote favorably about Hickok in a *Galaxy* magazine article and in his memoirs. Intentionally or not, Nichols and Custer used Hickok to shape the memory of the Civil War era.[1]

The war lingered in the West where many former Southern soldiers were reluctant to stand down. The nation wanted the war to have meant something monumental, so Hickok, the noble lawman figure, was among those plucked out of the war years to bring order and justice to upcoming towns and live out the romance of reunion. Hickok was identified with the Yankee marshals keeping the rowdy resister Texans in line in the cattle towns. Dime novels, *Buffalo Bill's Wild West,* and other entertainments provided diversion and escapism after the Civil War, but they could also be a reminder that the war didn't immediately bring order to the West; rather, it just opened it up to more conflict, stoking the war memory's embers into regular conflagrations.[2]

Hickok, too, was a reminder that borders and frontiers were dangerous places in an ongoing conflict. He left Illinois to make his way in Bleeding Kansas and stayed in the borderlands, disputed places such as Texas Street in Abilene. Cross Texas Street in one direction and you were in a peaceful part of town with churches and schools, but go the other way and you were in a war zone of saloons and brothels. Guns were banned, but hot blood and cheap whiskey could reignite the malice of the Civil War at any time. Ironically, the cattle towns may have been slowly uniting the warring sections in "mutually profitable commerce, an important step toward healing the ruptures caused by the Civil War," according to journalist and historian Christopher Knowlton. But before concord had been achieved, Hickok turned up in Deadwood, a lawless red zone not even legally part of the United States.[3]

Hickok could not easily be placed on a plinth to memorialize the Civil War veteran except on his home turf because his record was shadowy—he was said to have been a spy, sharpshooter, scout, teamster, outfitter, and courier. This part of the war was hard to document, unsuitable fodder for the memory industry unless invented and exaggerated. By the twenty-first century, the whole Civil War monument project had become problematic. Statues were toppled and names scrubbed from public buildings. The Confederacy was in the crosshairs, but so were the famous gunmen of the Wild West, even those on the war's winning side. Was Hickok just another indiscriminate Indian killer and lawman, quick with a truncheon and a gun? Whatever his actual Civil War record, his deeds attracted attention, first in the press and later in dime novels and popular culture.

Shifting the national focus westward was a safety valve that no doubt relieved some of the inevitable tensions east of the Mississippi. If anything, Northern victory exacerbated divisions and regional identity, as attested to in the shortcomings of Reconstruction, the rise of Jim Crow laws, the emergence of the Ku Klux Klan, and the affirmation of the Lost Cause mythology. In other words, there was no "national" idea in the air after the war. A national, unifying theme could be seen in the geographic expansion of the nation, the virtue of which all regions might agree. The idea emerges in the era of mass media and mass audiences after the war. "Americans did not embark on a positive 'mission' to change the world after the Civil War. There was no grand strategy for global reform, nor any deliberate policy to make any specific country in the liberal mold," according to historian Robert Kagan. That came later, after a period of recovery and reengagement. The immediate focus was on the West, the inland empire, along with opportunities for continental enlargement.[4]

Taming the Wild West provided common cause, personified in the invented characters of Hickok, Cody, and all the others who followed. Expansion and conquest have been fairly constant themes in the American story. But under a republican government, such an idea needs some level of public endorsement. To engage the unwashed mob in seizing upon this glittering promise, there must be some vehicle to convey the righteousness, whether moral or economic, of such an endeavor. Tracts on political philosophy could not do such a thing. Dime novels, pulp fiction, sensational journalism, and—later—films, television programs, shows, spectacles, and attractions could. Within a short time after the end of the war, conquest of the Wild West was not a question of "should" but of "how" and "when" and "who," the bailiwick of journalism. The Wild West that so engaged the public imagination in the postwar years, and which continues to do so, did not percolate up through the popular imagination and into political discourse and action via some imagined intellectual dynamic on the part of the semiliterate public. It began as entertainment, and it marinated the minds of a postwar generation in the glory of gunfights and subjugating Indians. Earlier, for Hickok, it had been bear fights and later—in pulp fiction and on screen—battles with a white buffalo.

Hickok's myth alone did not serve to work out anxieties about a loss of individualism after the war. Hickok had been a loner before and during the war, serving mostly as a scout. Even when he was in or near battle, according to legends, he was a sniper, shape-shifter, or spy off on secret assignments, never a representative soldier. After the war he was an itinerant lawman and gambler, hardly a reassuring character for dime-novel readers, although an entertaining one. He was always an individual, never part of the collective. He was an opportunist, a dreamer, and a gambler. As such, he fit the Western paradigm. He always measured the odds, cut the cards, and took a chance, brave and self-contained. He was a perfect trope for the Western story, always in contrast to the "folks back home" who stayed safe on the farm and read about their wayward son and sibling in the press. The West, as portrayed in the popular media, held the promise that free spirits like Hickok would thrive on the frontier. American audiences in the fully industrialized, militarized, outward-looking mid-twentieth century responded more viscerally to the laconic, enigmatic man on horseback, the cowboy who sleeps on the range and keeps his own counsel. At about the same time, the public renewed its interest in the character of the Civil War raider, like John Singleton Mosby, the Gray Ghost of the Confederacy, who had his own television program in 1957. Also, prominent on television amid the victory culture of the Eisenhower era were the rogue Civil War veterans like Lucas McCain, Bret and Bart Maverick, Johnny Yuma, Paladin, Yancy Derringer, and Wild Bill himself—individualists all. These and similar programs were more Westerns than Civil War sagas, as if war memory had been dragged into a Wild West context. The gravitational pull of the West was still strong. If individuals were still around, that is where they would be found.

The West

When frontier replaced wilderness, it meant people had arrived. Their first impulse was to subjugate and control what surrounded them, whether with plow, gun, or miner's pan. When people intruded upon and violated the untrammeled expanse, they needed to replace the lost savagery of the wilderness with something. In the Wild West, it was human savagery, as in Deadwood, which celebrated and commercialized a hard-drinking, fast-draw gambler and sometime lawman getting his brains blown out over a card table. In Eastern cities Hickok helped fulfill the savage fantasies of the overcivilized cultures. The violence he symbolized was a cultural blood-splatter pattern celebrated in everything from pulp fiction to literary masterworks, from B-grade Western cinema to award-winning films that made carnage an art. Just as Buffalo Bill drew on the mystique of the frontier and the Great Plains, Wild Bill was attached to a cultural fascination with wildness and wild men. The region's untamed energy was channeled—violently and dramatically—into a vital social order.[5]

Just as the frontier could not vanish from the national imagination, neither could the values it nurtured, especially individualism and egalitarianism. Postbellum America was a good time for popularizers of the wild—people such as John Muir, Aldo Leopold, and, especially, Theodore Roosevelt, who took his ideas about Western lands, character, and virility all the way to the bully pulpit. Cody elevated the frontier and the West in the national imagination to a lost paradise, a sacramental space. *Buffalo Bill's Wild West* in particular became "a passion play for the American frontier" according to Kasson.[6]

Violence as entertainment was nothing new, going back to the Greek tragedies and Shakespeare. But American violence was unlike anything out of a
European tradition, where there were no aboriginals to slay or crack-shots on
horseback to do so. Thus, as news, shootouts on horseback or on Main Street
fed the idea of American exceptionalism, even in killing. When Hickok was
touring in one of Buffalo Bill's theatrical shows in 1874, the Springfield, Massachusetts *Republican* credited him with being nothing short of "a terror to
evil-doers. Reckless characters whom no other man dared to tackle . . . and
in no case has he failed to make the desired arrest." Such observations about
Hickok were widespread, especially in the Kansas press of those years. An editor
at the Hays City *Sentinel* in 1877, the year after Hickok died, did get around to
noting that many of the stories of Hickok's heroics were outright lies—such as
the one that credited him with killing twelve men when he lived in Hays City.[7]

Cody defined the frontier as entertainment. Frederick Jackson Turner
deemed it the breeding ground of the American character and democracy.
Both were, in their own way, popularizers. The frontier was secure in place
and form in the American imagination, and Hickok was a colorful standout
in that mythic expanse. Turner, Roosevelt, and Muir may have identified and
defined the importance of the frontier, but the press and the media conveyed
the frontier idea and its images and heroes to the public. Without such a
conduit to the broader culture, no amount of pontification about the frontier
would have mattered in shaping the society in which the ideal of the wild has
thrived. It was not a coincidence that the West arose along with a mass, visual
culture. The powerful story merged with the powerful new kinds of media.[8]

The frontier ideal persisted in the national concept of democracy. The
disappearance of the frontier—and its representatives—inevitably would af-
fect that concept. So the frontier needed to be preserved, which was done in
several ways. One was the national park system, which set aside vast tracts of
wilderness, such as Yellowstone. There were obvious limitations because the
amount of land to save was finite. If it was "preserved," was it really wilderness?
The second way to preserve the frontier was with words and images.

The contemporary culture clung to the idea of the free-spirited citizen
venturing into the wild by reserving campsites at a national park, or hiking
along a maintained trail. With the construction of a transnational rail system
in the nineteenth century and interstate highways in the twentieth century,
more people could experience the frontier than ever and see this heart of the
American character. A more effective way to preserve wildness, in the interest
of preserving democracy, was to preserve it in the imagination, without the

bears, bugs, picnic baskets, and interstate highway traffic snarls. This eliminated any physical boundary and meant that frontier ideals about personal
heroism and civilization could be passed from one generation to another,
and not just within the United States. As Kasson pointed out, the "belief in
the triumph of European civilization in the struggle with savagery, which
derived from an amalgam of popular science and imperialist ideology, were
as attractive overseas as at home." This view gained even more currency after
the 1893 World's Columbian Exposition in Chicago.[9]

The vehicle to do that, then and now, was the press, the media. It worked,
and it continued in the twentieth century through political metaphors such
as the "space race" and "new frontiers." In the last few decades of the nineteenth century, when the frontier was in retreat, the press was booming, and
its reach continued to expand. The timing was good. In Turner's writing, the
wilderness engendered democracy and fostered the virtues of individualism
and independence—both at the core of democracy, and apparently critical
elements of the frontiersman.

The frontier itself became an alternative to the urbanization and industrialization that was occurring in postbellum America. Eastern cities—crowded
with immigrants, slum-ridden, pestilential, and dirty—meant factories, pollu-
tion, corruption, and discord. Although the frontier in reality was anything but
Eden, it was re-created in Eastern media in order to introduce an alternative to
such a flawed civilization. That meant that the virtuous agrarian republic, the
Jeffersonian ideal, had to be out there somewhere. The West with its wide-open
spaces represented the Other that could bring national salvation, an alternative
to the East. A good deal of hypocrisy was bound up in the false dichotomy,
but that's beside the point because it was a comprehensible Other with two
distinct dimensions. In Hickok's day, the Other in the West was the Native
American population. It was easy to find treachery in the Indians, who were
depicted in the press as uncivilized and barbaric in their conduct of war and
use of torture. When there was insufficient treachery, it was invented. After
the Civil War, the unrepentant South, the Other, had to be "reconstructed,"
monitored by occupation garrisons. The white South tried to control its Other,
the liberated slave. Elsewhere, the Other was the immigrant. It also took the
form of various threatening ideologies and philosophies that emerged over
time, including socialism, anarchism, communism, fascism, corporatism, and
unbridled capitalism. Campaigning for president in 1932, Franklin Roosevelt
told a San Francisco audience that the West could not save the country from
the ravages of the Depression. Summoning Turner even at that late date,

Roosevelt warned that there was "no safety valve in the form of a Western prairie to which those thrown out of work by the Eastern economic machines can go for a new start."[10]

There was, of course, an inevitable backlash to the Turner thesis, especially in the pages of the *New Republic,* a progressive journal coedited by Walter Weyl, whose influential *The New Democracy* was published in 1912. The idea of the West had "intoxicated the American," Weyl wrote. "It gave him an enlarged view of self. . . . It made the American mind a little sovereignty of its own, acknowledging no allegiances and but few obligations. It created an individualism, self-confident, short-sighted, lawless, doomed in the end to defeat itself, as the boundless opportunism which gave it birth became at last circumscribed." This exaggerated, self-absorbed individualism, in other words, worked against national and international thinking. The future would bring Wilsonian idealism and New Deal reforms. A country facing limits would have to confront modern life with social solutions and not an exhausted fantasy. The national intoxication induced by the West upon the national mind may be a valid criticism of the Turner thesis. But that criticism ignored the very strong undercurrent that the intoxication was attempting to hide—the rabid regionalism that infected the national ideal. Hickok and others like him were the bartenders at that national saloon, serving up common concerns, common cause, and common kinship. They were offering the Wild West. Then and now, everyone knew what it meant and generally accepted it as defining the American character and code.[11]

Weyl said nothing about Hickok, but he implied that the frontiersman's brand of individualism was done. "A new start" was what drew Hickok and others like him to the West, and if that door truly was closed, how could the economy, the hero, the code, and the West be recovered? And yet Hickok was so entrenched and accepted in the American story in 1953 that even President Eisenhower could invoke the hero of his youthful Abilene, which was planning (and would finish in 1958) "Old Abilene," a reconstruction of the heroic past to which Eisenhower referred. The Eisenhower incident showed what happens when memory is made to fit the Zeitgeist. Was Eisenhower remembering a real man, someone he had heard about in his hometown, or was he remembering a character he had seen at the movies or read about in books? What did "read your Westerns" really mean? Just as Joseph McCarthy was coming into his own with his posse of Red hunters, Hickok represented, to Eisenhower, the Code of the West: face your accuser, and fight fair. How did a common gunfighter with an uncommon talent for violence become, along with other such characters, a symbol for a national "code"? Hickok was shot in the back of his head. This told Americans that it didn't matter if one fought fair—the other guy wouldn't, like McCarthy. By extrapolation, they couldn't trust the "Other."

In 1953 it was the Soviet Union, and by the 1990s, the alien and the terrorist. In 1998, journalist Robert Kaplan visited Fort Leavenworth's Battle Command Training Program, where military personnel prepared to be dispatched as needed to potential global hot spots. A captain told Kaplan, "We know more about Honduras than about western Kansas during the Indian Wars. The intelligence on Honduras is more dense. Honduras is closer in time than western Kansas was, a few hours by plane rather than days on horseback." Scouts like Hickok had been replaced by advanced technology in an era when, according to Kaplan, the "Third World has become like the Old West. For the army, continental frontiers—of the kind that led to the building of Fort Leavenworth and of the nation—have grown dim."[12]

The Other was a necessity, helping define "us" via the antithesis, and had done so from Eden onward. In the 1950s, American democracy had to be good and virtuous in light of the communists, who were godless. Americans had to arm themselves like Hickok, dig a bomb shelter, and trust the military arsenal to protect the nation, but that wasn't enough. All the early biographies established Hickok as a superman—heroic, handsome, unstoppable, a magnificent shot. But in the end there was still Jack McCall, *not* the Other, just a punk who was a sore loser in a card game. The message was clear. Even if you held the good cards, they got you anyway. When Hickok took a seat with his back to the rear door, let down his guard, whatever cards he held no longer mattered. The side of justice and civility, in the West and in Eisenhower's day, needed to be armed, ready, and facing the Other, just as Hickok usually was until that errant, fatal moment.

Hickok was the ultimate individualist, but when he arrived in lawless, stateless Deadwood, his days were numbered. Hickok allegedly held a great hand but his killer did not follow the code in 1876. Hickok might as well have been holding Tarot cards—the cards spelled death. Although the "aces and eights" story was an invention, it has endured as an omen of bad ends, just a bad punch line. Professor Cosmo Fishhawk, a character in the syndicated cartoon strip *Shoe*, originated by Pulitzer Prize–winning journalist Jeff MacNelly, visited Deadwood in 2018. Cosmo was a columnist for the *Treetops Tattler-Tribune*, whose editorial staff and readers were birds (Cosmo was an osprey). In a February strip, Cosmo told waitress Roz that he saw Hickok's burial site on his trip. "I guess his death came as quite a surprise," said Roz. "No," responded Shoe, "it was in the cards."[13]

This works because what the wider audience remembers about Hickok is the death scene. Even the language used to describe Hickok's death was instructive. The word *assassinated* was prominent rather than *murdered* or *killed*. Maybe McCall foreshadowed the Gilded Age anarchists, the Haymarket bombings, Presidents Garfield, McKinley, and Kennedy, and the terrorists. The Other was always lurking out there. The mythic Hickok was in his media prime at the time of the Kennedy assassinations. By then newspapers, magazines, dime novels, movies, and television, had multiple pathways to the public imagination, as easy as a cowboy's saunter from saloon to bawdy house in frontier Abilene or Deadwood.[14]

Memory

Just how much memory of Wild Bill Hickok is still around? Even if Hickok has nothing much to do with ongoing gun debates, he has a lot to do with glamorized violence, the obsession with violence, the whole culture of violence that came out of the Civil War, the frontier, Prohibition, the movies, and television. Hickok was in the midst of an emerging celebrity culture in the nineteenth century that grew up around a mass media of penny newspapers and dime novels, theater, photography, and magazines. The press was powerful, but not always in the obvious ways: holding government officials to account; boosting cities and towns; promoting commerce and citizenship.

Just as the first order of business for a newspaper was to make a profit, so the journalist/writer had to make a living. With Hickok, the press was not so much chasing a legend as constructing one. Hickok was valuable to storytellers because he could embody the West's excitement, allure, danger, romance, and challenge. A good story, to a journalist, has multiple, easily grasped news values, including conflict, colorful characters, consonance, currency, consequence, action, irony, success/failure, or a mixture of all. Hickok's story resided comfortably for more than 150 years in the borderlands of a culture and its media that embraced violence and lawlessness as entertainment. So many versions of Hickok's story commend him as a civilizer who subdued secessionists, Indians, and outlaws and brought law and order to dusty cow towns. It was the image of a West civilized in a compelling landscape and not in the confines of a drab legislative hall or courtroom. This was in keeping with a West that wanted to define itself by its expanse, not the drudgery of lawmaking.

The gunfighter was one example of how celebrity and history were commodified. Audiences responded to the Wild West because they liked it, and media gilded the tale as a libertarian paradise where order was kept by fictional supermen like television's Wild Bill. Hickok cleaned up real life Abilene on the cheap, saving the citizenry the price of a police force. Controls were minimized, so what a paradise Deadwood must have been—no laws, no state, no nation. Hickok and other gunfighters possessed a certain dark power. If they wore a star, that power came with the ability to bring a semblance of order to the West. Their stories further reinforced individualism by showing how one person could make a difference either way—and, if both ways, even better. In 2018 a journalist in Springfield, where Hickok shot Davis Tutt in 1865, proclaimed a record-setting year for local tourism. Tourists, he said, learned about Springfield's exciting history and heard rich stories about the "outlaw Wild Bill Hickok." *Outlaw?* Did it really matter?[15]

The year Wild Bill died was a great year in which to get killed. It was the year America saw itself as conquering the frontier. The Philadelphia Exposition celebrated advances in science, manufacturing, communications technologies, agriculture, energy, and transportation. But the frontier and the border were still there, and still menacing. The major headline that summer was not Hickok's death but Custer's, at the Little Bighorn. Custer is remembered as an Indian fighter, eclipsing his significant reputation as a Civil War cavalry hero. The public Hickok could be used as both Indian fighter and gunfighter, as in the novel and film *The White Buffalo*. His supposed Civil War heroics occurred in the West, so they tended to be absorbed in a Western memory tableau. If neither was a great man, both were great stories, both recognizable types. "What charms us in them is partly their daring, skill, and invulnerability, partly their chivalry; but not to be overlooked is their impatience with all restraint, their freedom from social responsibility that [Michel-Guillaume-Jean de] Crèvecoeur admired in his citizen-farmer, and that on occasion bows the shoulders of every man born," according to Wallace Stegner.[16]

It did not matter that historians may have been critical of Hickok in his time and in subsequent generations because he prevailed in the public memory thanks to cultural values. The press found him on target with a fairly simple, straightforward idea that appealed to the audience. If writers so successfully inflated Hickok's deeds, it must be, as Allen Barra concluded, that "all of them saw in Hickok's deeds something worth exaggerating." The nineteenth-century press and dime novels seized on the essential parts of the Wild Bill story: individualism and dramatic, regenerative violence. The parts were fused into a character easily adapted into later media and fitted to a national mythology of American exceptionalism and triumph. *Buffalo Bill's Wild West* helped shape and prepare the country for such a national identity, and did so with the tools for national dissemination at hand—theatrics and the press.[17]

The real Wild Bill disappeared almost immediately, lost in the vacuum of primary sources about him. Instead, the sources for the legend become the sources for remembering the man. His legend became its own sort of reality. He was unlike Custer and Sherman because their myths could be weighed on the scales of judgment and memory against large bodies of primary documents. With Hickok, the scales were laden on one side—the mediated one—and light on the other. He was made so adaptable by the media that created him, a figure and symbol of what it took to civilize the West and assert American swagger in the wider world. Wild Bill was one of many characters who revealed the adaptability of the Western and Western figures to promoting American exceptionalism in an environment unique to the young nation. All these characters, ranging from scofflaws like Billy the Kid and Jesse James to sometime lawmen like Bat Masterson and Wyatt Earp, have in common a wide gap between their lives and legends. The media figure has about the same relation to the historical figure that a hologram has to a flesh-and-blood person. But each distortion serves a distinct audience expectation.

After the early episodes of the first season of *Deadwood*, Hickok practically vanished from television in the first two decades of the twenty-first century. Just one movie, and that a disappointment, portrayed the gunfighter in a leading role. In popular fiction, novels about Hickok kept coming until about 2006, somewhat in response to the popularity of *Deadwood*, and then vanished for a decade before a few titles appeared after 2015. With the death of Joseph Rosa in 2015 and James McLaird in 2017, two of the most important Hickok biographers left the field. Rosa had pretty much said all there was left to say about the life of Hickok. One of Rosa's last projects was a short volume for the juvenile library series. He left his young readers with a school book-report subject whose "name will live on and his reputation will not fade." Biographical works by Aaron Woodard, Bob Boze Bell, and Tom Clavin came along in 2018 and 2019. Travel writers, journalists, scholars of the West, and historical reenactors were continuing to show interest in Hickok, but some questioned how long he would last.[18]

On April 19, 2015, more than 1.5 million viewers tuned in to the Fox News Channel to see an episode about Hickok on *Legends & Lies: The Real West*, a dramatized documentary series produced by cable news personality

Bill O'Reilly. *James "Wild Bill" Hickok: Plains Justice* featured Brian Merrick in the title role. The companion volume to the series, written by journalist and author-ghostwriter David Fisher, devoted twenty-three lively pages to Hickok. While the series promised some debunking of its subjects, however, Hickok was described in the book as a man who "stood up for what was right," was, by reputation, the "perfect lawman," and "one of the best-known men in America" in his day, possibly rivaling the president (Grant?), while "credited with thirty-six righteous killings," before he was murdered in "Nutter and Mann's Saloon [*sic*]" holding aces and eights. Whether legends or lies—or one and the same—was not made clear, nor did it seem to matter. The book stayed high on the New York *Times* bestseller list for weeks. That might suggest people are at least interested in history even if they don't know much about it. The less they know, the easier it is to invent.[19]

Just how the memory of Hickok might evolve won't be limited by mainstream media. It was inevitable that Wild West stories would evolve into something beyond the print or film format. In 1996, *Deadlands: The Weird West*, an alternative history role-playing game, was introduced by Pinnacle Entertainment Group, followed by *Deadlands Reloaded* in 2006. This genre-mashing, horror-steampunk Western included *Deadlands: The Weird West Dime Novels*, a book series hybrid combining story and game-playing protocols. Steampunk is a science fiction or fantasy genre typically drawing on nineteenth-century themes or technology such as steam power. Game players engaged characters, such as a sheriff, to combat monsters and "undead" gunfighters who had arisen to menace the territory. Some supernatural characters pulled from the grave were called the Harrowed and may have been possessed by spiritual beings called manitous. As game scholar Rachel Mizsei Ward explained, "It allows players to experience the Wild West almost as a theme park; they can, for example, visit Deadwood and interact with Wild Bill Hickok in some form, even if it is an undead one." Hickok returned from the dead as a Harrowed to seek revenge on his killer or complete some other mission. "Harrowed" means, literally, pulled from the earth. Already granted immortality by the popular culture since his death in 1876, James Butler Hickok will be exhumed again and again to take on new missions he never imagined and never asked for because the theme park culture can't let him die.[20]

Epilogue: Hickok in Biography and History; An Essay on Sources

> Read no history; nothing but biography for that is life without theory.
>   —Benjamin Disraeli, 1832

> All history becomes subjective; in other words, there is properly no history; only biography.
>
>   —Ralph Waldo Emerson, 1841

Like histories of the West, Hickok biographies stretch to far-off horizons, meandering from nonsensical fabrication to insightful research. Like Custer, Hickok is amenable to mythmaking or mythbusting, and is therefore both vilified and glorified. Unlike Custer, at least for historians and biographers, Hickok has left us with few primary sources to work with—not many letters or family papers, no military records of substance—but a lot of secondary sources such as tall tales and dime novels. The ample secondary sources pander to audiences and market demand. The Hickok story that emerged in the nineteenth century appealed to people seeking entertainment, not critical readers checking sources. A generation or two after his death, biographies based on dubious sources, or no sources at all, came along. It was a long time before they were corrected or dismissed. Hickok is best understood not as a historical figure in his own right but as a myth contrived in the mass media. Why he has any presence at all in the history of American culture can only be comprehended in the context of the search for exceptionalism and individualism in the national imagination and the allure of violence as entertainment. His story brought to this entertainment theme a new kind of violence that amplified the mythic individualism. Duels were old hat. The Main Street walkdown as we know it started with Wild Bill.

Journalism is ephemeral, driven by audiences, formulaic and self-referential. History nods to permanence, fact, and interpretation. Hickok could never be "good" history, but he could be bad journalism, which is to say tabloid-style journalism. As in John Ford's classic 1962 Western film *The Man Who Shot Liberty Valence*, Jimmy Stewart's character, Sen. Ransom Stoddard, tried to tell the truth, which was that he did not shoot the notorious outlaw; John Wayne's character, Tom Doniphon, did. But a newspaper editor explained, "This is the West, sir. When the legend becomes fact, print the legend." The much-quoted phrase, according to Daniel Ford, is "cited today, with knowing irony, as a warning against mere myth-making. Somehow, though, we keep printing legends." The first Hickok biographers did just that, and, with few exceptions, the practice continued.[1]

The earliest biographies are awash in wild tales, some only a page removed from dime novels, which appear to have been the source for accounts of such things as the number of men he killed, his fantastic shooting ability, and his saintly deeds of charity. J. W. Buel, who wrote the first book-length account of Hickok's life, and William Connelley stood out. Joseph Rosa and James McLaird came later and offered more critical, evidence-based accounts of the gunslinger's life, separating myth and reality. Historians of the West, such as Richard W. Etulain and David Hamilton Murdoch, put Hickok in a broader context, usually with a chapter or two assessing his place in the region's history. They provided an extra dimension in attempting to understand Hickok's life, legend, and place in cultural values and myth. The expanse of material about Hickok shows why the stories about him slipped so easily into various media platforms. The Davis Tutt walkdown segued well into George Ward Nichols's and Richard T. Stanley's quasi-journalistic exaggerations of reality, then to dime novels, longer narrative, and cinema. Stories from history and fiction show that Hickok could be fitted to any number of roles.

Biography

The twentieth century began with a biographical homage to Hickok in *Everybody's Magazine* by Lt. Col. Edward Campbell (E. C.) Little, an Abilene, Kansas, lawyer and war hero. He did nothing to challenge the Rock Creek and Springfield stories as the signature elements in Hickok's legacy, but he built up Hickok's reputation as a Kansas lawman and savior of Abilene. He called for "a statelier history" than the dime novels had provided and thought Hickok worthy of an epic. Little had attended public schools in Abilene, graduated from the University of Kansas, practiced law in Lawrence, and then returned to Abilene in the role of county attorney. During the Spanish-American War and the Philippine Insurrection in 1898–99, he served as lieutenant colonel in the Twentieth Kansas Volunteer Regiment and won the Congressional Medal of Honor. He later served in Congress.[2]

Little said that, in 1901, Hickok's friends still remembered Abilene as "the wickedest town on earth" before the Coe shooting, after which the Texans left and Abilene remained "a law abiding city forever." Hickok, as marshal of this new frontier utopia, had set the standard for law-and-order police officers and shown that "he who keeps the peace is the most essential and valuable adjunct to civilization." Hickok was a "reincarnation of Lancelot, the renaissance of the knight-errant." Little's interest in Hickok as a civilizing symbol had political implications, too. Having a heroic Civil War veteran and Republican-leaning lawman in the party's pantheon boosted campaign rhetoric. Little exceeded even Buel and Nichols in spurious inventions and mangled metaphors. Hickok had killed eight men at Rock Creek, leaving the floor of the station "like the deck of a viking's warship after a glorious triumph," and its hero "[c]overed with wounds and freckled with bullet holes" and rendered "insensible and at the point of death."

Another Hickok booster who proved useful in establishing the Abilene connection for a national audience was Arthur Chapman. Born in Illinois in 1873, Chapman worked for Chicago and Denver newspapers before writing for the New York *Tribune* from 1919 to 1925. He was best known for a much-quoted, sentimental poem he wrote in 1910, "Out Where the West Begins," where handshakes were firmer and there was lots of laughter and singing, whiter snows, and a brighter sun. His account of Hickok's time in Abilene, "The Men That Tamed the Cowtowns," was published in 1904 in *Outing* magazine. Chapman quoted Stanley and emphasized Hickok's status as a "revolver expert" whose guns "seldom saw a week of silence." Were that true, Hickok's death toll in Abilene would have been staggering unless he was just shooting bottles. Chapman retold the Coe story and added the legend that Coe's mother vowed to pay $10,000 to anyone who could bring her the marshal's head, presumably on a platter. Chapman claimed that Hickok stood down Jesse James's gang in 1872 before they could steal the receipts from the city fair. "The very sight of the picturesque Marshal, with his death-dealing, ivory-handled revolvers aggressively displayed, was enough for the entire outfit and the gang decamped. . . ." Hickok wasn't even in Abilene in 1872, and the James gang took receipts from the Kansas City fair. Chapman should have stuck to poetry.[3]

Biographers in the 1920s and 1930s had only Buel to look to as a model, and as such they had reason to reconsider Buel's assessment of frontier violence. More needed to be said, and new sources were becoming available. Violence had intensified during World War I with the use of chemical weapons, aircraft, and trench and artillery warfare. The weapons were the products of industrialization, far more so than the six-shooter. Though handguns came out of a factory, an individual, not a military unit, pulled the trigger. Hickok meted out justice in one-on-one fashion. The industrial war machine crushed people indiscriminately in the ugliest possible fashion. Bodies were torn apart by artillery, chemically burned, or left hanging in barbed wire. Muddied corpses and mutilated bodies comprised the legacy of the Great War. Violence was not heroic, except for the relatively rare individual hero such as Sgt. Alvin York, who became an American film legend precisely because he was portrayed as a Tennessee frontiersman in France. By contrast, the Hickok legend was essentially nostalgic, recalling individualism and frontier virtues of self-reliance, purpose, and strength.

Many of the earliest Hickok biographies were undocumented or taken uncritically from dubious sources, including second- and thirdhand accounts, dime novels, and oral histories. Sometimes, the biographies sounded like dime novels—incredible shooting, exaggerated numbers of kills, gunfights in which Hickok overcame impossible odds. The feats attributed to Hickok in Buel's *The Life and Marvelous Adventures of Wild Bill* (1880) and *Heroes of the Plains* (1882) included shooting a crow out of the sky with his pistol, killing a grizzly with a knife, and roping a buffalo. Buel probably met Hickok in the early 1870s, when Buel was working as a journalist in St. Louis and Hickok was living there. Adding to the doubts about his work, Buel claimed to have drawn from Hickok's diary something Hickok's family was unaware of. Much of the biography was unverifiable. Though fairly worthless as history, the biography set the tone for much that followed. Buel's was the only biography of Hickok until several decades later, when a spate of similarly doting Hickok books came out. Those intervening decades saw the image of the Wild West emerge and coalesce. The Western saga—romantic and heroic—had arrived. The national culture eagerly embraced it.[4]

O. W. Coursey's *Wild Bill Hickok* (1924) originally was published in the Sioux Falls *Daily Argus-Leader*. The thin volume included an error-filled account of the Tutt walkdown and overstated Hickok's shooting ability. Wild Bill wept about killing, revealing a chivalric and tender soul. The dedication said it best: "To one of the few survivors of that grand galaxy of red-blooded men whose heroic sacrifice and unswerving devotion snatched the OLD WEST [caps, *sic*] from the throes of savage indolence and made it into the NEW WEST [caps, *sic*] of today, . . . 'Wild Bill' Hickok, 'Buffalo Bill' Cody, General Custer. . . ." That a signed first edition of the pocketsize bound eighty-page book is going for up to $325 is testament not to the quality of the history but to Hickok's popularity among collectors.[5]

In 1925, Frank Wilstach wrote an article about Hickok for the New York *Times* on the occasion of the fiftieth anniversary of the Deadwood boom. The article, under the headline TIME WIDENS WILD BILL HICKOK'S FAME, covered five columns and included a large photograph of Hickok wearing a fur hat. Wilstach concluded that Hickok was "not a bad man but a bad man to fool with." Wilstach got just about everything wrong in the article, claiming that Hickok killed ten men in the McCanles fight, killed a dozen men in Abilene, and was "said" to have killed at least forty men total. In 1926 Wilstach published *Wild Bill Hickok, the Prince of Pistoleers*, and though he dealt more with evidence than hearsay, the book still drew heavily on the latter and was a paean to the gunman. It was only the second book-length biography of Hickok. Wilstach was born in Lafayette, Indiana, in 1865. He had a journalistic background in San Francisco and New York. In Boston, he was an editor and worked as a publicist for a few local actors. He also worked as a theater manager in New York.[6]

Wilstach stated in the first sentence that it was not his purpose to "novelize Wild Bill Hickok." But by the second paragraph he was already turning up the stage lights. "His friends never ceased to chant his praises as an honest man, an incredibly accurate pistol shot, and an individual who was without fear in the presence of danger. . . ." He gave Hickok credit for fifteen to seventy-five killings, not counting Indians and the Civil War, but he at least admitted that the number was difficult to pin down. He contradicted himself a few pages later and said that the number would "naturally" include Indians and slayings as a military sharpshooter.[7]

Wilstach quoted the dime novelist Prentiss Ingraham on Hickok's membership in the Red Legs, a Union guerilla band in Kansas during the war, raising questions about other sources Wilstach may have used. However, he did confront some "mysteries," although whether or not he settled them is debatable, and those included the McCanles "slaughter," the origins of the Wild Bill name, and the Calamity Jane "canard." Wilstach demonstrated commendable skepticism in his research on the McCanles gunfight, contradicting what he had written in the New York *Times*. The author found only three killed, not the ten or more so often given in legend. He added that early Civil War animosities probably had a role in the fight, as well as horse theft and, maybe, a woman. As for sources, he drew on descendants and eyewitnesses through correspondence and interviews, but those did not always reveal lodes of information. He claimed to have located Sarah Shull, but he could not reveal her whereabouts "without violating confidences." She was, at the time, ninety-three years old and living back in North Carolina.[8]

He used the Nichols account of the Tutt shootout and drew on Buel, who claimed Tutt came to Springfield for the express purpose of killing Hickok. However, Wilstach concluded, it was "an old-time duel," and Hickok "left the field of honor victorious." The language is revealing, in that Wilstach was putting the shootout in the context of a "code of honor." As for Nichols including a woman in the incident, such was "idle twaddle." Throughout the book, Wilstach questioned conventional accounts, as well as some of his own sources, and acknowledged those points about which a range of opinion existed. He may have cleared up some confusion but added his own.[9]

The next Hickok biography appeared in 1931: Wilbert Edwin Eisele's *The Real Wild Bill Hickok: Famous Scout and Knight Chivalric—A True Story of Pioneer Life in the Far West.* Like the title, the 324-page book was an overly long epic of praise. Eisele drew heavily on Buel and Little and, as a result, made the "True Story" part of the title not true. Eisele found in Hickok the "powers of Samson and Hercules combined." Even when Eisele clung to the facts, he distorted by exaggeration: "[Hickok] was an unequaled horseman; he was a perfect marksman, he had a keen sight and constitution which had no limit of endurance. He was cool to audacity, brave to the point of rashness and always displayed great generalship under the most critical circumstances. . . . [H]e was always aligned on the side of law and order. . . . [N]ever indulged in liquor to the excess, . . . had the instincts of a gentleman. . . ." Hickok's horse even winked in response to a question from him, a buffoonery that had shown up in Nichols's article. Eisele even claimed that a "certain clique of writers" had revised the true story of the McCanles fight to discredit Hickok's high body count in what really was a border war with desperadoes. He said a fake account, limiting the death toll to three, was inspired by Southern sympathizers who resented Hickok's Civil War heroics and wanted to minimize his exploits.[10]

Connelley's *Wild Bill and His Era: The Life and Adventures of James Butler Hickok,* published in 1933 and reprinted in 1972, was also afflicted with the incredible. Connelley was born in Kentucky in 1855, worked in the lumber business in Springfield, Missouri, and had banking and oil interests in Kansas. His history writing was similar to what had come before. He added some information on Hickok's romances and a useful chronology of Hickok's life. In the preface, Charles M. Harger wrote, "No historian was so well qualified for this task as William Elsey Connelley. . . . Painstaking, sure of his statements, gifted with a pleasing style, and trained by his position as Secretary of the Kansas State Historical Society to allow no assertion to go unchallenged, he entered upon the writing of this book with a sincere purpose—to give an authoritative history of 'Wild Bill' Hickok. . . . He took nothing for granted and sought to create from original sources a delineation accurate in every detail." Harger was amiss. Connelley repeated the implausible and burdened his text with hero worship. His sources often were not evident. Having been secretary of the historical society for sixteen years, Connelley should have known better. Rosa put some of the blame on heavy-handed editing by Connelley's daughter. Connelley died in 1930, and the book was published three years later. Rosa called the result a "disaster" due to too much cutting. Equally unfortunate, his sources were subsequently scattered, and some of them disappeared. Even worse, as Murdoch and Kent Ladd Steckmesser charged, Connelley simply left out material that detracted from the worshipful portrait of Hickok.[11]

Connelley repeated exaggerations from Nichols and Stanley, among others, and made Hickok seem almost saintly at times, as if to absolve him of his sins. Hickok loved children, was moral, seldom drank, and never killed "without cause and justification." Hickok's marksmanship was near miraculous, and he killed one hundred men, a repetition of Stanley's bogus number. Fifty-three of those executions, an imposing body count, occurred when he was marshal of Abilene. He repeated the story that Hickok had killed a grizzly with a knife. Hickok's skill as a scout was enhanced by his ability to speak the language of every Plains tribe. Connelley's account of the shootout with Tutt exemplified the author's approach to his subject. Hickok was taunted into a shootout by Tutt and his friends. They tried to draw him into a fight, "but they could not provoke Bill into a row," eventually goading him into a duel. Connelley was even critical of Buel: "There was some truth in Buel's book, but much that he recorded was pure invention." And in one endnote he called Buel's statement that Hickok killed Benjamin McCulloch at Cross Timbers "preposterous." Connelley was not similarly critical of other sources, however.[12]

It's puzzling that early Hickok biographers were so gullible, especially when they recognized fabrications in other works and could acknowledge the limits of their own knowledge. The want of facts and plausibility speaks to the power of mythology. The audience wanted heroes, eschewing ambivalence and moral ambiguity. Complexity was not on the table unless it focused on unknowable details of shootouts, card games, and lovers' trysts. What cards was Hickok really holding when he was shot? How many men did he kill? Did Jack McCall act alone or was he part of an assassination conspiracy?

What did Wild Bill really think of Calamity Jane? David McCanles? John Wesley Hardin? The biographers had to decide if their man was the "gay and gallant gentleman" Connelley said he was or a "homicidal psychopath," which Richard O'Connor said he was not. Rather, O'Connor said, Hickok was "simply a man who went West and fell into a dangerous way of life," a story too simple to matter much to anyone.[13]

Bob Thompson encountered similar biographical bear dens when he wrote about Davy Crockett. His book was part travelogue, part historical inquiry by an experienced journalist who had developed his own history beat on the Washington *Post*. Thompson found himself being taken in by what he called the Legendary Davy Syndrome. "What had happened, I suddenly realized, was that I had started to see all those tales as utterly characteristic of the man I was trying to understand—even the ones I doubted were true." A similar Legendary Wild Bill Syndrome, the bear-in-the-woods of Hickok scholarship, afflicted those who tracked their quarry by following in the footsteps of Nichols and his credulous successors.[14]

The Ozark folklorist Vance Randolph, writing under the name Allison Hardy, broke the spell of infatuation in his short 1943 biography *Wild Bill Hickok: King of the Gun-Fighters*. At times he was even skeptical of his own sources, which may have been the best available or best known at the time. It was as much a critique of earlier biographies and sources as it was a biography of Hickok. In this sense, it was a good addition to Hickok and Western history. Randolph thought that Wilstach was the best biographer to date. Going back to the first Hickok biographies, Randolph pointed out that Nichols failed to identify his sources. Looking at Hickok's talent for killing, Randolph said the claim of fifty Indians killed by Hickok was a number from "imaginative historians" and writers of "Western thrillers."[15]

One instance of his laudable skepticism was the "standard version" of the McCanles shootout. "It is quite a thing for one man to whip 10 gun-fighters, and kill eight of them, all in the space of four or five minutes. Many Westerners regarded Bill Hickok's defeat of the McCandles [*sic*] gang as a sort of minor miracle, and one newspaper writer compared the fight to the Battle of Hastings and the fall of Troy." He provided an alternative version from a family descendent, who said there never was a gang and that the standard version was made up to bolster the Hickok legend. Randolph concluded that the traditional story was not true and cited, without complete commitment, his own dubious sources: dime-novel writer Ingraham; hero worshipper Wilstach, who drew on hero worshipper Buel; and Connelley, who drew on Wilstach and Buel. On Hickok, Randolph noted that it was "generally agreed he did not tell the whole truth," which he may not have known anyway.[16]

Randolph may have been trying to shake the habit of looking at Hickok stories as folklore rather than pastiche, or "fakelore"—stories that appear to come out of a comic, indigenous oral tradition but in reality are crassly media-manufactured pseudo-folklore intended to appeal to a mass audience. This, according to Crockett scholar Michael Lofaro, was part of what happened to the hero of the Alamo. The real man vanished, replaced by Walt Disney's coonskin-cap-wearing, sanitized *Davy Crockett* of the 1954–55 television season, watched by at least forty million people. The legendary frontiersman and congressman first was coopted by publishers of phony Crockett almanacs. These cheap booklets were full of homespun frontier aphorisms, often racist, misogynistic, warlike, and riddled with plagiarism and bogus biography featuring the trickster Davy channeling all the vulgar prejudices of the early nineteenth century as imagined by the Eastern publishing establishment. Wild Bill retained just enough corporality during his lifetime to avoid being stripped of his identity by the fakelore industry. A more mysterious death might have left him with a more ethereal legacy. He died at the right time and in the right place, a murder victim, not a martyr to a cause, and is buried in Deadwood. Crockett's remains were never conclusively identified.[17]

O'Connor's 1959 *Wild Bill Hickok* was among the next generation of Hickok biographies. O'Connor had worked as a journalist for the Los Angeles *Times*, the Chicago *Tribune*, the Boston *American*, and *Variety*. As a Hickok biographer, O'Connor was a little more critical and less worshipful. Among other falsehoods, "Nothing has been more exaggerated about Hickok than the number of men he killed, nothing more mendacious than the repeated assertions that 'Hickok got all his men by shooting them in the back or catching them unarmed.'" His opponents were armed and belligerent, usually in near-lawless environs, where "Hickok took them as they came." O'Connor's common sense made for a more plausible, if less fantastic, life story. For example, he recounted the wartime incident, told by Hickok, in which he and a dozen men in a supply train were attacked and pursued outside Leavenworth, Kansas. Hickok escaped, and when he made it to Independence, Missouri, he told the Union garrison that he had shot and killed four of the pursuers. "[H]ow he could have determined this while fleeing for his life was not made clear." At Pea Ridge, Hickok was credited for killing thirty-five Confederates, "although who counted the corpses for him was not stated." Similarly, after Hickok served as a spy and supposedly fled Confederate lines, a great shout arose from the Union side as he neared—"Here comes Wild Bill, the Union Scout!—but just how thousands of soldiers would simultaneously recognize Hickok in a ragged Confederate uniform was not explained." O'Connor's critical eye may have been due in part to his reliance on the press, which he used liberally. He did not use citations but listed fourteen period magazines and fifteen newspapers in the bibliography. He charged Nichols with "girlish enthusiasm." Although O'Connor repeated some of the legends from earlier biographers, he often was more dependable.[18]

Another 1959 biography, *Wild Bill Hickok: The Contemporary Portrait of a Civil War Hero,* expressed author Frank E. Irwin's desire to provide a balanced picture of Hickok, based more on evidence than dime novels. Irwin, also the publisher of this little book, had written for the Boston *Evening Transcript* and the New York *Times* before starting the Hillside Press in 1955 with nineteenth-century printing equipment. He wrote under the pseudonym Edward Knight. *Wild Bill Hickok* was the press's first book, a sign of the continuing widespread interest in Hickok in the 1950s. The author's difficulty ascertaining the facts illustrates the paucity of reliable reference material on Hickok as late as 1959. Irwin noted the inaccuracies of much of the Hickok legend. "Many of Wild Bill's experiences on the frontier and in the Civil War were real enough. They were the basis for the legend. The myth emerged, like the jinnee [*sic*] from a bottle, from the slight and fragile structure of direct evidence." However, the heroics and the sensation seemed inescapable. Irwin said that Hickok abided by a dueling code, and although he was not an "instinctive killer," he was the "best two-handed pistol shot on the frontier," which, Irwin acknowledged, was a matter of opinion. Irwin even said the dueling code underwent a "democratic revision" after the Civil War. He was oddly precise about the quickness of Wild Bill's draw. In trying to estimate the speed in the Tutt shootout, Irwin cited experimental psychologists' measurement of the "eyelid reflex" as "approximately 0.0418 seconds." It does not sound very approximate, but he went on to note that gunman Bill Tilghman estimated the time needed to get the best of an opponent would be only "slightly slower. . . . In this dimension, time, as a substantial period of duration, is difficult to imagine and even more difficult to describe." Although Irwin worked to overcome mythology, he still romanticized gunmen. Many were Civil War veterans, and some had been buffalo hunters. "They were all quick on the draw and deadly accurate marksmen. According to some authorities all of the ranking gun-fighters of the old west had blue or grey-blue eyes. . . ."[19]

Like others, Irwin gave gunfighting a patina of respectability with the endowment of a code and a sporting-style "ranking." In spite of his own fuzziness on many fantastic points, he was critical of those who did not even try to be balanced, such as Nichols, whom Irwin used as a source: "Colonel Nichols was certainly not a careful writer. Possibly he was a proper model of a historian telling tales akin to Mother Goose." He quoted Nichols at length about Hickok's experiences as a Union spy and concluded with Hickok's assassination: "The cards that slipped through his fingers and fell face upward on the floor of the bar were aces and eights."[20]

The improved biographies of Hickok probably did nothing to increase the general public's appreciation for more accurate history and citations, but they did help draw a sharper line between fact and fiction, which the earliest biographies did not do with their secondhand hearsay, oral accounts, and sensational journalism. Later history drew on more reliable records and tended to cast a colder eye upon accounts of fantastic feats in law enforcement, scouting, shooting, and debauchery. Journalists writing biographies typically had a sharp eye for a good, audience-pleasing story, but they often lacked the historians' appreciation for a mundane—but important—character. The best biographers, whether journalists or historians, could plod where necessary for depth and background and dazzle with entertaining stories when justified. Foremost among Hickok biographers was Joseph Rosa, who produced numerous volumes on the Wild West and its gunfighters, Hickok in particular. To Rosa's credit were two of the best books on Hickok: *Wild Bill Hickok: The Man and His Myth* (1996) and *They Called Him Wild Bill: The Life and Adventures of James Butler Hickok* (1964).

As one of the nation's great mythic figures of the West, Hickok merited a comprehensive volume on his myth. Rosa delivered. He noted that estimates varied widely and wildly on the number of men killed, which in reality, Rosa wrote, appeared to have been close to ten. He admitted that Hickok's own tall tales contributed to the distortion. Making extensive use of the press meant that Rosa also was able to trace the development of many Hickok myths, as well as follow the growth of the public persona into a legend. His work, therefore, consisted of much more than merely breaking down stories in the sense of exposing falsehoods. Providing one of the most extensively researched Hickok biographies, Rosa used court and legal documents, family records, and newspaper and magazine articles, many of which often were forgotten in biographies more intent on the incredible. As Rosa showed, reality was sufficiently fantastic to make for an exciting life story. The legend "was the creation of the fevered imagination of the press and the public." Rosa placed Hickok and frontier conflicts in the context of still-simmering Civil War tensions. Hickok emerged from the war "as a kind of demigod with superhuman strength and powers that place him in the forefront of frontier heroes."[21]

The 1974 revision of the volume had the most thorough vetting of documents from the years around Hickok's life. The historical records were not extensive. As in the *Myth*, Rosa took up much of the slack with newspaper and magazine articles and delved into family papers that apparently were unavailable to or just undiscovered by previous historians. The Englishman met several of Hickok's family members, including a nephew, the nephew's wife, and a niece. Rosa gained access to letters and other materials that, as far as he knew, had never been made public. He admitted in the introduction that the tall tales were problematic: "The proportion of truth in even the verifiable stories is hard to determine," as Hickok himself often "enlarged" upon his exploits, as did friends and enemies, who passed on "stories of doubtful validity, exaggerating the list of killings, asserting and denying his prowess as a pistoleer, plainsman, and persuader of women." Long ago, Rosa seemed to lament, Hickok was overshadowed by his own legend. Whether this made Hickok more marketable and more interesting remains part of the intrigue.[22]

Rosa was at his best when he was at his most pragmatic and commonsensical, as in the concluding pages where he pointed out that notching pistols, a cliché of Western print and cinematic fiction, was not a common practice among gunmen: "A notched gun was the weapon of the braggart, attracting nothing but trouble for its owner. Besides, notching destroyed the balance and comfortable grip, which were both vital factors in the game of life and death." Similar realism was handed to such incidents as the Tutt duel, the Rock Creek shootout, Hickok's stint in Wild West shows, and even his death. It remains the best Hickok biography, exhaustive and thorough, for the reader who prefers reality to fantasy.[23]

Rosa lived in Ruislip in Middlesex, England, where he died in 2015. His immersion in Western lore endeared him to many Hickok enthusiasts in the United States but also caused backlash from some Americans who believed they had a proprietary claim on Hickok's life. Rosa was a copywriter in England for a firm that printed stamps and bank notes, and he later worked in the communications industry. He wrote more than two dozen books on the West and Westerners. He said that he was drawn to Hickok and the American West purely by the adventure, romance, and tragedy of the subjects. He discovered the Wild West when he was a youngster after seeing the film

Wild Bill Hickok Rides (1941), with Bruce Cabot in the title role. Rosa recalled a scene when Wild Bill "foiled a train robbery by hiding his pistol inside a doll's dress and then shooting one of the robbers as he grabbed for the doll." He was pulled more deeply into Hickok and the West by watching Gary Cooper in *The Plainsman* (1936). He even dedicated *They Called Him Wild Bill* to Cooper. Like many Western historians, Rosa initially fell under the spell of Hollywood's version of history.[24]

In the mid-1950s Rosa began writing as many as four letters a month to the Kansas State Historical Society to get information on Hickok. Some of the information found its way into the *Kansas Historical Quarterly*. "The notes could not have come at a better time," according to Rosa. "The 'Western' was a staple in television programming worldwide. (British television, for example, featured *Gunsmoke*, *Maverick*, *Wagon Train*, *Rawhide*, *Bonanza*, and other Western programs each week . . . along with feature-length Western movies.)"[25]

Perhaps staying true to that youthful enthusiasm, Rosa in 2004 published *Wild Bill Hickok: Sharpshooter and U.S. Marshal of the Wild West*. The 112-page juvenile biography resurrected the heroic Hickok who had a useful foil in Rosa's earlier books. Distilling Hickok's story for youthful readers, Rosa concluded that Hickok "shot straight, asked favors of no one, and courageously faced his enemies in defense of himself and others." To paint him as a good role model for young readers, Rosa made excuses for Hickok's character flaws. He claimed that after the Nichols article "Hickok's fame spread and he became known as a fearsome mankiller. He resented this reputation, but he knew that his own sense of humor was to blame. By the summer of 1867, a frustrated Hickok refused to talk to journalists, hoping to dampen the firestorm of publicity he had created with his own tall tales. . . ." By Rosa's own earlier accounts and research, there was scant evidence for such an assertion. Rosa in earlier works did sometimes seem to feel obliged to defend Hickok and his mythmakers, no more so than when he wrote that Nichols "was unjustifiably condemned by later writers; only now is it known that much of what he wrote was true or in part based on fact."[26]

James McLaird, who taught history at Dakota Wesleyan University, specialized in the history of South Dakota and the West. In addition to *Wild Bill Hickok and Calamity Jane: Deadwood Legends* (2008), his work included *Calamity Jane: The Woman and the Legend* (2011) and *Hugh Glass: Grizzly Survivor* (2016). At the time of his death, McLaird was said to have been at work on a Hickok biography. McLaird, too, credited journalists, especially

Nichols and Stanley, with launching Hickok's fame, as well as inspiring magazines and dime novels, which made people take notice when he came to town. McLaird acknowledged numerous exaggerations in Hickok's story, in Nichols, and in early biographies in which the details were sketchy at best. Though the press was often the source of questionable information, McLaird believed that journalists saw through the nonsense in Nichols's article. For example, the editor of the Springfield, Missouri, *Patriot* wrote that Nichols "cuts it very fat" when describing Wild Bill's extraordinary feats with weapons, and pointed out other errors in the article, including the death of Hickok's companion Tom Martin during the war. Martin was in the editor's office at the time. Other newspapers were similarly critical. McLaird devoted much attention to where the tales originated, as opposed to trying to sort out the details of events that apparently were undocumented and unknowable for both Hickok and Calamity Jane. Though courteous, Hickok was a teller of tall tales, to put it charitably, an aimless drunkard and probably addicted to gambling. His impulses and wanderings tempered any heroism, and McLaird did not shy from citing such incidents as Hickok's arrest for vagrancy in Kansas City.[27]

Bob Boze Bell's *The Illustrated Life and Times of Wild Bill Hickok: The First Gunfighter* (2017) engaged readers with colorful photography and artwork while providing information and context for even the best-informed Hickok aficionados. Bell, executive editor of *True West* magazine, provided some biography as well as some lively anecdotes. He acknowledged what may be mere fancy, but at the same time he drew a few times on such dubious sources as Buel's biography. Bell offered trivia of interest not only to Hickok fans but also to those interested in popular culture—Wild Bill in film, television, and comic books. For example, nearly seventy actors have played Hickok or characters based on him, but any resemblance to him was apparently of little concern. That factoid is telling when considering the elevation of Wild Bill in the popular imagination and in entertainment. Bell's timeline was excellent context for Hickok's life, removing him from the role of a singular character of his own time and putting him in the broader history of America and the West. The illustrations were themselves worthy of study, particularly with regards as to how a myth develops, though Bell did not offer them in that fashion. In a culture enamored of the visual, these illustrations were especially insightful to the Wild Bill mythology, if not the biography per se.[28]

Aaron R. Woodard, who taught American history in Sioux Falls, South Dakota, and worked as an editorial writer for the Indianapolis *News*, brought out *The Revenger: The Life and Times of Wild Bill Hickok* in 2018. He explained the "times" but not so much the "life" of his subject. He did more with McCall. He claimed that his was the first biography to contain the "complete record of McCall's legal and political attempts to avoid the noose." That record comprised a twenty-four-page chapter and served to update Rosa's *Alias Jack McCall*. Despite expressing doubts about his sources, Woodard included lengthy excerpts from Buel, Nichols, and Calamity Jane. He cited a novelist as a factual source when better and more relevant information was available from Rosa and McLaird. He repeated preposterous stories—albeit with skepticism—that had turned up in the early Hickok literature. For example, that Hickok's battle with a bear went on for thirty minutes, as though it would have taken a grizzly that long to tear Hickok apart. Such "hand-to-hand" combat would more accurately be called hand-to-paw with loss of hand and life quickly to follow. Some psychobiography crept into the book along with counterfactual speculation, such as a discussion of what Hickok would have done if one of his friends had been shot in the back of the head.[29]

Tom Clavin's *Wild Bill: The True Story of America's First Gunfighter* came out in 2019 to amplify the interest in Hickok. Reviewers were enthusiastic, and the heavily promoted book merited a lot of attention. Clavin wrote for the New York *Times* for fifteen years. His many books focused on Western history and American sports. *Wild Bill* was a readable story because Clavin wrote well. The book offered few new insights about Hickok, but it did enrich the story with background on cow towns, some of the people who loomed large in the Hickok myth, and the border fighting in Kansas. The anecdotes on Hickok's exploits as a lawman were especially enlivening. But Clavin did not include much documentation, leaving a skeptical reader to wonder if what was being read was a rehash of early—and discounted—Hickok biographies. Clavin speculated that the fabled bear fight "may well be true." He called Rosa "surely a doubting Thomas about so many of the tales told about Hickok." That's because Rosa was a careful historian. Clavin was also overly inclined to delve into the minds of his subjects. He surmised what Hickok was thinking when he shot Williams, and Hickok may even have "sensed his lawman days were coming to an end." Elsewhere readers found out what Hickok must have been thinking as he lassoed and herded buffalo for a show. However, there is no evidence for thoughts, and small errors added up. Sarah Shull became Sandra Schull, and so on. Call it the curse of Ned Buntline. Something about Hickok seemed to bring out the dime novelist in the best of writers.[30]

History

Although some works on the West were not dedicated solely to Hickok, they merit attention because they placed Hickok in historical and mythical context. He was no longer the singular phenomenon he so often was in early biographies or in popular media. Instead, he became more substantive, placed in the larger history, and biography, of the American West. These books shed light not only on Hickok but also on the time and place in which he became an iconic figure. In *Re-Imagining the Modern American West* (1996), Etulain cited Theodore Roosevelt and Frederick Jackson Turner as having an especially strong influence on thinking about the West at the turn of the twentieth century. That the West was wild and needed civilizing was a common theme in the nineteenth century. At the time, newspapers, popular histories, magazines, and dime novels had launched and continued to promote heroes. The Wild West perspective dominated. Roosevelt, unlike Turner, was not a resident of the ivory tower. His history, the multivolume *The Winning of the West* (1905), was widely read and influential for more than a generation. Turner's thesis about the impact of region and section on American history was also important to popular history, which sometimes was enamored of region. Turner believed East Coast historians had little insight about the frontier and land west of the Appalachians. Roosevelt, however, saw history as being about men, not institutions, and the West as vital and masculine. Turner found such an approach to be romantic, emphasizing frontier heroism and elevating the brave deeds of individuals. His critique implied that popular media, an important driver of culture, could know little beyond their circulation or viewing area. Still, the implication was that journalists created a West according to established myths and mores of the East and imposed that vision on Western events and figures. Such a critique is not a defense of their skill as historians but an unintentional testament to their influence on American culture and myth.[31]

From the Civil War and well into the twentieth century, Eastern writers with little knowledge of the West found Cody, Canary, and Hickok great figures for heroic exploitation. The West could not be too wild for these characters, who needed only embellishment in order to subdue the even wilder West. Audiences loved it. So if Hickok killed a hundred men or so, rather than only ten, so much the better for the myth. The early biographies reflected many of the exaggerations of tabloid journalism and dime novels, repeating the outlandish tales of his prowess in marksmanship, romance, and Indian fighting.

Ultimately, this view was reflected in the Rooseveltian view of history as being driven by such supermen, a view that took root with troubling consequences.[32]

Further afield from Hickok per se but reflective of the special place he holds in American history and culture were volumes on the history of violence in America. A number of books did put violence in context. Two noteworthy ones were Richard Slotkin's *Gunfighter Nation: The Myth of the Frontier in Twentieth-Century America* (1993), and Richard Maxwell Brown's *No Duty to Retreat: Violence and Values in American History and Society* (1991). For example, the widely used term "fast-draw artist" suggested gunfighting was an "art or profession." Hickok, Earp, and Billy the Kid were "champions" in this arena, their images giving this form of homicide a sporting aura. In that limited sense, they were alike.[33]

According to Brown, Hickok was the first famous gunfighter of the West. The shootout in Springfield was the "effective beginning of the walkdown tradition, for it was the first to receive wide public recognition as such." Such a pronouncement gave the press as much credit as the individual—Hickok— for the walkdown ritual. When a jury found him not guilty of manslaughter, the walkdown made "no duty to retreat" a part of legal tradition. Brown differentiated between "incorporation" gunslingers, who were hired to kill or intimidate tenant farmers in the range wars, and "resister" gunmen, who were basically rebels, defending themselves, families, and communities. Neither was the sort of gunfighter glorified in later movies. Hickok and Earp were "incorporation gunfighters," a harsh reality buried in mythology and the ag- grandizement of the gunman.[34]

Slotkin attributed the interest in gunfighters to the press, entertainment, and tourism. "The upsurge of interest in the Plains that accompanied con- struction of the transcontinental railroads brought numerous tourists to the region, along with journalists, gentlemen hunters in search of big game, and dime novelists looking for material." Hickok and Cody both won early fame this way. *Buffalo Bill's Wild West* later provided a veneer of respectability via history and patriotic programs, in which the Wild West exemplified America, a theme partly in response to the show's European tour from 1887 to 1889. The 1886 program offered Buffalo Bill as "the representative" frontiersman, and he "would be almost a history of the middle West, and, though younger, equaling in terms of service and personal adventure Kit Carson, Old Jim Bridger, California Joe, Wild Bill, and the rest of his dead and gone associ- ates." Slotkin considered all of them as well or better known as dime-novel heroes than as historical figures.[35]

The noir crime and private eye genres in the early twentieth century complemented the early Hickok biographies. The noir formula gave rise to what Slotkin called the revenger, an inward-looking neurotic hero confronting the abyss in an ominous environment. "Like the revenger, the gunfighter is psychically troubled and isolated from normal society by something 'dark' in his nature and/or his past." As with the private eye, the gunfighter was a socially useful killer, usually professional. The existence of such a profession was itself a commentary on the nature of American society. Hickok and other gunmen embodied a paradox in the American self-image in the Cold War years, the sense of being both "supremely powerful and utterly vulnerable, politically dominant and yet helpless to shape the course of crucial events." The seminal film in the genre, according to Slotkin, was *The Gunfighter* (1950), in which the gunman, played by Gregory Peck, was both dangerous and heroic, a constant theme in biographies. "The image of the gunfighter as a professional of violence, for whom formalized killing was a calling and even an art, is an invention of movies like *The Gunfighter*, the reflection of Cold War–era ideas about professionalism and violence and not of the mores of the Old West."[36]

The film was inspired in part by Eugene Cunningham's *Triggernometry: A Gallery of Gunfighters* (1934), a collection of biographies of people, including Hickok, noted for skill with guns. Like boxing, gunfighting was a technical art, with rules. Like the boxer, the gunfighter could gain a reputation by defeating a better-known adversary and move up in the rankings. A subtitle to the book says it best: "With Technical Notes on Leather Slapping as a Fine Art, Gathered from Many a Loose Holstered Expert over the Years." Cunningham made no excuses or apologies for Hickok, stating without qualification that "[h]e was a killer" and asserting that in the McCanles shootout Hickok was guilty of murder. Embodying the paradox, Cunningham was an admirer. His chapter on Hickok is titled "The Magnificent." The author dissected the various versions of the McCanles shootout and decided a lot of hokum went into both sides' interpretation of events. The Hickok faction made its evidence "too good," and all of it could be interpreted to support the McCanles faction. For example, the detail about Hickok being behind a curtain was improbable because McCanles probably was armed and could have shot Hickok then, rather than demanding he come out from behind the curtain. Cunningham found that the Tutt killing was a justifiable one and did not involve any quick-draw artistry. Nevertheless, his book was dedicated to this dark "art," and he managed to repeat a few of the myths himself, such as the "dead man's hand." The final chapter was a study in techniques, as it detailed the technical and artistic aspects of such things as "the spin," "fanning," the "border shift," "rolls," and "pinwheeling," complete with illustrations. Any recognition of gunfighting as a skill, profession, or ritual must acknowledge Hickok, if not solely for his killing talent then at least for making it a spectacle.[37]

In *The Western Hero in History and Legend* (1965), Kent Ladd Steckmesser explored the Western hero mythology and reality, studying not only the differences but also how legend, fabrication, and history are symbiotic. Popular demand and repetition turn tall tales into history. In addition to Hickok, Steckmesser analyzed the hero via Custer and others. Their paths to national legend could hardly be more diverse, other than their living in a common era. Wild Bill ultimately became the "idealized gunfighter" of the Wild West as legend filled the vacuum when there was a lack of evidence, usually the case with Hickok.[38]

Steckmesser understood and charted the outsize role of journalists in building the Hickok celebrity. Dealing at length with the press was the foundation for a strong analysis of the historical sources and inconsistencies in various Hickok stories. In his autobiography, John Wesley Hardin remembered his 1871 confrontation with Hickok in Abilene as an occasion when Hickok backed down. There was no evidence for such a thing. Instead, it appeared that Hickok cooled the event with diplomacy, not bullets, and "arranged a truce with the untamed youngster" over a bottle of champagne. Such a peaceful resolution did not fit the legend, but it did fit the historical evidence, including the press reports.[39]

The Civil War loomed larger in Steckmesser's account than in many other Hickok histories and biographies. Integrating the war into a larger history of the West made the region more than a collection of dirt-street cow towns that littered the grasslands, a common image in popular entertainment, which cannot be burdened with historical or narrative complexity. When other biographers erred, Steckmesser went gunning for their flaws, which often fed the legend's narrative. Among the writers he excoriated was Buel, a journalist who knew what his audience wanted and must have absorbed the Nichols story and other sensational accounts of Hickok's life. Buel just added some anecdotes and wrote the book to fit the literary tastes of the era.[40]

Some of the anecdotes—without evidence—that Steckmesser cited included Hickok's dispensing with a dozen would-be lynchers in Independence, Missouri, gunning down an entire regiment as a Civil War sharpshooter, and slaying an Indian chief in a knife duel. There was no credible evidence for any of the feats. In another "preposterous tale accepted by most biographers," Hickok supposedly killed four rowdy cowboys in Jefferson County, Nebraska, in 1867. The evidence was Buel's statement that he consulted eyewitnesses. Steckmesser's assessment of Hickok's shooting skills was balanced, realistic, and not near-miraculous. There were credible reports of great accuracy, but Steckmesser gave more weight to fast reflexes and "readiness to kill." Steckmesser also administered a methodological caning to Wilstach, O'Connor, and Connelley.[41]

Another good volume on the West that includes Hickok was written by David Hamilton Murdoch. *The American West: The Invention of a Myth* insightfully mined the region's mythology and its place in the American imagination. He, too, credited journalists and dime novelists with creating the Wild Bill mythology. Because the United States was a "nation of change"—as declared by Cooper, who created the first Western hero—myth had to be constantly adapted to the ever-emerging culture. That, Murdoch believed, was why popular media were the creators of the Western myth.[42]

Murdoch put Hickok in the context of the larger West. He pointed out that the region was as much a place of the imagination as it was of history. In spite of the explosive growth after the Civil War, 87 percent of Americans still lived east of the Mississippi River in 1900. "Yet, the 'frontier heritage' has the status of an axiom of nationality." The frontier most Americans envisioned was not the one of Appalachian forests or Southern lowlands but the Great Plains and mountainous far West. The image was one of cowboys, wagon trains, and hostile Sioux and Apache. The characters that came to mind were not so much Boone or Crockett but Cody, James, Hickok, and Earp, among others. Murdoch called Buel's biography an "incredible farrago of nonsense [that] combined all the existing tales about Hickok with a series of wonderful inventions to illustrate his daring, courage and superhuman skill as a gunman."[43]

Murdoch also thought that Owen Wister invented the ritual main-street gunfight and that the closest thing in reality was the Hickok-Tutt walkdown, which became an attribute of heroism in national mythic narratives of Western heroes. For Murdoch, it was the act of a street thug. Maybe that was the enlightenment that the British scholar brought to Western history, a perspective less enamored of national myth and the cult of the frontier. Murdoch admitted to being captivated from an early age by Western movies. No admirer of Hickok, Murdoch noted caustically that the legend of cowboys and the West actually became bound up in national myth and that, "as for badmen, Wild Bill Hickok rated a reverential entry in *Encyclopedia Americana*."[44]

Murdoch contrasted Western myth and history, which were frequently at odds. The myth resided in the broader culture—generated in the nineteenth-century press and perpetuated in twentieth-century film and television—as well as Hickok biographies. Murdoch tied myth to nostalgia, especially at the hand of Theodore Roosevelt, Wister, and Frederic Remington. These three "convinced a majority of the nation that qualities which could save America were to be found on the last, vanishing frontier." According to Roosevelt, the "West contained a different breed of men: The men of the border reckon upon stern and unending struggles with their iron-bound sur-roundings; against the grim harshness of their existence they set the strength and abounding vitality that come with it. They run risks to life and limb that are unknown to the dwellers in cities. . . ." It sounds like the beginning of a Western pulp fiction novel. Remington saw the West as theater and heroism, "an existential world of tragedy and violence that resembled the literary world of Ernest Hemingway with its descriptions of bullfighters and tough-guy killers waiting for the end. It was a bleak world of cultural entropy," according to historian William Goetzmann. Remington did not record facts but events that the public wanted to see. As a mythmaker, he complemented Roosevelt in this role.[45]

Bad Boys of the Black Hills . . . and Some Wild Women, Too (2008), a largely undocumented volume of popular history by Barbara Fifer, is illustrative of any number of volumes that are not devoted to Hickok but included him out of necessity; it featured notable lawmen, gunmen extraordinaire, histories of violence and bloodshed in America, and the mythic West. Fifer included Custer, Sam Bass, Harry Longabaugh (the "Sundance Kid"), the Wild Bunch, Cody, Earp, Calamity Jane, and a number of other celebrities who came through Deadwood and the Black Hills. Fifer, too, was skeptical of the tall tales that attributed an outlandish number of killings to Hickok, noting that ten deaths could be confirmed; that he was a good shot whose ability was a matter of practice, not divine intervention; and that the truth about the McCanles gunfight was uncertain and undocumented as to whether it was "cowardly murder or Hickok defending himself and others in the station, including women." She condemned a history of killing, drinking, gambling, and frequenting brothels as she compiled Deadwood's infamous resume.[46]

Fifer attributed to Rosa's biography the dead man's hand, but *Wild Bill Hickok: The Man and His Myth* actually acknowledged the uncertainty of the aces-and-eights fable. Fifer only noted that debate surrounded the fifth card in the hand, not the aces and eights. Her assessment of Hickok was tough, fair, and concise: "Hickok lived as a law-and-order man who broke the law when he saw fit." The volume merits credit for understanding Hickok's time, place, and cohort.[47]

Biographies of Wild Bill and the histories of the West illustrate most vividly that the West and Hickok are much more than the myth. The legends persist, sometimes in revisionist guise, sometimes in the usual heroic formulas, which are useful—then and now—to the drivers of popular culture. The fact/myth divide is both artificial and highly complex. Hickok might now be an exhausted symbol, detached from any great themes. The earlier movie and television interpretations tended to be somewhat simple. As for those writing history, the public may be uncertain as to who can be called a historian—a journalist who writes popular (maybe footnoted) histories; the historian of public institutions, such as universities with their strict codes of scholarship; or the memoirist, who may compile personal, family, or community recollections. David W. Blight said that historians are the "custodians of the past. . . . History is what trained historians do. . . . Memory is often owned, history interpreted." Blight acknowledged that public history, the remembered past, must be engaged, however. Indeed it must, because although history, biography, and fiction are delineated neatly in citations and library shelves, the public imagination, and therefore public memory, is capacious. That kind of memory overwhelms history and often becomes fuel for myth.[48]

Three broad categories are employed here in discussing Hickok history: "wild tales," "Wild West," and "Wild Bill," the latter being the group truest to the label "biography." Although this is a taxonomy of convenience, most books, chapters, or articles about Hickok fit easily into one of the groups, from near-outright fiction to documented scholarship. The earliest biographies are exemplars of the wild tales, some only a step removed from dime novels. Buel and Connelley stand out. The Wild Bill designation is for genuine biographies, such as Rosa's, that are more critical, factual accounts of the gunslinger's life, separating myth and reality. The Wild West writers, such as Richard Etulain, put Hickok in that broader context, usually assessing his place in the region's history. They provide an important extra dimension, beyond just Hickok's story, in attempting to understand his life, legend, and place in cultural values and myth.

The taxonomy illustrates, too, why Hickok or the stories about him slip so easily into various media platforms. The Tutt walkdown is a great news story, which segues well into Nichols's and Stanley's quasi-journalistic exaggerations of reality, then to dime novels, and ultimately to longer narrative and cinematic drama. Although the gray areas between categories are expansive, they still lend understanding to Hickok the individual (Wild Bill), Hickok as prototype in a time and place (Wild West, Civil War), and the gunman as an entertaining, dramatic story (wild tales). Many Hickok histories and biographies explore a character of no intrinsic consequence, but a monumental figure in Western mythology. He may well have been the genesis of a critical part of thousands of story lines about the West, in which shootouts have become not just a mainstay but also an expectation.

Notes

Bibliography

Index

Notes

Introduction

1. For more on Sherman, see Matthew Carr, *Sherman's Ghosts: Soldiers, Civilians, and the American Way of War* (New York: New Press, 2015), 158, 209, 288. See also Edward Caudill and Paul Ashdown, *Sherman's March in Myth and Memory* (Lanham, MD: Rowman and Littlefield, 2008); *The Myth of Nathan Bedford Forrest* (Lanham, MD: Rowman and Littlefield, 2005); *The Mosby Myth: A Confederate Hero in Life and Legend* (Wilmington, DE: Scholarly Resources Inc., 2002); *Inventing Custer: The Making of an American Legend* (Lanham, MD: Rowman and Littlefield, 2015).

2. Durwood Ball, "Liberty, Empire, and Civil War in the American West," in *Empire and Liberty: The Civil War and the West*, ed. Virginia Scharff (Oakland: University of California Press, 2015), 68.

3. See, for example, Alvin M. Josephy Jr., *The Civil War in the American West* (New York: Alfred A. Knopf, 1991); Elliott West, *The Last Indian War: The Nez Perce Story* (New York: Oxford University Press, 2009); Richard Maxwell Brown, *No Duty to Retreat: Violence and Values in American History and Society* (New York: Oxford University Press, 1991), 44; William Pencak, "The American Civil War Did Not Take Place: With Apologies to Baudrillard," *Rethinking History* 6, no. 2 (2002): 217–21; Heather Cox Richardson, *West from Appomattox: The Reconstruction of America After the Civil War* (New Haven, CT: Yale University Press, 2007); Richard White, *"It's Your Misfortune and None of My Own": A New History of the American West* (Norman: University of Oklahoma Press, 1991); Patricia Limerick, *The Legacy of Conquest: The Unbroken Past of the American West* (New York: Norton, 1987); Stacey L. Smith, *Freedom's Frontier: California and the Struggle over Unfree Labor, Emancipation, and Reconstruction* (Chapel Hill: University of North Carolina Press, 2013); Stacey L. Smith, "Beyond North and South: Putting the West in the Civil War Era and Reconstruction," *Journal of the Civil War Era* 6, no. 4 (December 2016): 566–91.

4. Maurice Halbwachs, *The Collective Memory* (New York: Harper & Row, 1980); Pierre Nora, *Realms of Memory: Rethinking the French Past* (New York: Columbia University Press, 1996); Edward A Pollard, *The Lost Cause:*

A New Southern History of the War of the Confederates (New York: E. B. Treat & Co., 1866), iii; Robert Penn Warren, *The Legacy of the Civil War* (New York: Random House, 1961); David W. Blight, *Race and Reunion: The Civil War and American Memory* (Cambridge, MA: Harvard University Press, 2001); Caroline E. Janney, *Remembering the Civil War: Reunion and the Limits of Reconciliation* (Chapel Hill: University of North Carolina Press, 2013); Michael G. Kammen, *Mystic Chords of Memory: The Transformation of Tradition in American Culture* (New York: Alfred A. Knopf, 1991); Alice Fahs and Joan Waugh, *The Memory of the Civil War in American Culture* (Chapel Hill: University of North Carolina Press, 2005); Robert J. Cook, *Civil War Memories: Contesting the Past in the United States since 1865* (Baltimore, MD: Johns Hopkins University Press, 2017); Ari Kelman, *A Misplaced Massacre: Struggling Over the Memory of Sand Creek* (Cambridge, MA: Harvard University Press, 2013). For an overview of Civil War memory studies, see Stuart McConnell, "The Civil War and Historical Memory: A Historiographical Survey," *OAH Magazine of History* 8, no. 1, The Civil War (Fall 1993): 3–6; Matthew J. Grow, "The Shadow of the Civil War: A Historiography of Civil War Memory," *American Nineteenth Century History* 4, no. 2 (Summer 2003): 77–103.

5. See David W. Blight, "Historians and 'Memory,'" *Common-Place: The Interactive Journal of Early American Life* 2, no. 3 (April 2002): http://www.common-place-archives.org/vol-02/no-03/author/ (accessed May 25, 2019).

6. Matthew Christopher Hulbert, *The Ghosts of Guerrilla Memory: How Civil War Bushwhackers Became Gunslingers in the American West* (Athens: University of Georgia Press, 2016), 183.

7. Janice Hume, "Memory Matters: The Evolution of Scholarship in Collective Memory and Mass Communication," *Review of Communication* 10, no. 3 (2010): 181–98. See also Jill A. Edy, "Journalistic Uses of Collective Memory," *Journal of Communication* 49, no. 2 (June 2006): 71–87.

8. D. W. Pasulka, *American Cosmic: UFOs, Religion, Technology* (New York: Oxford University Press, 2019), 140; Roland Barthes, *Mythologies*, trans. Annette Lavers (London: Jonathan Cape, 1972); Marshall McLuhan, "Myth and Mass Media," *Daedalus* 88 (1959): 339–48. See Gaye Tuchman, "Myth and the Consciousness Industry," in *Mass Media and Social Change*, ed. Elihu Katz and Tamas Szecsko (Beverly Hills, CA: Sage, 1981), 90; Jack Lule, *Daily News, Eternal Stories: The Mythological Role of Journalism* (New York: Guilford Press, 2001).

9. Kent Ladd Steckmesser, *The Western Hero in History and Legend* (Norman: University of Oklahoma Press, 1965), 105.

10. Jenni Calder, *There Must Be a Lone Ranger: The American West in Film and Reality* (1974; New York: McGraw-Hill, 1977), 107.

11. See, for example, Paul G. Ashdown, "From Public Intellectuals to Technointellectuals: Gunslingers on the Cyberspace Frontier," *Soundings: An Interdisciplinary Journal* 82, nos. 1–2 (Spring/Summer 1999): 205–18; Alfred C. Yen, "Western Frontier or Feudal Society? Metaphors and Perceptions of Cyberspace," *Berkeley Technology Law Journal* 17 (2003): 1208, 1223.

12. Bob Thompson, *Born on a Mountaintop: On the Road with Davy Crockett and the Ghosts of the Wild Frontier* (New York: Crown, 2012), 52, 136–37; Robert Morgan, *Lions of the West: Heroes and Villains of the Westward Expansion* (Chapel Hill, NC: Algonquin, 2011), xxii; James Donovan, *The Blood of Heroes* (New York: Little, Brown and Co., 2012), 153; William C. Davis, *Three Roads to the Alamo: The Lives and Fortunes of David Crockett, James Bowie, and William Barret Travis* (New York: HarperCollins, 1998), 183–84.

13. Michael Crawford, "Action Figures," in *The Mythical West: An Encyclopedia of Legend, Lore, and Popular Culture*, ed. Richard W. Slatta (Santa Barbara, CA: ABC CLIO, 2001), 1–6.

14. Wallace Stegner, *The American West as Living Space* (Ann Arbor: University of Michigan Press, 1987), 65–75, esp. 65. Stegner discusses the "west of make believe," where this Western culture and character is easiest to identify. On aridity as the defining characteristic of the West, see part 1, "Living Dry."

15. Christopher Knowlton, "How Wild Was Wild Bill Hickok?" *New York Times*, February 14, 2019.

16. Joseph G. Rosa, *They Called Him Wild Bill: The Life and Adventures of James Butler Hickok* (1964; Norman: University of Oklahoma Press, 1974). Rosa's intention is quoted on the back cover of the book. Rosa's papers are held by the Kansas Historical Society in Topeka.

17. E. M. Forster, *Aspects of the Novel* (1927; New York: Harcourt, Brace and World, 1955), 27.

18. Camille Dautrich, "Ozarks Artist, Who Painted 'The Republican Club,' Working with History Museum," Springfield *News-Leader*, November 21, 2018.

1. Strange Ripples

1. Rosa, *They Called Him Wild Bill*, 9–13.

2. Benson Bobrick, *Testament: A Soldier's Story of the Civil War* (New York: Simon and Schuster, 2003), 16; Paul Angle and Richard L. Beyer, *Handbook of Illinois History* (Springfield: Illinois State Historical Society, 1943),

29; Orville Vernon Burton, *The Age of Lincoln* (New York: Hill and Wang, 2007), 104; Chris Brusatte, "Lincoln's Visits to La Salle County," La Salle County Historical Society, Ottawa, Illinois, *Times*, August 16, 2008, http://www.mywebtimes.com/life/lincoln-s-visits-to-lasalle-county/article _66dc7ed9–7ca6–5d95–81fb-3867634a4868.html (accessed May 29, 2017).

3. Owen W. Muelder, *The Underground Railroad in Western Illinois* (Jefferson, NC: McFarland, 2008), 12–13, 33; Rosa, *They Called Him Wild Bill*, 14–15; Charles L. Blockson, *The Underground Railroad* (New York: Prentice Hall Press, 1987), 202.

4. William E. Connelley, *Wild Bill and His Era* (New York: The Press of the Pioneers, 1933), 13; Richard O'Connor, *Wild Bill Hickok* (Garden City, NY: Doubleday, 1959), 35. Rosa, *They Called Him Wild Bill*, 13; Joseph G. Rosa, *The Gunfighter: Man or Myth?* (Norman: University of Oklahoma Press, 1969), 167, 171, 178.

5. Rosa, *They Called Him Wild Bill*, 17–20; Robert D. Kaplan, *An Empire Wilderness: Travels into America's Future* (New York: Random House, 1998), 5. Kenneth M. Stampp, *America in 1857: A Nation on the Brink* (New York: Oxford University Press, 1990), 144–46.

6. Rosa, *They Called Him Wild Bill*, 23, 27–33; Slatta, *Mythical West*, 280–82; Fred Reinfeld, *Pony Express* (1966; Lincoln: University of Nebraska Press, 1973).

7. Connelley, *Wild Bill and His Era*, 29–30.

8. J. W. Buel, *Life and Marvelous Adventures of Wild Bill, the Scout* (Chicago: Belford, Clarke and Co., 1880), 13; Rosa, *They Called Him Wild Bill*, 42–52; James D. McLaird, *Wild Bill Hickok and Calamity Jane* (Pierre: South Dakota State Historical Society Press, 2008), 9–12. Western historian Ramon F. Adams had no doubt about Hickok's role in the affair. "We now know that Wild Bill murdered three men in cold blood. . . . There was no fight because the three men Bill killed were not armed." But that hardly settles the matter. Ramon F. Adams, *Burs under the Saddle: A Second Look at Books and Histories of the West* (Norman: University of Oklahoma Press, 1964), 86–87; O'Connor, *Wild Bill Hickok*, 17, 27.

9. Edward Knight, *Wild Bill Hickok: The Contemporary Portrait of a Civil War Hero* (Franklin, NH: Hillside Press, 1959), 29–30.

10. David J. Eicher, *The Longest Night: A Military History of the Civil War* (New York: Simon and Schuster, 2002), 102–7; Rosa, *They Called Him Wild Bill*, 53.

11. Rosa, *They Called Him Wild Bill*, 53–56; "The Truth about Wild Bill," *Topeka Mail and Breeze*, December 20, 1901, quoted in Rosa, *They Called Him Wild Bill*, 54. Connelley, *Wild Bill and His Era*, 44–45; Connelley places this

incident in 1861, while Rosa, quoting a recollection by George W. Hance, puts it in 1862. O'Connor, channeling Connelley, places it in 1861, adding the dubious detail that the crowd in Independence melted away because they had heard that Hickok singlehandedly wiped out the McCanles "gang." O'Connor, *Wild Bill Hickok*, 59–60.

12. Connelley, *Wild Bill and His Era*, 51–66; Eicher, *Longest Night*, 185–93; Rosa, *They Called Him Wild Bill*, 58–60. Buel, *Life*, 20; Adams, *Burs under the Saddle*, 84.

13. Rosa, *They Called Him Wild Bill*, 64–65; Connelley, *Wild Bill and His Era*, 79; Eicher, *Longest Night*, 756.

14. Rosa, *They Called Him Wild Bill*, 69–70.

15. O'Connor, *Wild Bill Hickok*, 80; Rosa, *They Called Him Wild Bill*, 89. W. F. Cody, *An Autobiography of Buffalo Bill* (New York: Cosmopolitan Book Corp., 1920), 54.

16. Joseph G. Rosa, *Wild Bill Hickok, Gunfighter: An Account of Hickok's Gunfights* (Norman: University of Oklahoma Press, 2001), 86–90; Joseph G. Rosa, *Wild Bill Hickok: The Man and His Myth* (Lawrence: University Press of Kansas, 1996). The Nichols article is reproduced as an appendix, 214–40. The distance estimated by Nichols is on page 222. Rosa, *They Called Him Wild Bill*, 74–77. Some sources say the trial judge was Sempronius Hamilton Boyd. Rosa here appeared to make an error, citing the distance as fifty paces rather than the fifteen paces cited in the Nichols article. Steven Lubet, "Slap Leather! Legal Culture, Wild Bill Hickok, and the Gunslinger Myth," *Insights on Law and Society* 2, no. 2 (Winter 2002): 7–18.

17. Rosa, *They Called Him Wild Bill*, 72–81; Springfield, Missouri, *Weekly Patriot*, August 10, 1865.

18. Rosa, *They Called Him Wild Bill*, 86–93.

19. Sgt. Gilbert H. Bates walked from Vicksburg, Mississippi, to Washington, DC, in 1888, bearing an American flag to prove Nichols's point. He was generally well received, especially in the cities. Bates also carried the flag in *Buffalo Bill's Wild West* shows. Sherman visited Georgia in 1879. See Caudill and Ashdown, *Sherman's March*, 151–54; Rosa, *Wild Bill Hickok: The Man and His Myth*, 218–19; Thomas M. Spencer, ed., *The Other Missouri History: Populist, Prostitutes, and Regular Folk* (Columbia: University of Missouri Press, 2004), 46; Connie Sue Yen, "Horse-Stealing and Man-Hanging: An Examination of Vigilantism in the Missouri Ozarks" (master's thesis, Missouri State University, Summer 2015), 48–51, 65; Richard Maxwell Brown, *Strain of Violence: Historical Studies of American Violence and Vigilantism* (New York: Oxford University Press, 1975), 110; Jonathan Fairbanks and

Clyde Edwin Tuck, *Past and Present of Greene Country, Missouri* (Indianapolis: A. W. Bowen and Co., 1915), 226, quoted in Yen, "Horse-Stealing and Man-Hanging," 64.

20. Richardson, *West from Appomattox*, 221–22.

21. McLaird, *Wild Bill Hickok and Calamity Jane*, 34; Junction City, Kansas, *Weekly Union*, July 23, 1870, cited in Nyle H. Miller and Joseph W. Snell, *Why the West Was Wild: A Contemporary Look at the Antics of Some Highly Publicized Kansas City Cowtown Personalities* (Topeka: Kansas State Historical Society, 1963; repr., Norman: University of Oklahoma Press, 2003), 198.

22. Rosa, *They Called Him Wild Bill*, 135–71, 181; Jean Edward Smith, *Eisenhower in War and Peace* (New York: Random House, 2012), 9–10n; Samuel Eliot Morrison, *The Oxford History of the American People*, vol. 3, *1869–1963* (New York: New American Library, 1965, 1972), 64–69; Walter Prescott Webb, *The Great Plains* (Boston: Ginn and Co., 1931), 223.

23. Detroit, Kansas, *Western News*, February 11, 1870, quoted in Piers Brendon, *Ike: The Life and Times of Dwight D. Eisenhower* (London: Secker and Warburg, 1987), 16–17.

24. Robert Dykstra, "Wild Bill Hickok in Abilene," *Journal of the Central Mississippi Valley American Studies Association* 2, no. 2 (Fall 1961): 33; Brown, *No Duty to Retreat*, 41–43; Allen Barra, *Inventing Wyatt Earp: His Life and Many Legends* (1998; Lincoln: University of Nebraska Press, 2008), 41.

25. Rosa, *The Gunfighter*, 71–75. Rosa, *They Called Him Wild Bill*, 172–206; Christopher Knowlton, *Cattle Kingdom: The Hidden History of the Cowboy West* (Boston: Houghton Mifflin Harcourt, 2017), 50.

26. Rosa, *They Called Him Wild Bill*, 207–21, 243, 250–58; Brendon, *Ike*, 17. Russell Nye, *The Unembarrassed Muse: The Popular Arts in America* (New York: Dial Press, 1970), 148, 206;

27. Rosa, *They Called Him Wild Bill*, 262–65, 277–78; Topeka *Daily Commonwealth*, July 21, 1874; Kansas City *Times*, July 19, 1874; *Rocky Mountain News*, July 31, 1874; McLaird, *Wild Bill Hickok and Calamity Jane*, 43–45; Cheyenne, Wyoming, *Daily News*, December 3, 1874. Utter's sobriquet was spelled "Charlie" or "Charley."

28. New York *Herald*, June 25, 1876, quoted in Marc H. Abrams, *Sioux War Dispatches: Reports from the Field, 1876–1877* (Yardley, PA: Westholme, 2012), 114.

29. McLaird, *Will Bill Hickok and Calamity Jane*, 47–49, 109; Cheyenne, Wyoming, *Daily Leader*, March 15, 1874; *Daily News*, February 19, 1876; Rosa, *They Called Him Wild Bill*, 285–87. Some sources claim Calamity Jane was born in 1852. McLaird explicated the alleged connection between Hickok

and Martha Canary in numerous articles and books. He pointed out in *Wild Bill Hickok and Calamity Jane* that during the time between Hickok's death and Canary's death in 1903, "biographers relating Wild Bill's adventures did not even mention Calamity Jane. In fact, it is difficult to determine when stories linking the two first appeared." Just how Calamity Jane's legend became mixed up with Hickok's is better told by McLaird in the dual biography and in his *Calamity Jane: The Woman and the Legend* (Norman: University of Oklahoma Press, 2005). See also Richard W. Etulain, *The Life and Legends of Calamity Jane* (Norman: University of Oklahoma Press, 2014). For our purposes, there are enough underexplored twists and turns in the media invention of Wild Bill to warrant less attention to Calamity Jane, a character grafted on to Hickok lore primarily in pulp fiction and in the movies. Nevertheless, her name appears in this work more than sixty times.

30. Richardson, *West from Appomattox*, 165–66; John Ames, *The Real Deadwood: True Life Histories of Wild Bill Hickok, Calamity Jane, Outlaw Towns, and Other Characters of the Lawless West* (New York: Chamberlain Brothers, 2004), 6; Watson Parker, *Deadwood: The Golden Years* (Lincoln: University of Nebraska Press, 1981), 3–5, 12; Connelley, *Wild Bill and His Era*, 201, quoting O. W. Coursey, *Wild Bill* (Mitchell, SD: Educational Supply Co., 1924), n.p.; O'Connor, *Wild Bill Hickok*, 255, quotes the same story. Deadwood, Dakota Territory, *Black Hills Daily Pioneer*, July 28, 1886, quoted in McLaird, *Wild Bill Hickok and Calamity Jane*, 49; Rosa, *Wild Bill Hickok, Gunfighter*, 156.

31. Rosa, *They Called Him Wild Bill*, 288–90.

32. Rosa attributes the first publication of this letter to the Virginia City, Nevada, *Evening Chronicle*, August 4, 1877. Rosa, *They Called Him Wild Bill*, 296. It also appears in J. W. Buel's *Heroes of the Plains* (New York, 1882), 210–11; O'Connor, *Wild Bill Hickok*, 256, 268. He quotes the letter, the original of which Rosa says has disappeared. The saloon has various names. See Connelley, *Wild Bill and His Era*, 202–3.

33. Cheyenne *Daily Leader*, August 31, 1876; Rosa, *They Called Him Wild Bill*, 266, 319.

34. O'Connor, *Wild Bill Hickok*, 258–61, 274. Connelley, *Wild Bill and His Era*, 205; Rosa, *They Called Him Wild Bill*, 296–99. Details vary in all the biographies, including spelling of names and times. See Rosa, *Wild Bill Hickok: The Man and His Myth*, 187–213.

35. Rosa, *Wild Bill Hickok*, 200–201; See also Paul L. Hedren, ed., *Ho! For the Black Hills: Captain Jack Crawford Reports the Black Hills Gold Rush and Great Sioux War* (Pierre: South Dakota State Historical Society, 2012).

36. Baldwin, *History of La Salle County, Illinois*, 408.

2. Hickok and the Press

1. David Paul Nord, *Communities of Journalism: A History of American Newspaper and Their Readers* (Urbana: University of Illinois Press, 2001), 228–29.

2. McLaird, *Wild Bill and Calamity Jane*, 26; Rosa, *They Called Him Wild Bill*, 107–8. Nord, *Communities of Journalism*, 141.

3. Rosa, *Wild Bill Hickok: The Man and His Myth*, 50.

4. Chicago *Tribune*, August 5, 1861; Burlington, Iowa, *Weekly Hawk-Eye*, August 24, 1861.

5. Roderick Frazier Nash, *Wilderness and the American Mind*, 4th ed. (New Haven, CT: Yale University Press, 2001), 16, 51, 57.

6. Nord, *Communities of Journalism*, 228–29.

7. George Ward Nichols, *The Story of the Great March from the Diary of a Staff Officer* (New York: Harper and Bros., 1865); Edgar L. McCormick, Edward G. McGehee, and Marty Strahl, eds., *Sherman in Georgia* (Boston: D. C. Heath and Co., 1961, 30); Joseph G. Rosa, "George Ward Nichols and the Legend of Wild Bill Hickok," *Arizona and the West* 19, no. 2 (Summer 1977): 136; Irene M. Patten, "Of Noble Warriors and Maidens Chaste," *American Heritage* 22, no. 3 (April 1971): http://www.americanheritage.com/content/noble-warriors-and-maidens-chaste (accessed October 9, 2017); George Ward Nichols: "The Indian: What to Do with Him," *Harper's New Monthly Magazine* 40 (December 1869–May 1870): 372–79.

8. Nichols, *Story of the Great March*, 119.

9. "New Books: The Story of the Great March," New York *Times*, August 14, 1865, 124.

10. George Ward Nichols, *The Sanctuary: A Story of the Civil War* (New York: Harper and Brothers, 1866); Patten, "Of Noble Warriors."

11. George Ward Nichols, "Wild Bill," *Harper's New Monthly Magazine* 34 (February 1867): 274. Rosa, *Wild Bill Hickok: The Man and His Myth*, 214–40.

12. Rosa, *Wild Bill Hickok: The Man and His Myth*, 40–41, 233–34.

13. Ibid., 26–30; Richard W. Etulain, *Beyond the Missouri: The Story of the American West* (Albuquerque: University of New Mexico Press, 2006), 225; Springfield, Missouri, *Weekly Patriot*, January 31, 1867, quoted in Rosa, *They Called Him Wild Bill*, 37; "Harper's New Monthly Magazine," *American History through Literature 1820–1870*, Encyclopedia.com, http://www.encyclopedia.com (accessed July 9, 2018).

14. Richard Harwell and Philip N. Racine, eds. *The Fiery Trail: A Union Officer's Account of Sherman's Last Campaigns* (Knoxville: University of Tennessee Press, 1986), 153; Rachel Sherman Thorndike, ed., *The Sherman Letters:*

Correspondence between General and Senator Sherman from 1837 to 1891 (New York: Charles Scribner's Sons, 1894), 236. The letter was written June 9, 1864.

15. Rosa, *Wild Bill Hickok: The Man and His Myth*, 215–40.

16. Rosa, *They Called Him Wild Bill*, 4, 203–4; Jane Tompkins, *West of Everything: The Inner Life of Westerns* (New York: Oxford University Press, 1992), 50; Rosa, *Wild Bill Hickok: The Man and His Myth*, 233–37. Joseph Anderson, *I Buried Hickok: The Memoirs of White Eye Anderson*, ed. William B. Secrest (College Station, TX: Creative Pub., 1980).

17. Springfield, Missouri, *Weekly Patriot*, January 31, 1967, quoted by Rosa, *They Called Him Wild Bill*, 82–83.

18. Pamela Haag, *The Gunning of America: Business and the Making of American Gun Culture* (New York: Basic Books, 2016), 187; Rosa, *They Called Him Wild Bill*, 38–39, 106.

19. Chicago *Tribune*, January 31, 1867; Chicago *Tribune*, January 24, 1868; Columbus, Ohio, *Daily Ohio Statesman*, January 31, 1868; New York *Herald*, September 4, 1873; Salina, Kansas, *Saline County Journal*, January 18, 1872; Guildhall, Vermont, *Essex County Herald*, March 29, 1873; Chicago *Tribune*, March 25, 1872.

20. Haag, *Gunning of America*, 193; Frank Luther Mott, *A History of American Magazines*, vol. 2: *1860–1865* (Cambridge, MA: Belknap Press of Harvard University Press, 1957), 385–87, 390, 395–96, 405.

21. Rosa, *They Called Him Wild Bill*, 107–10; St. Louis, Missouri, *Weekly Democrat*, April 16, May 21, 1867; Steckmesser, *Western Hero*, 124; Rosa, *Wild Bill Hickok: The Man and His Myth*, 28, 51, 85, 100.

22. See John Bierman, *Dark Safari: The Life behind the Legend of Henry Morton Stanley* (Austin: University of Texas Press, 1993); Rosa, *Wild Bill Hickok: The Man and His Myth*, 100–101.

23. Jeff Guinn, *The Last Gunfight: The Real Story of the Shootout at the O.K. Corral—And How It Changed the American West* (New York: Simon and Schuster, 2011), 18–19.

24. Clarksville, Tennessee, *Chronicle*, September 16, 1871.

25. Atlanta *Constitution*, April 19, 1896.

26. Rosa, in *They Called Him Wild Bill*, cites court records, not press accounts, of 1865. A search of the Proquest newspaper database turned up no articles from July 21, 1865, to September 31, 1865, about the Tutt shooting; Chicago *Daily Tribune*, May 21, 1944.

27. Kansas City, Missouri, *Daily Journal of Commerce*, August 25, 1869, quoted in Rosa, *They Called Him Wild Bill*, 144; Leavenworth, Kansas,

Daily Commercial, October 3, 1869; quoted in Rosa, *They Called Him Wild Bill*, 148.

28. New York *Weekly*, December 23, 1869; Chicago *Daily Tribune*, December 15, 1869; Charleston, South Carolina, *Daily News*, December 15, 1869; Philadelphia *Evening Telegraph*, December 14, 1869; Richmond, Indiana, *Palladium*, December 21, 1869; Christine Bold, *Selling the Wild West: Popular Western Fiction, 1860 to 1960* (Bloomington: Indiana University Press, 1987), 11–12; Joy S. Kasson, *Buffalo Bill's Wild West: Celebrity, Memory, and Popular History* (New York: Hill and Wang, 2000), 20; David Hamilton Murdoch, *The American West: The Invention of a Myth* (Reno: University of Nevada Press, 2001), 38.

29. Leavenworth, Kansas, *Weekly Times*, October 12, 1871; White Cloud, Kansas, *Chief*, November 30, 1871, citing the Topeka, Kansas, *Commonwealth*; Ottawa, Illinois, *Free Trader*, December 2, 1871, citing the Chattanooga *Times*.

30. Delaware, Ohio, *Gazette*, November 12, 1869.

31. The Troy, Kansas, *Weekly Kansas Chief*, April 3, 1873; Independence, Iowa, *Buchanan County Bulletin*, May 17, 1872; Emporia, Kansas, *News*, May 16, 1873; Lancaster, Ohio, *Gazette*, November 18, 1869.

32. Jeffry D. Wert, *Custer: The Controversial Life of George Armstrong Custer* (New York: Simon and Schuster, 1996), 296.

33. George A. Custer, *My Life on the Plains* (1874; Lincoln: University of Nebraska Press, 1966), 68–71.

34. Elizabeth Bacon Custer, *Following the Guidon* (New York: Harper and Brothers, 1890), 161–62.

35. Goldhill, Nevada Territory, *Daily Times*, March 26, 1873; White Cloud, Kansas, *Chief*, March 20, 1873; Omaha, Nebraska, *Daily Bee*, July 20, 1873.

36. Richmond, Virginia, *Palladium*, March 22, 1873; Clarksville, Tennessee, *Weekly Chronicle*, March 29, 1873; Troy, Kansas, *Weekly Kansas Chief*, March 6, 1873; Lexington, Missouri, *Weekly Caucasian*, March 15, 1873; Guinn, *Last Gunfight*, 304–5, 308.

37. Rosa, *Wild Bill Hickok: The Man and His Myth*, 202; Deadwood *Black Hills Pioneer*, August 10, 1876, quoted in Rosa, *Wild Bill Hickok: The Man and His Myth*, 194; Dessem, Matthew, Slate.com, "Reading Deadwood's Newspaper: Here's How the Black Hills Pioneer Reported on Major Event in the HBO Series," June 2, 2019, accessed June 3, 2019.

38. Rosa, *Wild Bill Hickok: The Man and His Myth*, 10, 202, 203; Deadwood, *Black Hills Pioneer*, August 10, 1876, quoted in Rosa, *Wild Bill Hickok: The Man and His Myth*, 194.

39. Chicago *Daily Tribune*, August 25, 1876.

40. St. Louis *Post-Dispatch*, August 16, 1876.
41. Hays City, Kansas, *Ellis County Star*, August 17, 1876; Rosa, *Wild Bill Hickok: The Man and His Myth*, 202; Red Cloud, Kansas, *Chief*, September 7, 1876.
42. Boston *Daily Globe*, August 24, 1876; New York *Sun*, August 20, 1876.
43. The Kansas City, Missouri, *Times* account used here ran in the Memphis *Daily Appeal*, August 20, 1876; Milan, Tennessee, *Exchange*, August 24, 1876; and Jefferson City, Missouri, *State Journal*, August 18, 1876.
44. Plymouth, Indiana, *Marshall County Republic*, August 24, 1876, from the Denver *News*; the Chicago *Daily Tribune*, August 13, 1876; Paw, Michigan, *True Northerner*, September 15, 1876.
45. Bozeman, Montana, *Avant Courier*, September 1, 1876.
46. Such reports ran in many newspapers. Examples include: Barton, Vermont, *Orleans County Monitor*, August 21, 1876; Wheeling, West Virginia, *Daily Intelligencer*, August 14, 1876; Iola, Kansas, *Register*, August 19, 1876; Memphis *Daily Appeal*, August 13, 1876; Emporia, Kansas, *News*, August 25, 1876; Painesville, Ohio, *Northern Ohio Journal*, August 19, 1876; Chicago *Daily Tribune*, August 13, 1876.
47. Chicago *Daily Tribune*, August 25, 1876: Las Vegas *Gazette*, August 19, 1876; Abbeville, South Carolina, *Press and Banner*, October 4, 1876.
48. Cited in Rosa, *Wild Bill Hickok: The Man and His Myth*, 195. Jacks and Eights evidently was an earlier tradition designating an unlucky hand. It was easy to swap some cards and tailor the legend to fit Hickok or any ill-fated gambler.

3. Dime Novels

1. Clay Reynolds, "Introduction," in Ned Buntline, *The Hero of a Hundred Fights: Collected Stories from the Dime Novel King, from Buffalo Bill to Wild Bill Hickok*, ed. Clay Reynolds (New York: Sterling Publishing, 2011), xvi, xxxix; Nye, *Unembarrassed Muse*, 289; Daryl Jones, *The Dime Novel Western* (Bowling Green, OH: The Popular Press, 1978), 8.
2. G. K. Chesterton, "A Defense of Penny Dreadfuls," *The Speaker: The Liberal Review*, March 16, 1901.
3. Reynolds, "Introduction," xvi; Merle Curti, *The Growth of American Thought* (New York: Harper and Brothers, 1943), 346.
4. Curti, *Growth of American Thought*, 346–47, 599.
5. Michael Denning, *Mechanic Accents: Dime Novels and Working-Class Culture in America* (New York: Verso, 1987), 10–12; Murdoch, *American West*, 34.
6. Murdoch, *American West*, 52–53.
7. Reynolds, "Introduction," xv, xx; Murdoch, *American West*, 35.

8. Jones, *Dime Novel Western*, 7, 121; Murdoch, *American West*, 35; Rosa, *Gunfighter*, 65; Richard W. Etulain, *Re-imagining the Modern American West* (1966; Tucson: University of Arizona Press, 1996), viii–xxi.

9. Denning, *Mechanic Accents*, 27–30, 45–47; Edmund Pearson, *Dime Novels; Or, Following an Old Trail in Popular Literature* (Washington, NY: Kennikat Press, Inc., 1968), 49; Jay Monaghan, *The Great Rascal: The Life and Adventures of Ned Buntline* (Boston: Little, Brown and Co., 1952), 3.

10. Pearson, *Dime Novels*, 13–14, 46–55, 83; Denning, *Mechanic Accents*, 15; Rosa, *Gunfighter*, 65; Rosa cites, and we have used, Henry Nash Smith, *Virgin Land: The American West as Symbol and Myth* (Cambridge, MA: Harvard University Press, 1950), 123–24; Curti, *Growth of American Thought*, 506.

11. Paul Preston, *Wild Bill, the Indian-Slayer* (New York: Robert M. DeWitt, 1867), 15; Chris Forrest, ed., *Wild Bill's First Trail: As He Told It* (New York: Robert M. DeWitt, 1867), 15. William Osborn Stoddard, *Lincoln's White House Secretary: The Adventurous Life of William O. Stoddard*, ed. Harold Holzer (Carbondale: Southern Illinois University Press, 2007), 11; J. Randolph Cox, *The Dime Novel Companion: A Source Book* (Westport, CT: Greenwood Press, 2000), 251; Rosa, *They Called Him Wild Bill*, 118.

12. On the national culture of violence and its historical background, see Haag, *Gunning of America*; Brown, *No Duty to Retreat*, 52. The titles are from Monaghan, *Great Rascal*, 321–33.

13. Murdoch, *American West*, 93.

14. Murdoch, *American West*, 95, 96; Rosa, *Wild Bill Hickok: The Man and His Myth*, 107, 111, 131; Brown, *No Duty to Retreat*, 59–60; Nye, *Unembarrassed Muse*, 203

15. Albert Johannsen, *The House of Beadle and Adams and Its Dime and Nickel Novels: The Story of a Vanished Literature* (Norman: University of Oklahoma Press, 1950), 2:411. See the bibliography in Rosa, *They Called Him Wild Bill*, 262.

16. Buntline, *Hero of a Hundred Fights*, 365–419; Nye, *Unembarrassed Muse*, 207; Rosa, *They Called Him Wild Bill*, 243.

17. Rosa, *Wild Bill Hickok: The Man and His Myth*, 162–65.

18. Forrest, *Wild Bill's First Trail*, 9–10, 16.

19. Preston, *Wild Bill, the Indian-Slayer*; Buntline, *Wild Bill's Last Trail*, in *Hero of a Hundred Fights*, 361–419.

20. Murdoch, *American West*, 41.

21. Denning, *Mechanic Accents*, 50–51.

22. Nye, *Unembarrassed Muse*, 203.

23. The numbers of articles linking such crimes to dime novels numbered in the thousands in the postbellum press through the early part of the twentieth century. A ProQuest search for newspaper articles with "dime" and "novel" before January 1, 1900, turned up more than thirty-five hundred citations. Most of the articles were only a few paragraphs or less about a specific crime. The articles noted in the text were from: Atlanta *Constitution*, November 17, 1883; July 22, 1882; February 13, 1888; Chicago *Daily Tribune*, September 13, 1899, and August 25, 1879; New York *Times*, December 24, 1893; New York *Tribune*, December 12, 1883; San Francisco *Chronicle*, May 7, 1899.

24. Denning, *Mechanic Accents*, 22–23.

25. Ibid., 19–20, 22, 45–57, 168; Nye, *Unembarrassed Muse*, 206.

26. Nye, *Unembarrassed Muse*, 206, 286–87; Pearson, *Dime Novels*, 105.

27. Denning, *Mechanic Accents*, 22, 24.

28. Ibid., 24; Murdoch, *American West*, 35.

29. Reynolds, "Introduction," ix–x, xii, xviii; Monaghan, *Great Rascal*, 4, 9, 107–8.

30. Murdoch, *American West*, 38–42; Rosa, *Wild Bill Hickok: Gunfighter*, 197; Nye, *Unembarrassed Muse*, 207.

31. Reynolds, "Introduction," x, xix.

32. Stuart Lake, *Wyatt Earp: Frontier Marshal* (New York: Houghton Mifflin Co., 1931); Reynolds, "Introduction," xxi, xxv, 363; scc Monaghan, *Great Rascal*, 321–33, for a bibliography of Judson's work. The version in Buntline is from "The Nugget Library," Street and Smith, 1890, a reprint of the original from Street and Smith's New York *Weekly* (1880); Monaghan, *Great Rascal*, 75–77.

33. Johannsen, *House of Beadle and Adams*, 2:301–2.

34. Ibid., 2:156–57; Rosa, *They Called Him Wild Bill*, 61–62.

35. Robert W. Rydell and Rob Kroes, *Buffalo Bill in Bologna: The Americanization of the World, 1869–1922* (Chicago: University of Chicago Press, 2005), 105–11; Frank Christianson, ed., *The Popular Frontier: Buffalo Bill's Wild West and Transnational Mass Culture* (Norman: University of Oklahoma Press, 2017); Monaghan, *Great Rascal*, 6–7; Reynolds, "Introduction," xxi, xxxvii–xxxviii.

36. Monaghan, *Great Rascal*, 18; Reynolds, "Introduction," xxxv–xxxvi, 361–63; Murdoch, *American West*, 38–39.

37. John Plesent Gray, *When All Roads Led to Tombstone: A Memoir*, ed. W. Lane Rogers (Boise, ID: Tamarack Books, 1998), 131–32; "Bill Leonard," in Jay Robert Nash, ed., *Encyclopedia of Western Lawmen and Outlaws* (1992; New York: De Capo Press), 209.

38. Haag, *Gunning of America*, 187–92.

4. A Country in the Mind

1. Tompkins, *West of Everything*, 24. Tompkins took her title from a phrase in the novel *Hondo* by Louis L'Amour.

2. See, for example, Philip Durham, "Ernest Hemingway's Grace under Pressure: The Western Code," *Pacific Historical Review* 45, no. 3 (August 1976): 425–32; Alan Spiegel, *James Agee and the Legend of Himself: A Critical Study* (Columbia: University of Missouri Press, 1998), 89–90; James Agee, *A Death in the Family: A Restoration of the Author's Text*, ed. Michael A. Lofaro, *The Works of James Agee* (Knoxville: University of Tennessee Press, 2007), 1:145; See also "'From Almost as Early as I Can Remember': James Agee and the Civil War," in *Agee Agonistes*, ed. Michael A. Lofaro (Knoxville: University of Tennessee Press, 2007), 105–24; Carrie Adell Strahorn, *Fifteen Thousand Miles by Stage: A Woman's Unique Experience during Thirty Years of Path Finding and Pioneering from the Missouri to the Pacific and from Alaska to Mexico* (New York: G. P. Putnam's Sons, 1911), dedication page and 673, quoted in David M. Wrobel, *Promised Lands: Promotion, Memory, and the Creation of the American West* (Lawrence: University Press of Kansas, 2002), 114; Tompkins, *West of Everything*, 194, 199.

3. Archibald MacLeish, "Sweet Land of Liberty," *Collier's Weekly* (July 8, 1955): 44–57; Kent L. Steckmesser, "Lawmen and Outlaws," in *A Literary History of the American West* (Fort Worth: Texas Christian University Press, 1987), 123.

4. Bill Pronzini, "The Western Pulps," in *Wild West Show!* ed. Thomas W. Knowles and Joe R. Lansdale (New York: Wings Books, 1994), 92–97; Ed Hulse, *The Blood 'n' Thunder Guide to Collecting Pulps* (San Diego, CA: Murania Press, 2009), 137–41; Doug Ellis, John Locke, and John Gunnison, eds., *The Adventure House Guide to the Pulps* (Silver Spring, MD: Adventure House, 2000), 311–12; Alexandra Yancey, "Western Story Magazine," *The Pulp Magazine Project*, https://www.pulpmags.org/content/info/western -story-magazine.html (accessed February 7, 2018).

5. David M. Earle, *All Man! Hemingway, 1950s Men's Magazines, and the Masculine Persona* (Kent, OH: Kent State University Press, 2009), 84–85; Tompkins, *West of Everything*, 66–67.

6. Michael Schudson, *Discovering the News: A Social History of American Newspapers* (New York: Basic Books, 1978), 99; Scott Cupp, "Heaven in Four Colors: The Western in Comics Form," in Knowles and Lansdale, *Wild West Show!* 99–104; Nye, *Unembarrassed Muse*, 216–41.

7. *Wild Bill Hickok, Frontier Fighter* (New York: Avon, 1949).

8. Cupp, "Heaven in Four Colors"; Medio Iorio and Sal Trapani, *Wild Bill Hickok (Classics Illustrated)* (New York: Classics Illustrated Comics, 2017); David Hajdu, *The Ten-Cent Plague: The Great Comic-Book Scare and How It Changed America* (New York: Picador, 2008), 245–87, 326.

9. See "Notes for a Preface," Irwin R. Blacker, ed., *The Old West in Fiction* (New York: Ivan Obolensky, 1961); Andrew E. Mathis, *The King Arthur Myth in Modern American Literature* (W. Jefferson, NC: McFarland, 2001), 95; Curt Gentry "John Steinbeck: 'America's King Arthur Is Coming,'" San Francisco *Chronicle*, November 6, 1960; Steckmesser, *Western Hero*, 140–44.

10. See Harold Bloom, "Introduction: Don Quixote, Sancho Panza, and Miguel de Cervantes Saavedra," in Miguel de Cervantes, *Don Quixote* (New York: HarperCollins, 2003), xxi–xxxv.

11. Deeper comparisons might be made between Hickok and any of his contemporaries, but to what end? Billy the Kid arguably outrivals Hickok in Western lore and mythology. See Stephen Tatum, *Inventing Billy the Kid: Visions of the Outlaw in America: 1881–1981* (Albuquerque: University of New Mexico Press, 1982), and Jon Tuska, *Billy the Kid: His Life and Legend* (Albuquerque: University of New Mexico Press, 1994). Steckmesser notes that there are two Billy the Kids in legend, one a "tough little thug, a coward, a thief, and a cold-blooded murderer. The second is a romantic and sentimental hero, the brave and likable leader of an outnumbered band for justice." At the time of his writing (1965), Steckmesser thought the second characterization was dominant. Neither characterization suggests comparison with Hickok. The Kid had nothing to do with the Civil War, and his first killing occurred a year after Hickok's death. A more useful comparison might be made with the lawman Wyatt Earp, although Steckmesser notes that he was, in contrast to Hickok, a latecomer to gunfighter fame, and dates the origins of his legend to a 1933 biography. Unlike Hickok, Earp was too young for Civil War service (although he once tried to enlist). See Casey Tefertiller, *Wyatt Earp: The Life behind the Legend* (New York: Wiley, 1997); Barra, *Inventing Wyatt Earp*. Steckmesser, *Western Hero*, 57–58, 105, 247. We don't argue that Hickok is sui generis, but we defer to Steckmesser and others who examine the Western hero as a category amenable to such comparisons. What all Western heroes have in common is a wide gap between their life and legend. The media figure has about the same relation to the historical figure that a hologram has to a flesh-and-blood person. But each distortion serves a distinct audience expectation. Our primary interest is in the particular media creation of Wild Bill Hickok, not the generic Western hero or competitors.

12. Steckmesser, "Lawmen and Outlaws," 121, 125–26; Steckmesser, *Western Hero*, 141; Rosa, *Wild Bill Hickok: The Man and His Myth*, 150.

13. Joseph Montague, *Wild Bill: A Western Story* (New York: Chelsea House, 1926), 43; "J. Allan Dunn Dies; Author, Explorer," New York *Times*, March 26, 1941.

14. "John Peere Miles, Newspaper Man, Film Publicist, Cited for World War Record," New York *Times*, April 9, 1943; "Veteran Hollywood Publicity Man Dies," Los Angeles *Times*, April 9, 1943; John Peere Miles, IMDb (Internet Movie Database), http://www.imdb.com/name/nm0587158/bio (accessed February 12, 2018).

15. Steve Frazee, "One Evening in Abilene," in *Rawhiders and Renegades*, ed. Harry E. Maule (New York: Dell, 1960), 187–202, originally published in *The Fall Roundup* (New York: Random House, 1955).

16. Thomas Berger, *Little Big Man* (1964; New York: Dell, 1989); Brooks Landon, "Introduction: The Measure of *Little Big Man*," in Berger, *Little Big Man*, xi–xviii; Bob Herzberg, *Savages and Saints: The Changing Image of American Indians in Westerns* (Jefferson, NC: McFarland, 2008), 246–50; Allen Barra, "*The Little Big Man* Hoax," *True West*, November 4, 2014, https://truewestmagazine.com/the-little-big-man-hoax/ (accessed December 15, 2017); Michael Leigh Sinowitz, "The Western as Postmodern Satiric History: Thomas Berger's *Little Big Man*," *Clio* 28, no. 2 (1999): 129–243.

17. Berger, *Little Big Man*, 282, 288, 306–7.

18. Ibid., 302, 307, 312.

19. Berger, quoted in Barra, "Little Big Man Hoax"; Berger, *Little Big Man*, 303, 949.

20. Richard Sale "Dear Old Dad (Part 1)," *The Athenaeum*, May 22, 2015, http://turcopolier.typepad.com/the_athenaeum/2015/05/the-first-impression-of-my-father-that-i-can-still-vividly-recall-occurred-when-i-was-a-little-boy-living-with-my-sister-and.html (accessed October 24, 2017); "Richard Sale Is Dead; Film Director Was 80," New York *Times*, March 9, 1993.

21. Richard Sale, *The White Buffalo* (1975; New York: Bantam, 1977), 127, 173. Mari Sandoz, *Crazy Horse* (Lincoln: University of Nebraska Press, 1961); Mari Sandoz, *The Buffalo Hunters: The Story of the Hide Men* (New York: Hastings House, 1954). One story Sale takes from O'Connor, who got it from Buel, is that Hickok left Illinois because he thought he had killed a man in a fight. O'Connor, *Wild Bill Hickok*, 38; Rosa, *They Called Him Wild Bill*, 16.

22. Jane Veronica Charles Smith, "White Buffalo," in Slatta, *Mythical West*, 361–65; E. Douglas Branch, *The Hunting of the Buffalo* (Lincoln: University of Nebraska Press, 1962), 51; Kasson, *Buffalo Bill's Wild West*, 233.

23. Sale, *White Buffalo*, 14–17.

24. Ibid., 23, 26, 32–33, 74, 161.

25. Ibid., 50–51, 78–79, 90; Smith, "White Buffalo," 363.

26. Sale, *White Buffalo*, 168, 175, 200.

27. Ibid., 160.

28. Ibid., 169, 200.

29. Jerome Charyn, *Darlin' Bill: A Love Story of the Wild West* (New York: Arbor House, 1980), 75.

30. Charyn, *Darlin' Bill*, 161–62.

31. Ibid., 185.

32. Ibid., 232, 268, 271.

33. Loren D. Estleman, *Aces and Eights* (1981; New York: Tom Doherty, 1998), 179, 213–14; Connelley, *Wild Bill and His Era*, 71; McLaird, *Wild Bill Hickok and Calamity Jane*, 55–56; Rosa, *They Called Him Wild Bill*, 312–37.

34. Ellis E. Conklin, "Pete Dexter Lets It Bleed," Seattle *Weekly News*, October 25, 2011, http://archive.seattleweekly.com/2011–10–26/news/pete -dexter-lets-it-bleed/ (accessed October 13, 2017); Steve Volk, "Paper Man," Philadelphia *Weekly*, March 7, 2007, http://www.philadelphiaweekly.com /news/paper-man/article_900468ed-96a3–5147–9553–187258fd46ad.html (accessed October 13, 2017); Eric Konigsberg, "Write What You Know: Reflections of a Wayward Soul," New York *Times*, October 13, 2009; Glenn Collins, "From Memory to Page, or How Pete Dexter Wrote a Prize Winner," New York *Times*, December 5, 1988.

35. Conklin, "Pete Dexter Lets It Bleed"; Pete Dexter, *Paper Trails: True Stories of Confusion, Mindless Violence, and Forbidden Desires, a Surprising Number of Which Are Not about Marriage* (New York: Ecco/HarperCollins, 2007); John Avlon, Jesse Angelo, and Errol Louis, eds., *Deadline Artists: America's Greatest Newspaper Columns* (New York: Overlook, 2011).

36. Collins, "From Memory to Page." The name of the stage robber was Towle, and the story was that May dug up the head to claim the reward. But this would have happened after the time Hickok was in Deadwood. See Barbara Fifer, *Bad Boys of the Black Hills . . . and Some Wild Women, Too* (Helena, MT: Farcountry Press, 2008), 89–90.

37. Pete Dexter, *Deadwood* (New York: Vintage Books, 1986), 19–20.

38. Buzz Bissinger, "Philadelphia Stories," New York *Times Book Review*, March 4, 2007; Alex Belth, "Bronx Banter Interview: Pete Dexter," *Bronx Banter*, April 30, 2013, http://www.bronxbanterblog.com/2013/04/30/bronx -banter-interview-pete-dexter-2/ (accessed February 19, 2019); Conklin, "Pete Dexter Lets It Bleed."

39. Dexter, *Deadwood*, 68.

40. Ibid., 11, 20.

41. Ibid., 350.

42. Ibid., 136, 351; Dennis Drabelle, "Sex and Six-Guns: How the West Really Was," Washington *Post*, June 1, 1986.

44. Richard Matheson, *The Memoirs of Wild Bill Hickok* (1996; New York: Tom Doherty Associates, 2009), 200, 202; W. Joseph Campbell, *Yellow Journalism: Puncturing the Myths, Defining the Legacies* (Westport, CT: Praeger, 2001), 25–50.

45. His best known works are *I Am Legend*, a 1954 science fiction novel filmed as *The Omega Man* in 1971; the 1961 short story "Nightmare at 20,000 Feet," later adapted for *The Twilight Zone*; and the 1971 short story "Duel," the film version of which became Steven Spielberg's directorial debut.

46. Matheson, *Memoirs*, 6, 210–11.

47. Ibid., 8–9, 15, 72, 133.

48. Ibid., 36, 47.

49. Ibid., 70, 96, 102.

50. John Ames, *The Real Deadwood*, John Edward Ames Website, http://johnedwardames.tripod.com/index.html (accessed November 8, 2017); Judd Cole, *Wild Bill: Dead Man's Hand* (New York: Dorchester Publishing, 1999).

51. Richard Slotkin, *Gunfighter Nation: The Myth of the Frontier in Twentieth-Century America* (New York: HarperPerennial, 1993), 142–51.

52. Judd Cole, *Wild Bill: The Kinkaid County War* (New York: Dorchester Publishing, 1999), 9, 35, 86, 88, 135–36.

53. Judd Cole, *Wild Bill: Bleeding Kansas* (New York: Dorchester Publishing, 1999), 31, 60, 105.

54. Judd Cole, *Wild Bill: Yuma Bustout* (New York: Dorchester Publishing, 2000); Judd Cole, *Wild Bill: Santa Fe Death Trap* (New York: Dorchester Publishing, 2000), 7, 9, 145, 153.

55. Judd Cole, *Wild Bill: Black Hills Hellhole* (New York: Dorchester Publishing, 2000).

56. Judd Cole, *Wild Bill: Point Rider* (New York: Dorchester Publishing, 2001), 16, 23, 129.

57. Judd Cole, *Wild Bill: Gun Law* (New York: Dorchester Publishing, 2001), 167, 171.

58. Cole, *Wild Bill: Black Hills Hellhole*, 107; Cole, *Wild Bill: Santa Fe Death Trap*, 94, 128, 148; Cole, *Wild Bill: Gun Law*, 22, 126–27.

59. Matt Braun, *Hickok & Cody* (New York: St. Martin's, 2001).

60. Bill Brooks, *Law for Hire: Protecting Hickok* (New York: HarperCollins, 2003), 300.

61. Randy Lee Eickhoff, *And Not to Yield: A Novel of the Life and Times of Wild Bill Hickok* (New York: Tom Doherty, 2004).

62. Ibid., 130, 331, 448.

63. Johnny D. Boggs, *East of the Border* (2004; New York: Dorchester Publishing, 2006). See the author's note, 255–59.

64. Erie, Pennsylvania, *Morning Dispatch*, November 15, 1873; Terra Haute, Indiana, *Express*, October 8, 1873; Boggs, *East of the Border*, 211, 249.

65. Max McCoy, *A Breed Apart* (New York: Signet, 2004), 17, 154, 187–88.

66. Ibid., 141.

67. Joe R. Lansdale, *Paradise Sky* (New York: Little, Brown and Co., 2015), 3, 400. Nat Love, *The Life and Adventures of Nat Love* (1907; Lincoln: University of Nebraska Press, 1995). Slatta, *Mythical West*, 119–20; Steven C. Levi, *Deadwood Dick: A Biographical Novel* (Los Angeles: Holloway House, 1988); Harry Thomas, "Nat Love," Documenting the American South, University Library, University of North Carolina, http://docsouth.unc.edu/neh/natlove/summary.html (accessed April 28, 2018).

68. Lansdale, *Paradise Sky*, 198.

69. "Q and A with Joe R. Lansdale, Author of Paradise Sky," *CriminalElement*, September 26, 2017, https://www.criminalelement.com/qaa-with-joe-r-lansdale-author-of-paradise-sky/ (accessed April 30, 2018).

5. Box Office Bill

1. Paul Andrew Hutton, "A Fool's Errand," *True West* 65, no. 2 (February 2018): 32–34; Michael Bellesiles et al., "How the West Got Wild: American Media and Frontier Violence; A Roundtable," *Western Historical Quarterly* 31, no. 3 (Autumn 2000): 277–95. See especially Bellesiles, "Guns Don't Kill, Movies Kill: The Media's Promotion of Frontier Violence," *Western Historical Quarterly* 31, no. 3 (Autumn 2000): 284–90.

2. Buck Rainey, *Western Gunslingers in Fact and on Film: Hollywood's Famous Lawmen and Outlaws* (Jefferson, NC: McFarland, 1998), 177–86.

3. Hutton, "Fool's Errand," 32–33, 35.

4. Frank Jenners Wilstach Papers, New York Public Library, http://archives.nypl.org/mss/3355 (accessed February 12, 2018). Rosa, *Wild Bill Hickok: The Man and His Myth*, 182–83; Jon Tuska, *The American West in Film: Critical Approaches to the Western* (Westport, CT: Greenwood Press, 1985), 176–77; Rainey, *Western Gunslingers*, 186–87.

5. Rainey, *Western Gunslingers*, 188–201; Tuska, *American West in Film*, 177–79.

6. Robert Jay, "W2XBS Schedule, Week of April 21st, 1940," *Television Obscurities*, https://www.tvobscurities.com/2009/07/w2xbs-schedule-week-of-april-21st-1940/ (accessed July 24, 2018); "Notes on Television," New York *Times*, April 21, 1940.

7. Rainey, *Western Gunslingers*, 187–88.

8. Connelley, *Wild Bill and His Era*, 34–35; Nichols, in Rosa, *Wild Bill Hickok: The Man and His Myth*, 233.

9. Alanna Maclean, Canberra, Australia, *Times*, August 17, 2018.

10. "Jersey City Police Surround Movie House; Capture 3 Youths Who Fled Ohio Prison," New York *Times*, May 30, 1947.

11. Bruce Chadwick, *The Reel Civil War: Mythmaking in American Film* (New York: Vintage, 2001), 251.

12. Brian Steel Wills, *Gone with the Glory: The Civil War in Cinema* (Lanham, MD: Rowman and Littlefield, 2011), 84; Tuska, *American West in Film*, 179; Rainey, *Western Gunslingers*, 202–3.

13. Rainey, *Western Gunfighters*, 210–11; *Variety*, January 12, 1956, quoted by Rainey; "Tom Brown Dies at 75," New York *Times*, June 6, 1990.

14. Rosa, *They Called Him Wild Bill*, 165.

15. Tom Stockman, "My Favorite Movies: The One Where Charles Bronson Battles the Giant White Buffalo," *OnStl*, April 24, 2013, http://content.onstl .com/people/ron-stevens/item/541-my-favorite-movies-the-one-where -charles-bronson-battles-the-giant-white-buffalo/ (accessed November 3, 2017).

16. Roger Ebert, "Wild Bill," December 1, 1995, http://www.rogerebert.com /reviews/wild-bill-1995 (accessed October 11, 2017).

17. "Stage: 'Rebel Women,'" New York *Times*, June 4, 1976; "Thomas Babe; Wrote Plays Based on History," Los Angeles *Times*, December 17, 2000; "Thomas Babe, 59, Playwright For Papp's Public Theater," New York *Times*, December 15, 2000; Anne Sarah Rubin, *Through the Heart of Dixie: Sherman's March and American Memory* (Chapel Hill: University of North Carolina Press, 2014), 221–22; Jamie Diamond, "The 'Wild Bill' of History, Here Mostly Made Up," New York *Times*, November 26, 1995.

18. Thomas Babe, *Fathers and Sons* (New York: Dramatists Play Service, 1974), 6, 50; Diamond, "'Wild Bill' of History"; Cheyenne, Wyoming, *Daily Leader*, July 19, 1881; Rosa, *They Called Him Wild Bill*, 240–41.

19. Rosa, *Wild Bill Hickok: The Man and His Myth*, 184; Diamond, "'Wild Bill' of History."

20. Diamond, "'Wild Bill' of History"; Rosa, *Will Bill Hickok: The Man and His Myth*, 184–85.

21. This line from *Wild Bill* is an adaptation of words spoken in *Fathers and Sons* by Pacific Pete Tenison moments before he is shot to death in Carl Mann's saloon. Pete, an eloquent drifter infatuated with the West, says that if Hickok should be killed by McCall, his son's death would follow, and Pete would "miss the company of Wild Bill, his, well, biography delivered in steamy bits, and everytime there's a death out here, far away at the edge of civilization, far from the real Eastern world, we are all lessened. It drags down the morale...." This better suggests the precarious tension holding family, community, region, and myth in balance on the fringes of settlement. Babe, *Fathers and Sons*, 37.

22. Michael Wilmington, "Modernist 'Wild Bill' Is Good, but Misses Greatness," Chicago *Tribune*, December 1, 1995, http://articles.chicagotribune .com/1995-12-01/entertainment/9512010009_1_westerns (accessed October 10, 2017); Babe, *Fathers and Sons*, 50.

23. French, *Westerns*, 166–67.

24. Les D. Jensen, "Gatling Gun," and "Williams Rapid-Fire Gun," in *Historical Times Illustrated Encyclopedia of the Civil War*, ed. Patricia L. Faust (New York: Harper and Row, 1986), 302, 829–30; Herman Hattaway, "Engagement at Westport, Mo.," in Faust, *Historical Times Illustrated Encyclopedia*, 816; David J. Eicher, *The Longest Night: A Military History of the Civil War* (New York: Simon and Schuster, 2002), 754–57.

25. Rosa, *They Called Him Wild Bill*, 185.

26. Ibid., 194; Jay Robert Nash, *Encyclopedia of Western Lawmen and Outlaws* (1992; New York: Da Capo Press, 1994), 83, 301; according to Thompson's biographer, the Texans in town thought Hickok was on the take; William M. Walton, *Life and Adventures of Ben Thompson* (Austin, TX: privately published, 1884), 151, quoted by Steckmesser, *Western Hero*, 118.

27. Rosa, *They Called Him Wild Bill*, 185–88; Joseph Rosa, *The Taming of the West: Age of the Gunfighter* (New York: Smithmark, 1993), 52–53; Nash, *Encyclopedia of Western Lawmen*, 143–50; John Wesley Hardin, *The Life of John Wesley Hardin* (Seguin, TX: Smith and Moore, 1896), 44.

28. Rosa, *They Called Him Wild Bill*, 267–71.

29. Ibid., 8, 338.

6. Fancied Up Rooster

1. Dennis Devine, *Your Friend and Mine, Andy Devine* (Duncan, OK: Bear-Manor Media, 2012), 75–76; William Grimes, "Guy Madison, a Movie Actor and TV's Wild Bill, Dies at 74," New York *Times*, February 8, 1996; Myrna Oliver, "Guy Madison; Star of 'Wild Bill Hickok,'" Los Angeles *Times*, February 7, 1996.

2. J. Fred MacDonald, *One Nation under Television: The Rise and Decline of Network TV* (Chicago: Nelson-Hall, 1994), 126.

3. Rita Parks, *The Western Hero in Film and Television: Mass Media Mythology* (Ann Arbor, MI: UMI Research Press, 1982); Bob Burnham, "Wild Bill Hickok," in *Radio Rides the Range: A Reference Guide to Western Drama on the Air, 1929–1967*, ed. Jack French and David S. Siegel (Jefferson, NC: McFarland, 2013), 200–201; Wayne Hilinski, "Kellogg Company," *The Advertising Age Encyclopedia of Advertising*, ed. John McDonough and Karen Egolf (New York: Fitzroy Dearborn, 2003), v. 2, 891–3; James L. Baughman, *Same Time, Same Station: Creating American Television, 1948–1961* (Baltimore, MD: Johns Hopkins University Press, 2007), 206.

4. *TV Guide* 1:24, week of September 11–17, 1953, A-9, A-20–A-26; see *TV Guide* issues for May 28–June 3, 1954; June 18–24, 1954; and July 31–August 6, 1954.

5. Barbara Berch Jamison, "Portrait of a Guy Named Madison," New York *Times*, January 31, 1954.

6. Andrew L. Yarrow, *Measuring America: How Economic Growth Came to Define American Greatness in the Late Twentieth Century* (Amherst: University of Massachusetts Press, 2010), 108, quoted by Andrea Carosso, *Cold War Narratives: American Culture in the 1950s* (Bern: Peter Lang, 2012), 41, 84; Stephen R. Fox, *The Mirror Makers: A History of American Advertising and Its Creators* (New York: Morrow, 1984), 173; Lizabeth Cohen, *A Consumers' Republic: The Politics of Mass Consumption in Postwar America* (New York: Knopf, 2003), 4; MacDonald, *One Nation under Television*, 42; Bell, *Illustrated Life and Times*, 108–9.

7. Eric Barnouw, *The Image Empire: A History of Broadcasting in the United States* (New York: Oxford University Press, 1970), 3:18; Dwight D. Eisenhower, "Remarks upon Receiving the America's Democratic Legacy Award," November 23, 1953, The American Presidency Project, http://www.presidency.ucsb.edu/ws/index.php?pid=9770 (accessed July 16, 2018).

8. Smith, *Eisenhower*, 3–19; Rebecca Stefoff, *The Wild West* (Tarrytown, NY: Marshall Cavendish Benchmark, 2007), xv–xvii; New York *Times*, November 24, 1953; "Gen. Eisenhower on Americans' Code, 'Sneaking Up Behind' Deplored," *Times of London*, November 25, 1953; Merle Miller, *Ike the Soldier: As They Knew Him* (New York: G. P. Putnam's Sons, 1987), 72–73; Kenneth S. Davis, *Soldier of Democracy: A Biography of Dwight Eisenhower* (Garden City, NY: Doubleday, Doran, 1945), 72. On Eisenhower and McCarthy, see David A. Nichols, *Ike and McCarthy* (New York: Simon and Schuster, 2017); Barnouw, *Image Empire*, 8–19; Carosso, *Cold War Narratives*, 118–19; Brendon, *Ike*, 266–76.

9. Preston Lewis, "Ike Liked Westerns," *Roundup Magazine*, Western Writers of America (August 2016), 21–22; William E. Leuchtenburg, *The White House Looks South: Franklin D. Roosevelt, Harry S. Truman, Lyndon B. Johnson* (Baton Rouge: Louisiana State University Press, 2005), 148–49. Zane Grey, *Code of the West* (New York: Harper and Brother, 1934). Z. Ervin, "Zane Grey, and the Code of the West," in Slatta, *Mythical West*, 159–60; Richard T. Stanley, *The Eisenhower Years: A Social History of the 1950s* (Bloomington, IN: iUniverse, 2012), 148–49; Catharine Hamm, "In the Kansas Town That Was Home, the Astonishing Story of Eisenhower Lives On," Los Angeles *Times*, June 2, 2019.

10. Christine Bold, *The Frontier Club: Popular Westerns and Cultural Power, 1880–1924* (New York: Oxford University Press, 2013), 42–43. See also John F. Reiger, *American Sportsmen and the Origins of Conservation*, 3rd ed. (Corvallis: Oregon State University Press, 2001). Ramon F. Adams, *The Cowman and His Code of Ethics* (Austin, TX: Encino Press, 1970); Joe Wheeler, "Why You Should Read Zane Grey," Zane Grey's West Society, https://www.zgws.org/zgwsread.php (accessed August 1, 2018); Joseph Lawrence Wheeler, *Zane Grey's Impact on Life and Letters: A Study in the Popular Novel* (PhD diss., George Peabody College for Teachers, Nashville, Tennessee, 1982); Durham, "Hemingway's Grace Under Pressure," 425–32. Durham argued that Hemingway's famous code was an extension of the Code of the West, influenced by Raymond Chandler and Ernest Haycox. Hemingway was less impressed with Grey, according to biographer Carlos Baker, *Hemingway: A Life Story* (New York: Charles Scribner's Sons, 1969), 244, 271; Calder, *There Must Be a Lone Ranger*, 105.

11. Ron Soodalter, "Code of the West, History vs. Hollywood," *American Cowboy* 24, no. 1 (June/July 2017): 22; Guy Madison Official Website, http://www.guymadison.com (accessed May 13, 2017); Barnouw, *Image Empire*, 81.

12. Peter Pagnamenta, *Prairie Fever: British Aristocrats in the American West* (New York: W. W. Norton, 2012), 6–7, 12, 177–82, 221–31; Bob Stepno, "Frontier Gentleman," Newspaper Heroes on the Air, https://jheroes.com/adventure/westerns/frontier-gentleman/ (accessed April 23, 2017).

13. Jim Willard, "Western Writer Captured the Open Range," Loveland, Colorado *Reporter Herald*, March 21, 2013.

14. Tom Engelhardt, *The End of Victory Culture: Cold War America and the Disillusioning of a Generation* (1995; Amherst: University of Massachusetts Press, 1998), 150–53. David Foster Wallace, *A Supposedly Fun Thing I'll Never Do Again: Essays and Arguments* (1997; Boston: Back Bay Books, 1998), 22.

15. *Legend*, Richard Dean Anderson Website, http://www.rdanderson.com
/legend/legend.htm (accessed April 28, 2017).

16. Caryn James, "How the West Was Lost on TV," New York *Times*, September 15, 1996.

17. French, *Westerns*, 167–69.

18. Audio Commentary, *Deadwood: The Complete First Season*, HBO DVD
Video, 2015. "Making Deadwood," "The Real Deadwood," "The New Language of the Old West: A Conversation with David Milch and Keith Carradine," "An Imaginative Realty." David Milch, Audio Commentary, Episode 1: "Deadwood." See also Allen Barra, "The Man Who Made Deadwood,"
American Heritage 57, no. 3 (2006): 50–55.

19. Bill Carter, "HBO, Looking at 'Deadwood,' Sees Cavalry Riding to the Rescue," New York *Times*, June 16, 2004; Sadie Gennis, "NYPD Blue Creator
David Milch Is in Massive Debt after Gambling Away over $100 Million," *TV
Guide*, February 17, 2016, http://www.tvguide.com/news/nypd-blue-creator
-david-milch-gambling-debt/ (accessed June 28, 2018); Tim Walker, "Deadwood Creator Squandered $100 m Fortune on Gambling Habit," *Independent*,
February 18, 2018, https://www.independent.co.uk/news/people/david-milch
-deadwood-creator-squandered-100m-fortune-on-gambling-habit-a6882336.
html (accessed June 28, 2018); Barra, "Man Who Made Deadwood." See also
Paul Stasi and Jennifer Greiman, eds., *The Last Western: Deadwood and the
End of American Empire* (New York: Bloomsbury, 2013). Paul A. Cantor, *The
Invisible Hand in Popular Culture: Liberty vs. Authority in American Film and
TV* (Lexington: University Press of Kentucky, 2012), 97–127; David Milch,
Deadwood: Stories of the Black Hills (New York: Bloomsbury USA, 2006).

20. Audio Commentary, Episode 1, "Deadwood," and Episode 4, "Here Was
a Man"; Brown, *No Duty to Retreat*, 199.

21. Audio Commentary, Episode 1. Wendy Witherspoon, "The Final Stamp:
Deadwood and the Gothic American Frontier," in *Dirty Words in Deadwood: Literature and the Postwestern*, ed. Melody Graulich and Nicholas S.
Witschi (Lincoln: University of Nebraska Press, 2014), 104–5.

7. Scribes and Tourists

1. Chicago *Tribune*, October 18, 2008.

2. Alfred D. Richardson, *Beyond the Mississippi* (Hartford, CT: American
Publishing Co., 1867). James D. McLaird, "'I Know . . . Because I Was
There': Leander P. Richardson Reports the Black Hills Gold Rush," *South
Dakota History* 3-4 (Fall/Winter 2001): 239–48. Leander Richardson, "A
Trip to the Black Hills," *Scribner's Monthly* 13 (April 1877): 755.

3. New York *Times*, July 27, 1876; Chicago *Daily Tribune*, July 27, 1876; Cheyenne, Wyoming, *Daily Leader*, August 17, 1876; McLaird, "'I Know,'" 245; Wrobel, *Promised Lands*, 170.

4. Altoona, Pennsylvania, *Tribune*, March 31, 1891; Daniel J. Czitrom, *Media and the American Mind: From Morse to McLuhan* (Chapel Hill: University of North Carolina Press, 1982), 21–27; See also Paul Starr, *The Creation of Media: Political Origins of Modern Communications* (New York: Bargain Books, 2005). There had been criticism of Richardson's negative views of Deadwood from business interests. Some claimed Richardson was never in Deadwood. *Black Hills Daily Times*, April 29, 1878, cited in McLaird, "'I Know.'"

5. Richardson, "Trip to the Black Hills," 749, 751–52.

6. Ibid., 755–56.

7. New York *Times*, February 3, 1918; William Richard Cutter, ed., *American Biography: A New Cyclopedia* (New York: American Historical Society, 1919), 6:53–54.

8. McLaird, "'I Know,'" 250–54; St. Paul, Minnesota, *Pioneer Press*, March 12, 1894; Rosa, *They Called Him Wild Bill*, 291–95.

9. New York *Tribune*, May 10, May 15, 1894; New York *Evening World*, May 14, 1894; Leander Richardson, "Typical Frontiersman, The True Story of Wild Bill," Christchurch, New Zealand, *Weekly Press*, February 17, 1894; Leander Richardson, "Last Days of a Plainsman," *True West* 13 (November–December 1965): 22; Agnes Wright Spring, *Colorado Charlie, Wild Bill's Pard* (Boulder, CO: Pruett Press, 1968), 98–101; McLaird, "'I Know,'" 239.

10. Richardson, "Typical Frontiersman."

11. Ibid.

12. Leander P. Richardson, *Captain Kate, the Heroine of Deadwood Gulch* (New York: Street and Smith, 1896); Leander P. Richardson, *The Road Agents: A Tale of Black Hills Life* (New York: Street and Smith, 1889); McLaird, "'I Know,'" 264–65.

13. Gary Forney, "Montana's Pioneer Editor: The Epic Career of Bozeman's First Newspaper Man," *Montana Pioneer* (June 2011), https://montanapioneer.com/montanas-pioneer-editor/ (accessed June 26, 2017); James Bruce Putnam, "The Evolution of a Frontier Town: Bozeman, Montana, and Its Search for Economic Stability, 1864–1877" (master's thesis, Montana State University, 1973), 36.

14. H. N. Maguire, *The Coming Empire: A Complete and Reliable Treatise on the Black Hills, Yellowstone and Big Horn Regions* (Sioux City, IA: Watkins and Smead, 1878), 61–62.

15. H. N. Maguire, *The Black Hills and American Wonderland: From Personal Explorations* (Chicago: Donnelley, Lloyd and Co., 1877), 304; H. N. Maguire, *The Black Hills of Dakota: A Miniature History of Their Settlement, Resources, Population, and Prospects, with Accurate Tables of Local Distances, and a General Business Directory of Principal Towns* (Rapid City, Dakota Territory: J. S. Gantz, 1879). McLaird, *Wild Bill Hickok and Calamity Jane*, 85–86.

16. Maguire, *Coming Empire*, 70, 131–32.

17. "Deadwood in the Spring of 1877," in *Deadwood: The Best Writings on the Most Notorious Town in the West*, ed. T. D. Griffith (Guilford, CT: Globe Pequot Press, 2010), 23–25.

18. Ibid.

19. Fred Ellsworth Sutton, "Turbulent Deadwood, Once Wild and Wooly Mine Camp Will Observe Fiftieth Birthday by Reviving Its Reckless Youth," Dallas *Morning News*, August 8, 1926.

20. Fred Ellsworth Sutton and A. B. MacDonald, *Hands Up! Stories of the Six-Gun Fighters of the Old Wild West* (Indianapolis: Bobbs-Merrill, 1927); Adams, *Burs under the Saddle*, 498–503; Elizabeth A. Brennan and Elizabeth C. Clarage, *Who's Who of Pulitzer Prize Winners* (Westport, CT: Greenwood, 1999), 555.

21. Edward L. Senn, "Deadwood—A Modern Sodom Needs Another Renovation," *Senn's Forum*, December 1938, in Griffith, *Deadwood*, 72–78; Denise M. Karst Faehnrich, "Edward Louis Senn's Half-Century on the Last Frontier," *South Dakota History* 29, no. 1 (Spring 1999): 1–22; Chuck Cecil, *Prohibition in South Dakota: Astride the White Mule* (Mt. Pleasant, SC: History Press, 2016), 41.

22. Michael Watkins, "The New Pioneers of Deadwood," *Times of London*, May 22, 1982.

23. Rosa, *They Called Him Wild Bill*, 4.

24. Bill Bryson, *The Lost Continent: Travels in Small-Town America* (New York: Harper and Row, 1989), 12, 288–89.

25. Kathleen Norris, *Dakota: A Spiritual Geography* (New York: Ticknor and Fields, 1993), 33–34.

26. Bernard-Henri Lévy, *American Vertigo: Traveling America in the Footsteps of Tocqueville* (New York: Random House, 2006), 238–39.

27. Fraser Harrison, "Yankton: Portrait of a River City," *South Dakota History* 44, no. 1 (2014): 27.

28. Laurie Taylor, "Irony in the Soul," *Times of London*, January 22, 1994; Fraser Harrison, *Infinite West: Travels in South Dakota* (Pierre: South Dakota Historical Society Press, 2012), 2–6, 129.

29. Harrison, *Infinite West*, 130–45.

30. Rosa, *They Called Him Wild Bill*, 288–89. Agnes had permitted publication of the letter in several newspapers in 1877; Harrison, *Infinite West*, 145–49.

31. Harrison, *Infinite West*, 150–56.

32. The Warhol remark can be found in *The Oxford Dictionary of Thematic Quotations*, ed. Susan Ratcliffe (New York: Oxford University Press, 2000), 114.

33. Harrison, "Yankton," 12–14, 26–28; Harrison, *Infinite West*, 146.

34. Emilie Rusch, "Searching for the Ghosts of Old Deadwood in the Black Hills," Denver *Post*, May 21, 2015; Robert Sullivan, *Cross Country* (New York: Bloomsbury, 2006), 148.

35. Chandra Lahiri, "Days 22 & 23: Sin and Debauchery," Muscat *Daily*, June 20, 2018, https://www.muscatdaily.com/Archive/Stories-Files/Days-22–23-Sin-Debauchery!-59po (accessed June 22, 2018).

36. T. D. Griffith, "Historic-Preservation Officer Works to Keep Deadwood's Vibrant Past Alive," Rapid City, South Dakota, *Journal*, January 2, 2019; Marilyn Johnson, *This Book Is Overdue! How Librarians and Cybrarians Can Save Us All*, New York: HarperCollins, 2010, 1–5. "Deadwood 1876—Second Life," YouTube, May 24, 2008, https://www.youtube.com/watch?v=hi122Xf-iSc (accessed January 10, 2019).

37. Johnson, *This Book Is Overdue!* 7.

8. Conclusions

1. Kasson, *Buffalo Bill's Wild West*, 238.

2. Robert Wooster, *The Military and United States Indian Policy, 1865–1903* (Lincoln: University of Nebraska Press, 1988), 74, quoted in Kasson, *Buffalo Bill's Wild West*, 237–38; Brown, *No Duty to Retreat*, 44–45.

3. Knowlton, *Cattle Kingdom*, 59.

4. See Greg Grandin, *The End of the Myth: From the Frontier to the Border Wall in the Mind of America* (New York, Henry Holt, 2019). In chapter 4, Grandin vets the safety valve idea. Robert Kagan, *Dangerous Nation* (New York: Knopf, 2006), 286.

5. Kasson, *Buffalo Bill's Wild West*, 235–38; 256.

6. Ibid., 62

7. Rosa, *Wild Bill Hickok: The Man and His Myth*, 145–48; Springfield, Massachusetts, *Republican*, February 21, 1874; Hays City, Kansas, *Sentinel*, February 2, 1877.

8. On the role of Turner in popularizing the frontier, see Gary J. Hausladen, ed., *Western Places, American Myths: How We Think about the West* (Reno: University of Nevada Press, 2003), 3–4. For a summary of the reaction against Turner and contemporary border issues, see Grandin, *End of the Myth*.

9. Kasson, *Buffalo Bill's Wild West*, 65, 97–102, 197; R. Reid Badger, "Chicago 1893, World's Columbian Exposition," in *Historical Dictionary of World's Fairs and Expositions, 1851–1988*, ed. John E. Findling and Kimberly D. Peele (New York: Greenwood Press, 1990), 122–32.

10. Roosevelt spoke to the Commonwealth Club in San Francisco, September 23, 1932.

11. Walter Weyl, *The New Democracy*, rev. ed. (New York: Macmillan, 1914), 36; Grandin, *End of the Myth*, 168–69.

12. Kaplan, *Empire Wilderness*, 7.

13. Blount County, Tennessee, *Daily Times*, February 22, 2018.

14. See, for example, Rosa's chapter 16 title, "A Fitting Death for an Assassin," in *They Called Him Wild Bill*; Buel, *Life*, 71.

15. Rusty Worley, "Opinion: The Case for Downtown as Recreational Hub," Springfield, Missouri, *Business Journal*, June 4, 2018, http://sbj.net/stories /opinion-the-case-for-downtown-as-recreational-hub,59079 (accessed August 1, 2018).

16. Wallace Stegner, *Where the Bluebird Sings to the Lemonade Springs: Living and Writing in the West* (1995; New York: Modern Library, 2002), 106–7.

17. Barra, *Inventing Wyatt Earp*, 389; Kasson, *Buffalo Bill's Wild West*, 265.

18. Rosa, *Wild Bill Hickok: Sharpshooter and U.S. Marshal of the Wild West*, 99.

19. David Fisher, *Bill O'Reilly's Legends & Lies: The Real West* (New York: Henry Holt and Co., 2015), 93, 99, 104, 112; "Fox News Channel's 'Legends and Lies: The Real West' Sees Big Gains in Second Week," TV by the Numbers, https://tvbythenumbers.zap2it.com/cable-news/fox-news-channels -legends-and-lies-the-real-west-sees-big-gains-in-second-week/ (accessed October 15, 2018); "Combined Print & E-Book Nonfiction," New York *Times*, May 21, 2015; "Books: Hardcover Nonfiction," New York *Times*, June 28, 2015.

20. Rachel Mizsei Ward, "Genre Mashing in the Role-Playing Game *Deadlands: The Weird West, the Horror Steampunk Western*," in *Undead in the West II: They Just Keep Coming*, ed. Cynthia J. Miller and A. Bowdoin Van Riper (Lanham, MD: Scarecrow Press, 2013), 269–85. See "The Harrowed," *Deadlands*, Pinnacle Entertainment Group, https://deadlandsridersonthestorm .obsidianportal.com/wikis/the-harrowed (accessed January 30, 2018).

Epilogue

1. Philip French, *Westerns: Aspects of a Movie Genre and Westerns Revisited* (Manchester: Carcanet Press, 2005), 96; Daniel Ford, "Boom Times for Jet Pilots," *Wall Street Journal*, July 28–29, 2018.

2. Kansas Historical Society, *kansapedia*, https://www.kshs.org/kansapedia /edward-campbell-little/16976 (accessed July 18, 2018); E. C. Little, "A Son of the Border," *Everybody's Magazine* 4 (June 1901): 578–87; Steckmesser, *Western Hero*, 140; Dykstra, "Wild Bill Hickok in Abilene," 20–48.

3. Arthur Chapman, "The Man Who Tamed the Cow-Towns," *Outing* 45 (November 1904): 131–39; Adams, *Burs under the Saddle*, 503–6.

4. Buel, *Life*; Rosa, *Wild Bill Hickok: The Man and His Myth*, 47, 53.

5. Coursey, *Wild Bill*; on Coursey, see www.southdakotamagazine.com (accessed January 1, 2018). The entry is revised from the September/October 2012 *South Dakota Magazine* article on Coursey. The price on Amazon. com was as of January 2, 2018.

6. Frank J. Wilstach, "Time Widens Wild Bill Hickok's Fame: Indian Scout and Tamer of Bad Men Had Forty Notches on His Gun; Yet He Was Shy before an Audience," New York *Times*, September 13, 1925; "Frank J. Wilstach Dies in Hospital," New York *Times*, November 29, 1933.

7. Frank J. Wilstach, *Wild Bill Hickok: The Prince of Pistoleers* (Garden City, NY: Doubleday, Page and Co., 1926), vii, x, 3. The information on Wilstach is via http://archives.nypl.org/mss/3355 (accessed February 28, 2017).

8. Wilstach, *Wild Bill Hickok*, xv, 4, 69. Rosa, *They Called Him Wild Bill*, 44; Steckmesser, *Western Hero*, 143.

9. Ibid., 131–36, 253.

10. Wilbert Edwin Eisele, *The Real Wild Bill Hickok: Famous Scout and Knight Chivalric—A True Story of Pioneer Life in the Far West* (Denver, CO: William H. Andre, 1931), 119, 116, 5, 52; Adams, *Burs under the Saddle*, 163.

11. Dykstra, "Wild Bill Hickok in Abilene"; Connelley, *Wild Bill and His Era*, xii; Rosa, *They Called Him Wild Bill*, x–xii.

12. William E. Connelley, *Wild Bill and His Era* (New York: Cooper Square Publishers, 1972), xii, 5–7, 8–20, 29–30, 85–86, 113, 153, 217–18.

13. Buel, *Life*, 5; Connelley, *Wild Bill and His Era* (1972), 7; O'Connor, *Wild Bill Hickok*, 9; Wilstach, *Wild Bill Hickok: The Prince of Pistoleers*.

14. Thompson, *Born on a Mountaintop*, 89–90.

15. Allison Hardy, *Wild Bill Hickok: King of the Gun-Fighters* (Girard, KS: Haldman-Julius Publications, 1943), 4–12; "Vance Randolph, 1892–1980" *Encyclopedia of Arkansas History and Culture*, http://www.encyclopediaof arkansas.net/encyclopedia/entry-detail.aspx?entryID=2265 (accessed May 2, 2018). Robert Cochran, *Vance Randolph: An Ozark Life* (Champaign: University of Illinois Press, 1985).

16. Hardy, *Wild Bill Hickok*.

17. For more on fakelore, see Richard M. Dorson, *American Folklore* (1959; Chicago: University of Chicago Press, 1977), 4. Dorson first used the term in 1950. Thompson, *On the Road*, 198–208, 223; Michael A. Lofaro, ed., *Davy Crockett: The Man, the Legend, the Legacy, 1786–1986* (Knoxville: University of Tennessee Press, 1985); Lofaro, quoted in Thompson, 198–208 passim; Steckmesser, *Western Hero*, 131.

18. O'Connor, Wild Bill Hickok, 12, 59, 70–71, 73, 81; "Richard O'Connor, 59, A Writer of 60 Nonfiction Books, Is Dead," New York Times, February 21, 1975.

19. Knight, *Wild Bill Hickok*, 10–13; Philip John Schwarz, "The Contemporary Private Press," *Journal of Library History (1966–1972)* 5, no. 4 (October 1970): 314; *Catalog of Copyright Entries*, 3rd series: January–June 1959 (Washington, DC: Copyright Office, Library of Congress, 1960), 340. Eleanor Irwin with Ann Bahar, "The Hillside Press: Adventures of a Miniature Book Publisher," *Miniature Book Society Newsletter* (April 1992): 4–5. On the accuracy of the book, see Adams, *Burs under the Saddle*, 312–13.

20. Knight, *Wild Bill Hickok*, 39–40, 23–27, 59.

21. Rosa, *Wild Bill Hickok: The Man and His Myth*, xvi.

22. Rosa, *They Called Him Wild Bill*, vii, 9, 99.

23. Ibid., 349.

24. Thadd M. Turner, "Joseph Rosa: On Obsession, Possession, and Wild Bill," *True West*, August 1, 2001, https://truewestmagazine.com/joseph-rosa/ (accessed January 20, 2018); Rosa, *Wild Bill Hickok: The Man and His Myth*, 183.

25. Joseph G. Rosa, "Foreword," in Miller and Snell, *Why the West Was Wild*, xii.

26. Joseph G. Rosa, *Wild Bill Hickok: Sharpshooter and U.S. Marshal of the Wild West* (New York: Rosen Publishing Group, 2004), 9; Joseph G. Rosa, *The West of Wild Bill Hickok* (1982; Norman: University of Oklahoma Press, 1994), 66.

27. McLaird, *Wild Bill Hickok and Calamity Jane*, 3, 11–23, 41–42.

28. Bob Boze Bell, *The Illustrated Life and Times of Wild Bill Hickok: The First Gunfighter* (Cave Creek, AZ: Two Roads West, 2017).

29. Aaron Woodard, *The Revenger: The Life and Times of Wild Bill Hickok* (Lanham, MD: Rowman and Littlefield, 2018), 11, 113–37, 154; Joseph Rosa, *Alias Jack McCall* (Kansas City, MO: Lowell Press, 1967.)

30. Tom Clavin, *Wild Bill: The True Story of America's First Gunfighter* (New York: St. Martin's Press, 2019), 38, 44, 118, 201–2, 216.

31. Etulain, *Re-Imagining*, xix–xx, 32–34.

32. Ibid., xix–xxi.

33. Slotkin, *Gunfighter Nation*, 383–90. Slotkin cited Brown, *No Duty to Retreat*, and Rosa, *The Gunfighter.*

34. Brown, *No Duty to Retreat*, 49–51, 45–46; see also Springfield, Missouri, *Weekly Patriot*, August 10, 1865.

35. Slotkin, *Gunfighter Nation*, 69, 75.

36. Ibid., 381–84.

37. Eugene Cunningham, *Triggernometry: A Gallery of Gunfighters* (New York: The Press of the Pioneers, 1934), 251–57, 260–61, 233, 414–25.

38. Steckmesser, *Western Hero*, 105.

39. Ibid., 115, 123–24, 136–37.

40. Ibid., passim. On Wilstach, see 142–43, 156, 130; Steckmesser finds Wilstach an "important landmark," however.

41. Ibid., on O'Connor, see 144, 149, 134–35; on Connelley (1972), see 108–10, 121–23, 126–27, 133, 145–49, 155.

42. Murdoch, *American West*, 13, 93

43. Ibid., viii–ix, 2, 93–95.

44. Ibid., 76, 105.

45. Ibid., 63–75; see chapter 5 on myth and nostalgia. Murdoch quotes Goetzmann. See p. 80 on Roosevelt, Wister, and Remington; Nye, *Unembarrassed Muse*, 289.

46. Fifer, *Bad Boys*, 23, 25, 31.

47. Ibid., 31, 34, 123–32.

48. Blight, "Historians and Memory," 1.

Bibliography

Books

Abbott, Carl. *Frontiers Past and Future: Science Fiction and the American West.* Lawrence: University Press of Kansas, 2006.

Abrams, Marc H. *Sioux War Dispatches: Reports from the Field, 1876–1877.* Yardley, PA: Westholme, 2012.

Adams, Ramon F. *Burs under the Saddle: A Second Look at Books and Histories of the West.* Norman: University of Oklahoma Press, 1964.

———. *The Cowman and His Code of Ethics.* Austin, TX: Encino Press, 1970.

Agee, James. *A Death in the Family: A Restoration of the Author's Text.* Edited by Michael A. Lofaro. *The Works of James Agee.* Vol. 1. Knoxville: University of Tennessee Press, 2007.

Ames, John. *The Real Deadwood: True Life Histories of Wild Bill Hickok, Calamity Jane, Outlaw Towns, and Other Characters of the Lawless West.* New York: Chamberlain Brothers, 2004.

Anderson, Joseph. *I Buried Hickok: The Memoirs of White Eye Anderson.* Edited by William B. Secrest. College Station, TX: Creative Pub., 1980.

Angle, Paul, and Richard L. Beyer. *Handbook of Illinois History.* Springfield: Illinois State Historical Society, 1943.

Ashdown, Paul. "'From Almost as Early as I Can Remember': James Agee and the Civil War." In *Agee Agonistes*, edited by Michael A. Lofaro, 105–24. Knoxville: University of Tennessee Press, 2007.

Ashdown, Paul, and Edward Caudill. *The Mosby Myth: A Confederate Hero in Life and Legend.* Wilmington, DE: Scholarly Resources Inc., 2002).

———. *The Myth of Nathan Bedford Forrest.* Lanham, MD: Rowman and Littlefield, 2005.

Avlon, John, Jesse Angelo, and Errol Louis, eds. *Deadline Artists: America's Greatest Newspaper Columns.* New York: Overlook, 2011.

Babe, Thomas. *Fathers and Sons.* New York: Dramatists Play Service, 1974.

Baker, Carlos. *Hemingway: A Life Story.* New York: Charles Scribner's Sons, 1969.

Barnouw, Eric. *The Image Empire: A History of Broadcasting in the United States.* Vol. 3. New York: Oxford University Press, 1970.

Barra, Allen. *Inventing Wyatt Earp: His Life and Many Legends.* 1998. Lincoln: University of Nebraska Press, 2008.

Barthes, Roland. *Mythologies.* Translated by Annette Lavers. London: Jonathan Cape, 1972.

Baughman, James L. *Same Time, Same Station: Creating American Television, 1948–1961.* Baltimore, MD: Johns Hopkins University Press, 2007.

Bell, Bob Boze. *The Illustrated Life and Times of Wild Bill Hickok: The First Gunfighter.* Cave Creek, AZ: Two Roads West, 2017.

Berger, Thomas. *Little Big Man.* 1964. New York: Dell, 1989.

Bierman, John. *Dark Safari: The Life behind the Legend of Henry Morton Stanley.* Austin: University of Texas Press, 1993.

Blacker, Irwin R., ed. *The Old West in Fiction.* New York: Ivan Obolensky, 1961.

Blight, David W. *Race and Reunion: The Civil War and American Memory.* Cambridge, MA: Harvard University Press, 2001.

Blockson, Charles L. *The Underground Railroad.* New York: Prentice Hall Press, 1987.

Bobrick, Benson. *Testament: A Soldier's Story of the Civil War.* New York: Simon and Schuster, 2003.

Boggs, Johnny D. *East of the Border.* 2004. New York: Dorchester Publishing, 2006.

Bold, Christine. *The Frontier Club: Popular Westerns and Cultural Power, 1880–1924.* New York: Oxford University Press, 2013.

———. *Selling the Wild West: Popular Western Fiction, 1860 to 1960.* Bloomington: Indiana University Press, 1987.

Branch, E. Douglas. *The Hunting of the Buffalo.* Lincoln: University of Nebraska Press, 1962.

Braun, Matt. *Hickok & Cody.* New York: St. Martin's, 2001.

Brendon, Piers. *Ike: The Life and Times of Dwight D. Eisenhower.* London: Secker and Warburg, 1987.

Brennan, Elizabeth A., and Elizabeth C. Clarage. *Who's Who of Pulitzer Prize Winners.* Westport, CT: Greenwood, 1999.

Brooks, Bill. *Law for Hire: Protecting Hickok.* New York: HarperCollins, 2003.

Brown, Richard Maxwell. *No Duty to Retreat: Violence and Values in American History and Society.* New York: Oxford University Press, 1991.

———. *Strain of Violence: Historical Studies of American Violence and Vigilantism.* New York: Oxford University Press, 1975.

Bryson, Bill. *The Lost Continent: Travels in Small-Town America.* New York: Harper and Row, 1989.

Buel, J. W. *Heroes of the Plains.* New York, 1882.

————. *Life and Marvelous Adventures of Wild Bill, the Scout.* Chicago: Belford, Clarke and Co., 1880.

Buntline, Ned. *The Hero of a Hundred Fights: Collected Stories from the Dime Novel King, From Buffalo Bill to Wild Bill Hickok.* Edited and with an introduction by Clay Reynolds. New York: Sterling Publishing, 2011.

Burton, Orville Vernon. *The Age of Lincoln.* New York: Hill and Wang, 2007.

Calder, Jenni. *There Must Be a Lone Ranger: The American West in Film and Reality.* 1974. New York: McGraw-Hill, 1977.

Campbell, Joseph W. *Yellow Journalism: Puncturing the Myths, Defining the Legacies.* Westport, CT: Praeger, 2001.

Cantor, Paul A. *The Invisible Hand in Popular Culture: Liberty vs. Authority in American Film and TV.* Lexington: University Press of Kentucky, 2012.

Carosso, Andrea. *Cold War Narratives: American Culture in the 1950s.* Bern: Peter Lang, 2012.

Carr, Matthew. *Sherman's Ghosts: Soldiers, Civilians, and the American Way of War.* New York: New Press, 2015.

Castel, Albert. *Civil War Kansas: Reaping the Whirlwind.* Lawrence: University Press of Kansas, 1997.

Caudill, Edward, and Paul Ashdown. *Inventing Custer: The Making of an American Legend.* Lanham, MD: Rowman and Littlefield, 2015.

————. *Sherman's March in Myth and Memory.* Lanham, MD: Rowman and Littlefield, 2008.

Cecil, Chuck. *Prohibition in South Dakota: Astride the White Mule.* Mt. Pleasant, SC: History Press, 2016.

Chadwick, Bruce. *The Reel Civil War: Mythmaking in American Film.* New York: Vintage, 2001.

Charyn, Jerome. *Darlin' Bill: A Love Story of the Wild West.* New York: Arbor House, 1980.

Christianson, Frank, ed. *The Popular Frontier: Buffalo Bill's Wild West and Transnational Mass Culture* (Norman: University of Oklahoma Press, 2017).

Clavin, Tom. *Wild Bill: The True Story of America's First Gunfighter.* New York: St. Martin's Press, 2019.

Cochran, Robert. *Vance Randolph: An Ozark Life.* Champaign: University of Illinois Press, 1985.

Cody, W. F. *An Autobiography of Buffalo Bill.* New York: Cosmopolitan Book Corp., 1920.

Cohen, Lizabeth. *A Consumers' Republic: The Politics of Mass Consumption in Postwar America.* New York: Knopf, 2003.

Cole, Judd. *Wild Bill: Black Hills Hellhole.* New York: Dorchester Publishing, 2000.

——. *Wild Bill: Bleeding Kansas.* New York: Dorchester Publishing, 1999.

——. *Wild Bill: Dead Man's Hand.* New York: Dorchester Publishing. 1999.

——. *Wild Bill: Gun Law.* New York: Dorchester Publishing, 2001.

——. *Wild Bill: The Kinkaid County War.* New York: Dorchester Publishing, 1999.

——. *Wild Bill: Point Rider.* New York: Dorchester Publishing, 2001.

——. *Wild Bill: Santa Fe Death Trap.* New York: Dorchester Publishing, 2000.

——. *Wild Bill: Yuma Bustout.* New York: Dorchester Publishing, 2000.

Connelley, William E. *Wild Bill and His Era: The Life and Adventures of James Butler Hickok.* New York: Cooper Square Publishers, 1972.

——. *Wild Bill and His Era: The Life and Adventures of James Butler Hickok.* New York: The Press of the Pioneers, 1933.

Cook, Robert J. *Civil War Memories: Contesting the Past in the United States since 1865.* Baltimore, MD: Johns Hopkins University Press, 2017.

Coursey, O. W. *Wild Bill.* Mitchell, SD: Educational Supply Co., 1924.

Cox, J. Randolph. *The Dime Novel Companion: A Source Book.* Westport, CT: Greenwood Press, 2000.

Cunningham, Eugene. *Triggernometry: A Gallery of Gunfighters.* New York: The Press of the Pioneers, 1934.

Curti, Merle. *The Growth of American Thought.* New York: Harper and Brothers, 1943.

Custer, Elizabeth Bacon, *Following the Guidon.* New York: Harper and Brothers, 1890.

Custer, George A. *My Life on the Plains.* 1874. Lincoln: University of Nebraska Press, 1966.

Cutter, William Richard, ed. *American Biography: A New Cyclopedia.* Vol. 6. New York: American Historical Society, 1919.

Czitrom, Daniel J. *Media and the American Mind: From Morse to McLuhan.* Chapel Hill: University of North Carolina Press, 1982.

Davis, Kenneth S. *Soldier of Democracy: A Biography of Dwight Eisenhower.* Garden City, NY: Doubleday, Doran, 1945.

Davis, William C. *Three Roads to the Alamo: The Lives and Fortunes of David Crockett, James Bowie, and William Barret Travis.* New York: HarperCollins, 1998.

Denning, Michael. *Mechanic Accents: Dime Novels and Working-Class Culture in America.* New York: Verso, 1987.

Devine, Dennis. *Your Friend and Mine, Andy Devine.* Duncan, OK: BearManor Media, 2012.

Dexter, Pete. *Deadwood.* New York: Vintage Books, 1986.

———. *Paper Trails: True Stories of Confusion, Mindless Violence, and Forbidden Desires, a Surprising Number of Which Are Not about Marriage.* New York: Ecco/HarperCollins, 2007.

Donovan, James. *The Blood of Heroes.* New York: Little, Brown and Co., 2012.

Dorson, Richard M. *American Folklore.* 1959. Chicago: University of Chicago Press, 1977.

Earle, David M. *All Man! Hemingway, 1950s Men's Magazines, and the Masculine Persona.* Kent, OH: Kent State University Press, 2009.

Eicher, David J. *The Longest Night: A Military History of the Civil War.* New York: Simon and Schuster, 2002.

Eickhoff, Randy Lee. *And Not to Yield: A Novel of the Life and Times of Wild Bill Hickok.* New York: Tom Doherty, 2004.

Eisele, Wilbert Edwin. *The Real Wild Bill Hickok: Famous Scout and Knight Chivalric—A True Story of Pioneer Life in the Far West.* Denver, CO: William H. Andre, 1931.

Ellis, Doug, John Locke, and John Gunnison, eds. *The Adventure House Guide to the Pulps.* Silver Spring, MD: Adventure House, 2000.

Engelhardt, Tom. *The End of Victory Culture: Cold War America and the Disillusioning of a Generation.* 1995. Amherst: University of Massachusetts Press, 1998.

Estleman, Loren D. *Aces and Eights.* 1981. New York: Tom Doherty, 1998.

Etulain, Richard W. *Beyond the Missouri: The Story of the American West.* Albuquerque: University of New Mexico Press, 2006.

———. *The Life and Legends of Calamity Jane.* Norman: University of Oklahoma Press, 2014.

———. *Re-imagining the Modern American West.* 1966. Tucson: University of Arizona Press, 1996.

Fahs, Alice, and Joan Waugh. *The Memory of the Civil War in American Culture.* Chapel Hill: University of North Carolina Press, 2005.

Fairbanks, Jonathan, and Clyde Edwin Tuck. *Past and Present of Greene Country, Missouri.* Indianapolis: A. W. Bowen and Co., 1915.

Fifer, Barbara. *Bad Boys of the Black Hills . . . and Some Wild Women, Too.* Helena, MT: Farcountry Press, 2008.

Fisher, David. *Bill O'Reilly's Legends & Lies: The Real West.* New York: Henry Holt and Co., 2015.

Forrest, Chris, ed. *Wild Bill's First Trail: As He Told It.* New York: Robert M. DeWitt, 1867.

Forster, E. M. *Aspects of the Novel.* 1927. New York: Harcourt, Brace and World, 1955.

Fox, Stephen R. *The Mirror Makers: A History of American Advertising and Its Creators.* New York: Morrow, 1984.

French, Philip. *Westerns: Aspects of a Movie Genre and Westerns Revisited.* Manchester: Carcanet Press, 2005.

Grandin, Greg. *The End of the Myth: From the Frontier to the Border Wall in the Mind of America.* New York: Henry Holt, 2019.

Gray, John Plesent. *When All Roads Led to Tombstone: A Memoir.* Edited by W. Lane Rogers. Boise, ID: Tamarack Books, 1998.

Grey, Zane. *Code of the West.* New York: Harper and Brother, 1934.

Griffith, T. D., ed. *Deadwood: The Best Writings on the Most Notorious Town in the West.* Guilford, CT: Globe Pequot Press, 2010.

Guinn, Jeff. *The Last Gunfight: The Real Story of the Shootout at the O.K. Corral—And How It Changed the American West.* New York: Simon and Schuster, 2011.

Haag, Pamela. *The Gunning of America: Business and the Making of American Gun Culture.* New York: Basic Books, 2016.

Hajdu, David. *The Ten-Cent Plague: The Great Comic-Book Scare and How It Changed America.* New York: Picador, 2008.

Halbwachs, Maurice. *The Collective Memory.* New York: Harper & Row, 1980.

Hardy, Allison. *Wild Bill Hickok: King of the Gun-Fighters.* Girard, KS: Haldman-Julius Publications, 1943.

Hardin, John Wesley. *The Life of John Wesley Hardin.* Seguin, TX: Smith and Moore, 1896.

Harrison, Fraser. *Infinite West: Travels in South Dakota.* Pierre: South Dakota Historical Society Press, 2012.

Harwell, Richard, and Philip N. Racine, eds. *The Fiery Trail: A Union Officer's Account of Sherman's Last Campaigns.* Knoxville: University of Tennessee Press, 1986.

Hausladen, Gary J., ed. *Western Places, American Myths: How We Think about the West.* Reno: University of Nevada Press, 2003.

Hedren, Paul L., ed. *Ho! For the Black Hills: Captain Jack Crawford Reports the Black Hills Gold Rush and Great Sioux War.* Pierre: South Dakota State Historical Society, 2012.

Herzberg, Bob. *Savages and Saints: The Changing Image of American Indians in Westerns.* Jefferson, NC: McFarland, 2008.

Hulbert, Matthew Christopher. *The Ghosts of Guerrilla Memory: How Civil War Bushwhackers Became Gunslingers in the American West.* Athens: University of Georgia Press, 2016.

Hulse, Ed. *The Blood 'n' Thunder Guide to Collecting Pulps.* San Diego, CA: Murania Press, 2009.

Janney, Caroline E. *Remembering the Civil War: Reunion and the Limits of Reconciliation.* Chapel Hill: University of North Carolina Press. 2013.

Johannsen, Albert. *The House of Beadle and Adams and Its Dime and Nickel Novels: The Story of a Vanished Literature.* Vol. 2. Norman: University of Oklahoma Press, 1950.

Johnson, Marilyn. *This Book Is Overdue! How Librarians and Cybrarians Can Save Us All.* New York: HarperCollins, 2010.

Jones, Daryl. *The Dime Novel Western.* Bowling Green, OH: The Popular Press, 1978.

Josephy, Alvin M., Jr. *The Civil War in the American West.* New York: Alfred A. Knopf, 1991.

Kagan, Robert. *Dangerous Nation.* New York: Knopf, 2006.

Kammen, Michael G. *Mystic Chords of Memory: The Transformation of Tradition in American Culture.* New York: Alfred A. Knopf, 1991.

Kaplan, Robert D. *An Empire Wilderness: Travels into America's Future.* New York: Random House, 1998.

Kasson, Joy S. *Buffalo Bill's Wild West: Celebrity, Memory, and Popular History.* New York: Hill and Wang, 2000.

Kelman, Ari. *A Misplaced Massacre: Struggling Over the Memory of Sand Creek.* Cambridge, MA: Harvard University Press, 2013.

Knight, Edward. *Wild Bill Hickok: The Contemporary Portrait of a Civil War Hero.* Franklin, NH: Hillside Press, 1959.

Knowlton, Christopher. *Cattle Kingdom: The Hidden History of the Cowboy West.* Boston: Houghton Mifflin Harcourt, 2017.

Lake, Stuart. *Wyatt Earp: Frontier Marshal.* New York: Houghton Mifflin Co., 1931.

Lansdale, Joe R. *Paradise Sky.* New York: Little, Brown and Co., 2015.

Latham, Aaron. *Code of the West.* New York: Simon and Schuster, 2001.

Leuchtenburg, William E. *The White House Looks South: Franklin D. Roosevelt, Harry S. Truman, Lyndon B. Johnson.* Baton Rouge: Louisiana State University Press, 2005.

Levi, Steven C. *Deadwood Dick: A Biographical Novel.* Los Angeles: Holloway House, 1988.

Lévy, Bernard-Henri. *American Vertigo: Traveling America in the Footsteps of Tocqueville.* New York: Random House, 2006.

Limerick, Patricia. *The Legacy of Conquest: The Unbroken Past of the American West.* New York: Norton, 1987.

———. *Something in the Soil: Legacies and Reckonings in the New West.* New York: Norton, 2000.

Lofaro, Michael A., ed. *Davy Crockett: The Man, the Legend, the Legacy, 1786–1986.* Knoxville: University of Tennessee Press, 1985.

Logan, Jake. *Slocum and Wild Bill's Lady.* New York: Jove Books, 2000.

Love, Nat. *The Life and Adventures of Nat Love.* 1907. Lincoln: University of Nebraska Press, 1995.

Lule, Jack. *Daily News, Eternal Stories: The Mythological Role of Journalism.* New York: Guilford Press, 2001.

MacDonald, J. Fred. *One Nation under Television: The Rise and Decline of Network TV.* Chicago: Nelson-Hall, 1994.

Maguire, H. N. *The Black Hills and American Wonderland: From Personal Explorations, the Lakeside Library.* Chicago: Donnelley, Lloyd and Co., 1877.

———. *The Black Hills of Dakota: A Miniature History of Their Settlement, Resources, Population, and Prospects, with Accurate Tables of Local Distances, and a General Business Directory of Principal Towns.* Rapid City, Dakota Territory: J. S. Gantz, 1879.

———. *The Coming Empire: A Complete and Reliable Treatise on the Black Hills, Yellowstone and Big Horn Regions.* Sioux City, IA: Watkins and Smead, 1878.

Matheson, Richard. *The Memoirs of Wild Bill Hickok.* 1996. New York: Tom Doherty Associates, 2009.

Mathis, Andrew E. *The King Arthur Myth in Modern American Literature.* W. Jefferson, NC: McFarland, 2001.

McCormick, Edgar L., Edward G. McGehee, and Marty Strahl, eds. *Sherman in Georgia* Boston: D. C. Heath and Co., 1961.

McCoy, Max. *A Breed Apart.* New York: Signet, 2004.

McLaird, James D. *Wild Bill Hickok and Calamity Jane.* Pierre: South Dakota State Historical Society Press, 2008.

Milch, David. *Deadwood: Stories of the Black Hills.* New York: Bloomsbury USA, 2006.

Miller, Merle. *Ike the Soldier: As They Knew Him.* New York: G. P. Putnam's Sons, 1987.

Miller, Nyle H., and Joseph W. Snell. *Why the West Was Wild: A Contemporary Look at the Antics of Some Highly Publicized Kansas Cowtown Personalities.* Topeka: Kansas State Historical Society. Reprint, Norman: University of Oklahoma Press, 2003.

Monaghan, Jay. *The Great Rascal: The Life and Adventures of Ned Buntline.* Boston: Little, Brown and Co., 1952.

Montague, Joseph. *Wild Bill: A Western Story.* New York: Chelsea House, 1926.

Morgan, Robert. *Lions of the West: Heroes and Villains of the Westward Expansion.* Chapel Hill, NC: Algonquin, 2011.

Morrison, Michael A. *Slavery and the American West: The Eclipse of Manifest Destiny and the Coming of the Civil War*. Chapel Hill: University of North Carolina Press, 1997.

Morrison, Samuel Eliot. *The Oxford History of the American People*. Vol. 3: *1869–1963*. New York: New American Library, 1965, 1972.

Mott, Frank Luther. *A History of American Magazines*. Vol. 2: *1860–1865*. Cambridge, MA: Belknap Press of Harvard University Press, 1957.

Muelder, Owen W. *The Underground Railroad in Western Illinois*. Jefferson, NC: McFarland, 2008.

Murdoch, David Hamilton. *The American West: The Invention of a Myth*. Reno: University of Nevada Press, 2001.

Nash, Jay Robert. *Encyclopedia of Western Lawmen and Outlaws*. 1992. New York: Da Capo Press, 1994.

Nash, Roderick Frazier. *Wilderness and the American Mind*. 4th ed. New Haven, CT: Yale University Press, 2001.

Nichols, David A. *Ike and McCarthy*. New York: Simon and Schuster, 2017.

Nichols, George Ward. *The Sanctuary: A Story of the Civil War*. New York: Harper and Brothers, 1866.

———. *The Story of the Great March from the Diary of a Staff Officer*. New York: Harper and Bros., 1865.

Nora, Pierre. *Realms of Memory: Rethinking the French Past*. New York: Columbia University Press, 1996.

Nord, David Paul. *Communities of Journalism: A History of American Newspaper and Their Readers*. Urbana: University of Illinois Press, 2001.

Norris, Kathleen. *Dakota: A Spiritual Geography*. New York: Ticknor and Fields, 1993.

Nye, Russell. *The Unembarrassed Muse: The Popular Arts in America*. New York: Dial Press, 1970.

O'Connor, Richard. *Wild Bill Hickok*. Garden City, NY: Doubleday, 1959.

Pagnamenta, Peter. *Prairie Fever: British Aristocrats in the American West*. New York: W. W. Norton, 2012.

Parker, Watson. *Deadwood: The Golden Years*. Lincoln: University of Nebraska Press, 1981.

Parks, Rita. *The Western Hero in Film and Television: Mass Media Mythology*. Ann Arbor, MI: UMI Research Press, 1982.

Pasulka, D. W. *American Cosmic: UFOs, Religion, Technology*. New York: Oxford University Press, 2019.

Pearson, Edmond. *Dime Novels; or, Following an Old Trail in Popular Literature*. Washington, NY: Kennikat Press, Inc., 1968.

Pollard, Edward A. *The Lost Cause: A New Southern History of the War of the Confederates*. New York: E. B. Treat & Co., 1866.

Preston, Paul. *Wild Bill, the Indian-Slayer*. New York: Robert M. DeWitt, 1867.

Rainey, Buck. *Western Gunslingers in Fact and on Film: Hollywood's Famous Lawmen and Outlaws*. Jefferson, NC: McFarland, 1998.

Reiger, John F. *American Sportsmen and the Origins of Conservation*. 3rd ed. Corvallis: Oregon State University Press, 2001.

Reinfeld, Fred. *Pony Express*. 1966. Lincoln: University of Nebraska Press, 1973.

Richardson, Alfred D. *Beyond the Mississippi*. Hartford, CT: American Publishing Co., 1867.

Richardson, Heather Cox. *West from Appomattox: The Reconstruction of America after the Civil War*. New Haven, CT: Yale University Press, 2007.

Richardson, Leander P. *Captain Kate, the Heroine of Deadwood Gulch*. New York: Street and Smith, 1896.

———. *The Road Agents: A Tale of Black Hills Life*. New York: Street and Smith, 1889.

Rosa, Joseph G. *Alias Jack McCall*. Kansas City, MO: Lowell Press, 1967.

———. *The Gunfighter: Man or Myth?* Norman: University of Oklahoma Press, 1969.

———. *The Taming of the West: Age of the Gunfighter*. New York: Smithmark, 1993.

———. *They Called Him Wild Bill: The Life and Adventures of James Butler Hickok*. 1964. Norman: University of Oklahoma Press, 1974.

———. *The West of Wild Bill Hickok*. 1982. Norman: University of Oklahoma Press, 1994.

———. *Wild Bill Hickok: The Man and His Myth*. Lawrence: University Press of Kansas, 1996.

———. *Wild Bill Hickok: Sharpshooter and U.S. Marshal of the Wild West* (New York: Rosen Publishing Group, 2004.

———. *Wild Bill Hickok, Gunfighter: An Account of Hickok's Gunfights*. Norman: University of Oklahoma Press, 2001.

Rubin, Anne Sarah. *Through the Heart of Dixie: Sherman's March and American Memory*. Chapel Hill: University of North Carolina Press, 2014.

Rydell, Robert W., and Rob Kroes, *Buffalo Bill in Bologna: The Americanization of the World, 1869–1922*. Chicago: University of Chicago Press, 2005.

Sale, Richard. *The White Buffalo*. 1975. New York: Bantam, 1977.

Sandoz, Mari. *The Buffalo Hunters: The Story of the Hide Men*. New York: Hastings House, 1954.

———. *Crazy Horse*. Lincoln: University of Nebraska Press, 1961.

Scharff, Virginia, ed. *Empire and Liberty: The Civil War and the West.* Oakland: University of California Press, 2015.

Schudson, Michael. *Discovering the News: A Social History of American Newspapers.* New York: Basic Books, 1978.

Schwartz, Barry. *Abraham Lincoln in the Post-Heroic Era: History and Memory in Late Twentieth-Century America.* Chicago: University of Chicago Press, 2008.

Slatta, Richard W., ed. *The Mythical West: An Encyclopedia of Legend, Lore, and Popular Culture.* Santa Barbara, CA: ABC CLIO, 2001.

Slotkin, Richard. *Gunfighter Nation: The Myth of the Frontier in Twentieth-Century America.* New York: HarperPerennial, 1993.

Smith, Henry Nash. *Virgin Land: The American West as Symbol and Myth.* Cambridge, MA: Harvard University Press, 1950.

Smith, Jean Edward. *Eisenhower in War and Peace.* New York: Random House, 2012.

Smith, Stacey L. *Freedom's Frontier: California and the Struggle over Unfree Labor, Emancipation, and Reconstruction.* Chapel Hill: University of North Carolina Press, 2013.

Spencer, Thomas M., ed. *The Other Missouri History: Populist, Prostitutes, and Regular Folk.* Columbia: University of Missouri Press, 2004.

Spiegel, Alan. *James Agee and the Legend of Himself: A Critical Study.* Columbia: University of Missouri Press, 1998.

Spring, Agnes Wright. *Colorado Charlie, Wild Bill's Pard.* Boulder, CO: Pruett Press, 1968.

Stampp, Kenneth M. *America in 1857: A Nation on the Brink.* New York: Oxford University Press, 1990.

Stanley, Richard T. *The Eisenhower Years: A Social History of the 1950s.* Bloomington, IN: iUniverse, 2012.

Starr, Paul. *The Creation of Media: Political Origins of Modern Communications.* New York: Bargain Books, 2005.

Stasi, Paul, and Jennifer Greiman, eds. *The Last Western: Deadwood and the End of American Empire.* New York: Bloomsbury, 2013.

Steckmesser, Kent Ladd. *The Western Hero in History and Legend.* Norman: University of Oklahoma Press, 1965.

Stefoff, Rebecca. *The Wild West.* Tarrytown, NY: Marshall Cavendish Benchmark, 2007.

Stegner, Wallace. *The American West as Living Space.* Ann Arbor: University of Michigan Press, 1987.

———. *Where the Bluebird Sings to the Lemonade Springs: Living and Writing in the West.* 1995. New York: Modern Library, 2002.

Stoddard, William Osborn. *Lincoln's White House Secretary: The Adventurous Life of William O. Stoddard.* Edited by Harold Holzer. Carbondale: Southern Illinois University Press, 2007.

Strahorn, Carrie Adell. *Fifteen Thousand Miles by Stage: A Woman's Unique Experience during Thirty Years of Path Finding and Pioneering from the Missouri to the Pacific and from Alaska to Mexico.* New York: G. P. Putnam's Sons, 1911.

Sullivan, Robert. *Cross Country.* New York: Bloomsbury, 2006.

Sutton, Fred Ellsworth, and A. B. MacDonald. *Hands Up! Stories of the Six-Gun Fighters of the Old Wild West.* Indianapolis: Bobbs-Merrill, 1927.

Tatum, Stephen. *Inventing Billy the Kid: Visions of the Outlaw in America: 1881–1981.* Albuquerque: University of New Mexico Press, 1982.

Tefertiller, Casey. *Wyatt Earp: The Life behind the Legend.* New York: Wiley, 1997.

Thompson, Bob. *Born on a Mountaintop: On the Road with Davy Crockett and the Ghosts of the Wild Frontier.* New York: Crown, 2012.

Thorndike, Rachel Sherman, ed. *The Sherman Letters: Correspondence between General and Senator Sherman from 1837 to 1891.* New York: Charles Scribner's Sons, 1894.

Tompkins, Jane. *West of Everything: The Inner Life of Westerns.* New York: Oxford University Press, 1992.

Tuska, Jon. *The American West in Film: Critical Approaches to the Western.* Westport, CT: Greenwood Press, 1985.

———. *Billy the Kid: His Life and Legend.* Albuquerque: University of New Mexico Press, 1994.

Wallace, David Foster. *A Supposedly Fun Thing I'll Never Do Again: Essays and Arguments.* 1997. Boston: Back Bay Books, 1998.

Warren, Robert Penn. *The Legacy of the Civil War.* New York: Random House, 1961.

Webb, Walter Prescott. *The Great Plains.* Boston: Ginn and Co., 1931.

Wert, Jeffry D. *Custer: The Controversial Life of George Armstrong Custer.* New York: Simon and Schuster, 1996.

West, Elliott. *The Last Indian War: The Nez Perce Story.* New York: Oxford University Press, 2009.

Weyl, Walter. *The New Democracy.* Revised ed. New York: Macmillan, 1914.

Wheeler, Joseph Lawrence. *Zane Grey's Impact on Life and Letters: A Study in the Popular Novel.* PhD diss., George Peabody College for Teachers, Nashville, Tennessee, 1982.

White, Richard. *"It's Your Misfortune and None of My Own": A New History of the American West.* Norman: University of Oklahoma Press, 1991.

Wills, Brian Steel. *Gone with the Glory: The Civil War in Cinema.* Lanham, MD: Rowman and Littlefield, 2011.

Wilstach, Frank J. *Wild Bill Hickok: The Prince of Pistoleers*. Garden City, NY: Doubleday, Page and Co., 1926.

Woodard, Aaron. *The Revenger: The Life and Times of Wild Bill Hickok*. Lanham, MD: Rowman and Littlefield, 2018.

Wooster, Robert. *The Military and United States Indian Policy, 1865–1903*. Lincoln: University of Nebraska Press, 1988.

Wrobel, David M. *Promised Lands: Promotion, Memory, and the Creation of the American West*. Lawrence: University Press of Kansas, 2002.

Yarrow, Andrew L. *Measuring America: How Economic Growth Came to Define American Greatness in the Late Twentieth Century*. Amherst: University of Massachusetts Press, 2010.

Newspapers and Periodicals

Abbeville, South Carolina, *Press and Banner*, 1876.

Altoona, Pennsylvania, *Tribune*, 1891.

Atlanta *Constitution*, 1883, 1888, 1896.

Barton, Vermont, *Orleans County Monitor*, 1876.

Black Hills Daily Times, 1878.

Boston *Daily Globe*, 1876.

Bozeman, Montana, *Avant Courier*, 1876.

Burlington, Iowa, *Weekly Hawk-Eye*, 1861.

Canberra, Australia, *Times*, 2018.

Charleston, South Carolina, *Daily News*, 1869.

Cheyenne, Wyoming, *Daily Leader*, 1874, 1876, 1881.

Cheyenne, Wyoming, *Daily News*, 1874, 1876.

Chicago *Daily Tribune*, 1869, 1876, 1879, 1899, 1944.

Chicago *Tribune*, 1861, 1867, 1868, 1872, 1995.

Christchurch, New Zealand, *Weekly Press*, 1894.

Clarksville, Tennessee, *Chronicle*, 1871.

Clarksville, Tennessee, *Weekly Chronicle*, 1873.

Columbus, Ohio, *Daily Ohio Statesman*, 1868.

Dallas *Morning News*, 1926.

Denver *Post*, 2015.

Deadwood, Dakota Territory, *Black Hills Daily Pioneer*, 1876, 1886.

Delaware, Ohio, *Gazette*, 1869.

Denver, Colorado, *Rocky Mountain News*, 1874.

Detroit, Kansas, *Western News*, 1870.

Emporia, Kansas, *News*, 1873, 1876.

Erie, Pennsylvania, *Morning Dispatch*, 1873.

Everybody's Magazine, 1901.

Goldhill, Nevada Territory, *Daily Times,* 1873.

Guildhall, Vermont, *Essex County Herald,* 1873.

Harper's New Monthly Magazine, 1867, 1869, 1870.

Hays City, Kansas, *Ellis County Star,* 1876.

Independence, Iowa, *Buchanan County Bulletin,* 1872.

Iola, Kansas, *Register,* 1876.

Junction City, Kansas, *Weekly Union,* 1870.

Kansas City, Missouri, *Daily Journal of Commerce,* 1869.

Kansas City, Missouri, *Times,* 1874, 1876.

Jefferson City, Missouri, *State Journal,* 1876.

Lancaster, Ohio, *Gazette,* 1869.

Las Vegas *Gazette,* 1876.

Leavenworth, Kansas, *Daily Commercial,* 1869.

Leavenworth, Kansas, *Weekly Times,* 1871.

Lexington, Missouri, *The Weekly Caucasian,* 1873.

Los Angeles *Times,* 1943, 1996, 2000.

Loveland, Colorado, *Reporter Herald,* 2013.

Memphis *Daily Appeal,* 1876.

Milan, Tennessee, *Exchange,* 1876.

New York *Evening World,* 1894.

New York *Herald,* 1873, 1876.

New York *Times,* 1865, 1876, 1893, 1918, 1925, 1933, 1940, 1941, 1943, 1953, 1954,
    1947, 1974–76, 1988, 1990, 1993, 1995, 1996, 2000, 2009, 2015.

New York *Times Book Review,* 2007.

New York *Tribune,* 1883, 1894.

New York *Sun,* 1876.

New York *Weekly,* 1869.

Omaha, Nebraska, *Daily Bee,* 1873.

Ottawa, Illinois, *Free Trader,* 1871.

Outing, 1904.

Painesville, Ohio, *Northern Ohio Journal,* 1876.

Paw, Michigan, *True Northerner,* 1876.

Philadelphia *Evening Telegraph,* 1869.

Philadelphia *Weekly,* 2007.

Plymouth, Indiana, Marshall County *Republic,* 1876.

Rapid City, South Dakota, *Journal,* 2019.

Red Cloud, Kansas, *Chief,* 1876.

Richmond, Indiana, *Palladium,* 1869, 1873.

Saint Paul, Minnesota, *Pioneer Press,* 1894.

Salina, Kansas, *Saline County Journal,* 1872.

San Francisco *Chronicle,* 1899, 1960.

Seattle *Weekly News,* 2011.

Springfield, Missouri, *Weekly Patriot,* 1865, 1867, 1967.

St. Louis, Missouri, *Weekly Democrat,* 1867.

St. Louis *Post-Dispatch,* 1876.

Terra Haute, Indiana, *Express,* 1873.

Times of London, 1953, 1982.

Topeka, Kansas, *Daily Commonwealth,* 1874.

Troy, Kansas, *Weekly Kansas Chief,* 1873.

TV Guide, 1953, 1954.

Virginia City, Nevada, *Evening Chronicle,* 1877.

Wall Street Journal, 1992, 2018.

Washington *Post,* 1986.

Wheeling, West Virginia, *Daily Intelligencer,* 1876.

White Cloud, Kansas, *Chief,* 1871, 1873.

Articles and Chapters

Alter, Judy. "The Market for Popular Western Fiction." In *Updating the Literary West,* edited by Thomas J. Lyon, 893–97. Fort Worth: Texas Christian University Press, 1997.

Ashdown, Paul G. "From Public Intellectuals to Technointellectuals: Gunslingers on the Cyberspace Frontier." *Soundings: An Interdisciplinary Journal* 82, nos. 1–2 (Spring/Summer 1999): 205–18.

Badger, R. Reid. "Chicago 1893, World's Columbian Exposition." In *Historical Dictionary of World's Fairs and Expositions, 1851–1988,* edited by John E. Findling and Kimberly D. Peele, 122–32. New York: Greenwood Press, 1990.

Ball, Durwood. "Liberty, Empire, and Civil War in the American West." In *Empire and Liberty: The Civil War and the West,* edited by Virginia Scharff, 66–86. Oakland: University of California Press, 2015.

Barra, Allen. "The Man Who Made Deadwood." *American Heritage* 57, no. 3 (2006): 50–55.

Bellesiles, Michael, et al. "How the West Got Wild: American Media and Frontier Violence; A Roundtable." *Western Historical Quarterly* 31, no. 3 (Autumn 2000): 277–95.

Blacker, Irwin R., ed. "Notes for a Preface." *The Old West in Fiction.* New York: Ivan Obolensky, 1961, n.p.

Blight, David W. "Historians and 'Memory.'" *Common-Place: The Interactive Journal of Early American Life* 2, no. 3 (April 2002): http://www.common -place-archives.org/vol-02/no-03/author/. Accessed May 25, 2019.

Brooks, Landon. "Introduction: The Measure of *Little Big Man*." In Thomas Berger, *Little Big Man*, xi–xviii. 1964. New York: Dell, 1989.

Burnham, Bob. "Wild Bill Hickok." In *Radio Rides the Range: A Reference Guide to Western Drama on the Air, 1929–1967*, edited by Jack French and David S. Siegel, 200–201. Jefferson, NC: McFarland, 2013.

Chapman, Arthur. "The Man Who Tamed the Cow-Towns." *Outing* 45 (November 1904): 131–39.

Crawford, Michael. "Action Figures." In *The Mythical West: An Encyclopedia of Legend, Lore, and Popular Culture*, edited by Richard W. Slatta, 1–6. Santa Barbara, CA: ABC CLIO, 2001.

Cupp, Scott. "Heaven in Four Colors: The Western in Comics Form." In *Wild West Show!* edited by Thomas W. Knowles and Joe R. Lansdale, 99–104. New York: Wings Books, 1994.

"Deadwood in the Spring of 1877." In *Deadwood: The Best Writings on the Most Notorious Town in the West*, edited by T. D. Griffith, 23–25. Guilford, CT: Globe Pequot Press, 2010.

Durham, Philip. "Ernest Hemingway's Grace under Pressure: The Western Code." *Pacific Historical Review* 45, no. 3 (August 1976): 425–32.

Dykstra, Robert. "Wild Bill Hickok in Abilene." *Journal of the Central Mississippi Valley* 2, no. 2 (Fall 1961): 33.

Edy, Jill A. "Journalistic Uses of Collective Memory." *Journal of Communication* 49, no. 2 (June 2006): 71–87.

Ervin, Z. "Zane Grey, and the Code of the West." In *The Mythical West: An Encyclopedia of Legend, Lore, and Popular Culture*, edited by Richard W. Slatta, 159–60. Santa Barbara, CA: ABC CLIO, 2001.

Faehnrich, Denise M. Karst. "Edward Louis Senn's Half-Century on the Last Frontier." *South Dakota History* 29, no. 1 (Spring 1999): 1–22.

Frazee, Steve. "One Evening in Abilene." In *Rawhiders and Renegades*, edited by Harry E. Maule, 187–202. New York: Dell, 1960.

Grow, Matthew J. "The Shadow of the Civil War: A Historiography of Civil War Memory." *American Nineteenth Century History* 4, no. 2 (Summer 2003): 77–103.

Harrison, Fraser. "Yankton: Portrait of a River City." *South Dakota History* 44, no. 1 (2014): 1–96.

Hattaway, Herman. "Engagement at Westport, Mo." In *Historical Times Illustrated Encyclopedia of the Civil War*, edited by Patricia L. Faust, 816. New York: Harper and Row, 1986.

Hilinski, Wayne. "Kellogg Company." In *The Advertising Age Encyclopedia of Advertising*, edited by John McDonough and Karen Egolf, 2:891–93. New York: Fitzroy Dearborn, 2003.

Hume, Janice. "Memory Matters: The Evolution of Scholarship in Collective Memory and Mass Communication." *Review of Communication* 10, no. 3 (2010): 181–98.

Hutton, Paul Andrew. "A Fool's Errand." *True West* 65, no. 2 (February 2018): 32–34.

Iorio, Medio, and Sal Trapani. *Wild Bill Hickok (Classics Illustrated)*. New York: Classics Illustrated Comics, 2017.

Irwin, Eleanor, with Ann Bahar. "The Hillside Press: Adventures of a Miniature Book Publisher." *Miniature Book Society Newsletter* (April 1992): 4–5.

Jensen, Les D. "Gatling Gun," and "Williams Rapid-Fire Gun." In *Historical Times Illustrated Encyclopedia of the Civil War*, edited by Patricia L. Faust, 302, 829–30. New York: Harper and Row, 1986.

Lewis, Preston. "Ike Liked Westerns." *Roundup Magazine*, Western Writers of America (August 2016): 21–22.

Little, E. C. "A Son of the Border." *Everybody's Magazine* (June 1901): 578–87.

Lubet, Steven. "Slap Leather! Legal Culture, Wild Bill Hickok, and the Gunslinger Myth." *Insights on Law and Society* 2, no. 2 (Winter 2002): 7–18.

MacLeish, Archibald. "Sweet Land of Liberty." *Collier's Weekly* (July 8, 1955): 44–57.

McConnell, Stuart. "The Civil War and Historical Memory: A Historiographical Survey." *OAH Magazine of History* 8, no. 1, The Civil War (Fall 1993): 3–6.

McLaird, James D. "'I Know . . . Because I Was There': Leander P. Richardson Reports the Black Hills Gold Rush." *South Dakota History* 3–4 (Fall/Winter 2001): 239–48.

McLuhan, Marshall. "Myth and Mass Media." *Daedalus* 88 (1959): 339–48.

Morrison, Samuel Eliot. *The Oxford History of the American People*. Vol. 3: *1869–1963*. New York: New American Library, 1965, 1972.

Nash, Jay Robert. "Bill Leonard." In *Encyclopedia of Western Lawmen and Outlaws*, 209. 1992. New York: De Capo Press, 1994.

Nichols, George Ward. "The Indian: What to Do with Him," *Harper's New Monthly Magazine* 40 (December 1869–May 1870): 372–79.

———. "Wild Bill." *Harper's New Monthly Magazine* 34 (February 1867): 273–85.

Pencak, William. "The American Civil War Did Not Take Place: With Apologies to Baudrillard." *Rethinking History* 6, no. 2 (2002): 217–21.

Pronzini, Bill. "The Western Pulps." In *Wild West Show!* edited by Thomas W. Knowles and Joe R. Lansdale, 92–97. New York: Wings Books, 1994.

Putnam. James Bruce. "The Evolution of a Frontier Town: Bozeman, Montana, and Its Search for Economic Stability, 1864–1877." Master's thesis, Montana State University, 1973.

Richardson, Leander. "Last Days of a Plainsman." *True West* 13 (November–December 1965): 22.

———. "A Trip to the Black Hills." *Scribner's Monthly* 13 (April 1977), 755.

Rosa, Joseph G. "Foreword." In Nyle H. Miller and Joseph W. Snell. *Why the West Was Wild: A Contemporary Look at the Antics of Some Highly Publicized Kansas Cowtown Personalities.* Topeka: Kansas State Historical Society, 1963. Reprint Norman: University of Oklahoma Press, 2003.

———. "George Ward Nichols and the Legend of Wild Bill Hickok." *Arizona and the West* 19, no. 2 (Summer 1977): 136.

Sale, Richard. "Dear Old Dad (Part 1)." *The Athenaeum,* May 22, 2015.

Senn, Edward L. "Deadwood—A Modern Sodom Needs Another Renovation." *Senn's Forum,* December 1938. In *Deadwood: The Best Writings on the Most Notorious Town in the West,* ed. T. D. Griffith, 72–78. Guilford, CT: Globe Pequot Press, 2010.

Schwartz, Philip John. "The Contemporary Private Press." *Journal of Library History (1966–1972)* 5, no. 4 (October 1970): 297–322.

Sinowitz, Michael Leigh. "The Western as Postmodern Satiric History: Thomas Berger's *Little Big Man.*" *Clio* 28, no. 2 (1999): 129–243.

Smith, Stacey L. "Beyond North and South: Putting the West in the Civil War Era and Reconstruction." *Journal of the Civil War Era* 6, no. 4 (December 2016): 566–91.

Steckmesser, Kent L. "Lawmen and Outlaws." In *A Literary History of the American West.* Fort Worth: Texas Christian University Press, 1987.

Tuchman, Gaye. "Myth and the Consciousness Industry." In *Mass Media and Social Change,* edited by Elihu Katz and Tamas Szecsko, 83–100. Beverly Hills, CA: Sage, 1981.

Ward, Rachel Mizsei. "Genre Mashing in the Role-Playing Game *Deadlands: The Weird West, the Horror Steampunk Western,*" in *Undead in the West II: They Just Keep Coming.* Edited by Cynthia J. Miller and A. Bowdoin Van Riper, 269–85. Lanham, MD: Scarecrow Press, 2013.

White, Lynn, Jr. "The Legacy of the Middle Ages in the American Wild West." *Speculum* 40:2 (April 1965): 91.

Wild Bill Hickok, Frontier Fighter 1, no. 1: 99–104. New York: Avon, 1949.

Witherspoon, Wendy. "The Final Stamp: Deadwood and the Gothic American Frontier." In *Dirty Words in Deadwood: Literature and the Post Western,* edited by Melody Graulich and Nicholas S. Witschi, 104–5. Lincoln: University of Nebraska Press.

Web Pages

Ames, John. *The Real Deadwood.* John Edward Ames Website. http://
johnedwardames.tripod.com/index.html. Accessed November 8, 2017.

Anderson, Richard Dean. Website. *Legend.* http://www.rdanderson.com
/legend/legend.htm. Accessed April 28, 2017.

Barra, Allen, "The Little Big Man Hoax." *True West,* November 4, 2014.
https://truewestmagazine.com/the-little-big-man-hoax/. Accessed December 15, 2017.

Belth, Alex. "Bronx Banter Interview: Pete Dexter." *Bronx Banter,* April 30,
2013. http://www.bronxbanterblog.com/2013/04/30/bronx-banter
-interview-pete-dexter-2/. Accessed February 19, 2019.

Brusatte, Chris. "Lincoln's Visits to La Salle County." La Salle County Historical Society, Ottawa, Illinois, *Times,* August 16, 2008. http://www.
mywebtimes.com/life/lincoln-s-visits-to-lasalle-county/article
_66dc7ed9–7ca6–5d95–81fb-3867634a4868.html. Accessed May 29, 2017.

Ebert, Roger. "Wild Bill." December 1, 1995. http://www.rogerebert.com
/reviews/wild-bill-1995. Accessed October 11, 2017.

Eisenhower, Dwight D. "Remarks upon Receiving the America's Democratic
Legacy Award." The American Presidency Project, November 23, 1953. http://
www.presidency.ucsb.edu/ws/index.php?pid=9770. Accessed July 16, 2018.

Forney, Gary. "Montana's Pioneer Editor: The Epic Career of Bozeman's First
Newspaper Man." *Montana Pioneer,* June 2011. https://montanapioneer
.com/montanas-pioneer-editor/. Accessed June 26, 2017.

Gennis, Sadie. "NYPD Blue Creator David Milch Is in Massive Debt after
Gambling Away over $100 Million." *TV Guide,* February 17, 2016. http://
www.tvguide.com/news/nypd-blue-creator-david-milch-gambling-debt/.
Accessed June 28, 2018.

Guy Madison Official Website. http://www.guymadison.com. Accessed May
13, 2017.

"Harper's New Monthly Magazine." *American History through Literature
1820–1870,* Encyclopedia.com. http://www.encyclopedia.com. Accessed
July 9, 2018.

"The Harrowed." *Deadlands,* Pinnacle Entertainment Group. https://
deadlandsridersonthestorm.obsidianportal.com/wikis/the-harrowed.
Accessed January 30, 2018.

Jay, Robert. "W2XBS Schedule, Week of April 21st, 1940." *Television Obscurities,* https://www.tvobscurities.com/2009/07/w2xbs-schedule-week-of
-april-21st-1940/. Accessed July 24, 2018.

Kansas Historical Society, *kansapedia,* https://www.kshs.org/kansapedia /edward-campbell-little/16976. Accessed July 18, 2018).

Lahiri, Chandra. "Days 22 & 23: Sin and Debauchery." Muscat *Daily,* June 20, 2018. https://www.muscatdaily.com/Archive/Stories-Files/Days -22–23-Sin-Debauchery!-59po. Accessed June 22, 2018.

Miles, John Peere. IMDb (Internet Movie Database). http://www.imdb .com/name/nm0587158/bio. Accessed Feb. 12, 2018.

Patten, Irene M. "Of Noble Warriors and Maidens Chaste." *American Heritage* 22, no. 3 (April 1971): http://www.americanheritage.com/content /noble-warriors-and-maidens-chaste. Accessed October 9, 2017.

"Q and A with Joe R. Lansdale, Author of Paradise Sky." *CriminalElement,* September 26, 2017. https://www.criminalelement.com/qaa-with-joe-r -lansdale-author-of-paradise-sky/. Accessed April 30, 2018.

Soodalter, Ron. "Code of the West, History vs. Hollywood." *American Cowboy* 24, no. 1 (June/July 2017).

Stepno, Bob. "Frontier Gentleman." Newspaper Heroes on the Air, https:// jheroes.com/adventure/westerns/frontier-gentleman/. Accessed April 23, 2017.

Stockman, Tom. "My Favorite Movies: The One Where Charles Bronson Battles the Giant White Buffalo." *OnStl,* April 24, 2013. http://content .onstl.com/people/ron-stevens/item/541-my-favorite-movies-the-one -where-charles-bronson-battles-the-giant-white-buffalo/. Accessed November 3, 2017.

Thomas, Harry. "Nat Love." *Documenting the American South,* University Library, University of North Carolina. http://docsouth.unc.edu/neh /natlove/summary.html. Accessed April 28, 2018.

"Vance Randolph, 1892–1980." *Encyclopedia of Arkansas History and Culture.* http://www.encyclopediaofarkansas.net/encyclopedia/entry-detail.aspx ?entryID=2265. Accessed May 2, 2018.

Walker, Tim. "Deadwood Creator Squandered $100 m Fortune on Gambling Habit." *Independent,* February18, 2018. https://www.independent .co.uk/news/people/david-milch-deadwood-creator-squandered-100m -fortune-on-gambling-habit-a6882336.html. Accessed June 28, 2018.

Wheeler, Joe. "Why You Should Read Zane Grey." Zane Grey's West Society, https://www.zgws.org/zgwsread.php. Accessed Aug. 1, 2018.

Wilstach, Frank J. *Wild Bill Hickok: The Prince of Pistoleers* (Garden City, NY: Doubleday, Page and Co., 1926). http://archives.nypl.org/mss/3355. Accessed February 28, 2017.

Wilstach, Frank Jenners. Papers. New York Public Library. http://archives
.nypl.org/mss/3355. Accessed February 12, 2018.

Worley, Rusty. "Opinion: The Case for Downtown as Recreational Hub."
Springfield, Missouri, *Business Journal*, June 4, 2018. http://sbj.net/stories
/opinion-the-case-for-downtown-as-recreational-hub,59079. Accessed
August 1, 2018.

Yancey, Alexandra. "Western Story Magazine." *The Pulp Magazine Project*,
https://www.pulpmags.org/content/info/western-story-magazine.html.
Accessed February 7, 2018.

Yen, Alfred C. "Western Frontier or Feudal Society? Metaphors and Perceptions of Cyberspace." *Berkeley Technology Law Journal* 17 (2003): 1207–61.

Index

A range of pages indicates that an entry is cited continuously on those pages (e.g., 91–99). Where other information intervenes, a comma separates page numbers (e.g., 90, 91).

Paul Ashdown is a professor emeritus of journalism at the University of Tennessee, Knoxville. He previously worked as a newspaper and wire service reporter. In addition to his interest in the memory of the Civil War era, he specializes in literary journalism, international communication, and popular culture.

Edward Caudill is a professor emeritus of journalism at the University of Tennessee, Knoxville. He previously worked as a newspaper and wire service editor. His scholarship primarily has focused on media history, the Civil War era, and the history of ideas in public memory and the press.

ENGAGING
—*the*—
CIVIL WAR

Engaging the Civil War, a series founded by the historians at the blog Emerging Civil War (www.emergingcivilwar.com), adopts the sensibility and accessibility of public history while adhering to the standards of academic scholarship. To engage readers and bring them to a new understanding of America's great story, series authors draw on insights they gained while working with the public—walking the ground where history happened at battlefields and historic sites, talking with visitors in museums, and educating students in classrooms. With fresh perspectives, field-tested ideas, and in-depth research, volumes in the series connect readers with the story of the Civil War in ways that make history meaningful to them while underscoring the continued relevance of the war, its causes, and its effects. All Americans can claim the Civil War as part of their history. This series , which was cofounded by Chris Mackowski and Kristopher D. White, helps them engage with it.

Chris Mackowski and Brian Matthew Jordan, Series Editors

Queries and submissions
emergingcivilwar@gmail.com